Narrative and Truth

PREVIOUS PUBLICATION

Richard Wagner and the Centrality of Love (2010)

NARRATIVE AND TRUTH

AN ETHICAL AND DYNAMIC PARADIGM FOR THE HUMANITIES

BARRY EMSLIE

NARRATIVE AND TRUTH

First published in 2012 by
PALGRAVE MACMILLAN®
in the United States—a division of St. Martin's Press LLC,
175 Fifth Avenue, New York, NY 10010.

Where this book is distributed in the UK, Europe and the rest of the world,
this is by Palgrave Macmillan, a division of Macmillan Publishers Limited,
registered in England, company number 785998, of Houndmills,
Basingstoke, Hampshire RG21 6XS.

Palgrave Macmillan is the global academic imprint of the above companies
and has companies and representatives throughout the world.

Palgrave® and Macmillan® are registered trademarks in the United States,
the United Kingdom, Europe and other countries.

ISBN: 978–1–137–27544–8

Library of Congress Cataloging-in-Publication Data

Emslie, Barry.
    Narrative and truth : an ethical and dynamic paradigm for the
humanities / Barry Emslie.
        p. cm.
    Includes bibliographical references.
    ISBN 978–1–137–27544–8 (alk. paper)
        1. Humanities—Moral and ethical aspects. 2. Narration (Rhetoric)—
Moral and ethical aspects. 3. Knowledge, Theory of, in literature.
    4. Literature—Philosophy. I. Title.

AZ103.E47 2012
001.3—dc23   2012016611

A catalogue record of the book is available from the British Library.

Design by Newgen Imaging Systems (P) Ltd., Chennai, India.

First edition: October 2012

10 9 8 7 6 5 4 3 2 1

Printed in the United States of America.

Contents

Acknowledgments

I would like in particular to thank Herta Frenzel who helped with the preparation of the text, and Dr Falk Schmidt whose comments and encouragement were invaluable. Both are protected by the usual disclaimers and are in no way responsible for the shortcomings of this book.

I am also grateful for the help of the librarians at the Bertolt Brecht Archives in Berlin and, in particular, for their permission to quote from the archive material used in chapter 6.

Chapter 1

An Overview

"Madame," declares Ernest Hemingway to his imaginary interlocutor at the end of the eleventh chapter of *Death in the Afternoon*, "all stories, if continued far enough, end in death." And so they do. This simple but universally experienced fact is customarily dismissed as so crudely self-evident as not to be worth troubling about, or is circumvented by theories of resurrection and reincarnation, none of which—even on their own terms—are able to gainsay death as an event. Hemingway is well aware of this and finishes his sentence with "...and he is no true-story teller who would keep that from you." And although there is never but one true story, true storytelling is what this book is about.

Not surprisingly, the fundamental categories of death and narrative generate a plethora of eclectic themes, and the specific thematic material out of which the epistemological and normative claims of this book are constructed are dealt with in a free manner in this chapter. It should also give the reader a better idea of how the general argument will play out in detail in the following six chapters.

Death is the notion that, paradoxically, most powerfully affects our lives. It compels us to acknowledge that we are narrative creatures. Moreover, we can in the most personal manner physically chart the unfolding of just that narrative. Adorno, for instance, is remorseless:

> What death does to what is socially condemned, is anticipated biologically in beloved human beings of great age; not only their bodies but their ego, everything which determines them as human beings, crumbles without illness and violent intervention.[1]

But even in the face of Adorno's grim picture of degeneration, it may seem unfortunate that, in an age that has sanitized death and left the individual in technologically advanced societies victim to a machine dependent demise, we have lost that feeling for its presence, which Benjamin had in mind when he wrote that once "there wasn't a house, hardly a room, in which someone hadn't died."[2]

The great deathbed scene, whether serious as in *War and Peace* when the illegitimate Pierre is allowed in to see his dying father or comic as when Gianni Schicchi or Volpone rob the greedy relatives, is hardly possible in Western fiction any more. The dying are not at home, and anyway they are too far gone to talk. Instead, in our entertainment culture death is often served up as mass, computer-generated slaughter or transmitted as raw newsreel film of Third World disasters. Its meaning is altered in both cases—in the first because it has become kitsch and in the second because we are forced into strategies of detachment in the face of gratuitous horrors that, we may feel, have no place in our living rooms.

Nonetheless, it does not matter how convinced we may be that the sun will daily seem to rise above the horizon, or how enamored we may become of the returning seasons, we know that following birth, our lives are ostensibly linear: we grow, possibly procreate, and then, assuming we get to run the full course, degenerate and die. We are in our commonsense understanding of ourselves and the societies we make, not cyclical, but teleological. And no matter that it may seem morbid or pessimistic, our prosaic death-shaped teleology is unmistakably goal fixed.

Yet, it need not be pessimistic. Even if we forgo the consolations of religions that either purport to offer eternal life or "transcend" death by taking us round and round the course of existence ad infinitum, the greater narrative that we call history—a narrative that by its very character transcends the fortunes and potential nihilism of the individual or the single generation—holds out the possibility of progress. Paul Ricoeur's observation that "what is ultimately at stake in the case of the structural identity of the narrative function as well as in that of the truth claim of every narrative work, is the temporal character of human experience" would be incomplete if that temporal experience were restricted to either a single individual or generation.[3] When, for instance, he rhetorically asks "What is more intimate to life, more part of it, than death, or rather dying?"[4] only half of the matter has been broached. Later the missing element surfaces, but he regards it as, in part, a rationalization. Death indicates "that the replacement of generations is the euphemism by which we signify that the living take the place of the dead." Hence "the idea of a generation is the insistent reminder that history is the history of mortals. But death is also thereby superseded . . . In history, death, as the end of every individual life, is only dealt with by allusion, to the profit of those entities that outlast the cadavers—a people, nation, state, class, civilization."[5] With respect to death and what might be inferred normatively from it, it is—among other things—the task of this book to arrive at conclusions that will escape euphemism and deliver more than this.

Given that teleology and the role of a utopian telos will turn out to be central considerations, one turns to Benjamin to take the first step. When he observes that "the notion of eternity has always been most strongly rooted in Death"[6] we are reminded of the dialectical contradiction that death is the source of the idea that transcends it. That "eternity"—which is the projection of history into the future—with its *multiple* linearity confronts us with a more complex reality than that focused on the death of the individual and his generation, and suggests the possibility of a more optimistic, even utopian, epistemology.

Detlev J. K. Peukert, tracing the mentality that led the Nazis to the "Final Solution", argues that utopian thought attempts to banish death in respect of the individual, substituting a corporeal notion of the folk ("Volkskörper"), which can then be regarded as eternal.[7] However this is, as is customarily the case with fascist arguments, a simplification. Instead it is exactly the individual death and its epistemological status *within* a collective history that is critical. For above all, it is the collective that changes the temporal parameters of death. And this dialectic equation made up of the (opposed) claims of the subject and the whole is a consideration that will repeatedly surface in a variety of guises during the coming chapters. It will, for instance, emerge as a necessary element in arguments underpinning utopian thinking.

In general, we can see that the task of explicating history has seldom been more pejoratively regarded than now. The optimistic and positivist Weltanschauungen of the nineteenth century are, after the horrors of the twentieth, mockingly held up as examples of grand interpretations gone mad on their own conceited assumptions. Sweeping historical teleology, usually implying—at the very least—a utopian telos, has never had a worse press. And with the collapse of one monolithic block devoted to one partial Weltanschauung, history itself has been dismissed as a transcended and redundant category.

But the collapse of the nominally Marxist bloc made it easy, and seemingly logical, to toss out the baby of Marxist humanism with the bathwater of totalitarian Marxism. While the lamentable cost and consequence of this will be examined in the next chapter, we can note now how this radical change has thrown up unlikely parallels. In declaring the end of history, Francis Fukuyama reproduces the Marxist pattern of a prehistory transcended by a new phase in which the anomalies of the "past" are resolved...finally. Liberal democracy, declares Fukuyama, is "free from...fundamental internal contradictions."[8] But the great leap in

Marxism from capitalist to communist societies implies a radical transformation in both epistemological and ontological categories. An entirely new subject of history is in play and all the tensions between it and the objective world are erased in a benign community where everybody lives his or her life to the abundant full. Fukuyama, however, ends history in the most complacent and constricted manner. "Events" do go on but the triumph of liberal democracy is so radiantly clear that all grand debates are resolved. He of course claims, like Marx, to be a Hegelian (in his case mediated by Kojève), however he is a weak one. History may be "directional" but, except for the continued spread of the global market and the dominance of liberal democracies, it is by no means clear where this direction leads. It is a teleology without a telos.

In fact Fukuyama is a structuralist with a formal model of society, which he can explain in nuts and bolts terms but into which he has also, somewhat slyly, injected a vague dynamic. Essentially, the best he can offer is but more of the same. This seems an unlikely scenario given that history has always turned out to be more confused and multifarious than we had anticipated, something that is central to the elaborate interpretation of Fukuyama's teacher Samuel P. Huntington. He explains the present historical dynamic on the basis of a multipolar, and highly discordant, model. Still, there is a neat dialectical switch in *The End of History*. Vice emerges as the agent of virtue. It turns out that striving for recognition ("thymos")— which can be traced back through Hegel to Plato— becomes the motor of history and thereby "thymic pride" enables greed to work out its benevolent potential without being skewered into behavior more appropriate to the Hobbesian jungle. In spirit this is a wholly Marxist solution; in content it is a glib rationalization.

Fukuyama can be placed alongside the optimistic Lukács. He too is committed to Hegelian "totality" but on a much more sophisticated level. In his idealist account of history, progress is an inevitable expression of the raised consciousness of the proletariat. Class warfare may be the motor in the classic Marxist sense, but it is expressed as conscious wisdom in that it uniquely resolves a host of antinomies: subject/object, theory/praxis, and self-interest/universal good. It is a measure of Lukács's boldness that his paradigmatic account has been so fruitful. That it has been (as must always be the case) overtaken by the narratives of history itself and that it has (as Lukács was not surprised to observe) collapsed through its own contradictions and omissions does not invalidate its contemporary challenge. For if Lukács is also "idealistic" in the popular pejorative sense of being impractical, in working out Marxist theory in such a sophisticated manner he does put on center stage an optimistic Weltanschauung and the utopian promise. Above all, he also reminds us of the difficulty of understanding history. For history—which demands of us a deep-seated engagement with the future—is, when not reduced to random events, likely to be the site where analytical and normative values are most intimately coupled. It is, moreover, a noble undertaking, no matter how often pessimism or determinist arrogance exposes it as a forlorn one. It is certainly not appropriate for the historian when speculating about the future to flunk because he is worried about getting it wrong. As Hayden White points out, the historian is well-nigh synonymous with the philosopher of history.[9]

Structuralist forms may be safer and a great many games can be played putting together topologies (as Hayden White, most notably, does), but they are ineluctably exposed as impotent when confronted by the flux of events. Perhaps the only dynamic alternative to teleological accounts implying normative values and a utopian telos, is that of arbitrary (though quite possibly racially based) theories celebrating belligerence, the indulgence of the ego, and the superiority of the tribe. However, such explanations tend to debase history epistemologically because, above all, they are utterly in hock to struggle as a virtue in itself. For instance, the fascist Weltanschauung certainly has a temporal character in that it celebrates the acquisition of *growing* power over those deemed inferior. But its narrative is jejune. Nonetheless, it must be given its due and we will return to its teleological poverty in the last chapter. However, it should be acknowledged now that fascism's inability to deal substantively with the notion of a goal (telos) encourages us to address the virtues, and not just the dangers, of utopian thinking.

Implicit is a further question, which will grow in importance throughout the following chapters. It relates directly to the two title terms of the book. In the first instance, narrative is foregrounded because it is more "truthful" in the sense that it best enables us to understand the world. It is, to put it simply, more "realistic" and it will be argued in chapter 6 that narrative, realism, and truth are, in effect, synonyms. However, that is not the end of the matter. The question surfaces whether narrative is also more "truthful" in that it is generative of normative values that are logically necessary and not mere arbitrary assumptions. Clearly for those of us who are not fascists, the prospect of inferring, or even perhaps deducing, from a narrative epistemology enlightened normative values is attractive. And this temptation will not go away in these pages. Furthermore, any move in this direction will raise another ubiquitous consideration, one which has already been touched on in the context of utopian thinking: namely, the theoretical reconciliation in the grand historical context of the rival claims of the class (or collective) and the individual subject. It is axiomatic that such a reconciliation must be theoretically possible if the (enlightened or humanist) normative agenda is to be realized. As this will place great weight on the notion of telos, and of narratives that express it in utopian terms, one is grateful—at this early point—that Lukács's account of history and class consciousness also reminds us of Fredric Jameson's assertion that "all class consciousness is in its very nature utopian."[10]

And indeed one of the most ubiquitous dichotomies behind grand accounts of history is that posed by the competing claims of the subject and the systems in which he is placed. It is a dichotomy that cannot be avoided. Although it is not to be wondered at that grand theoreticians disposed to explain history in terms of generic types and tropes do not bother much with the subject, it is striking that even *narrative* metacommentaries are often likewise distrustful of the same category. The subject is then rejected in favor of grander "scientific" notions of historical agency. The matter has been the site of serious battles. Norman Geras, placing the subject center stage, trenchantly argued in 1983 that Marx did not abandon a notion of human nature in the *Theses on Feuerbach* while, on the other hand, Althusser insisted that he could not give any ground in claiming that "man" was absent from a true Marxist account, for to begin with man would be to begin with a bourgeois and humanist idea of man[11]—a difficulty that has troubled many left- wing thinkers.[12]

What is evoked by the Subject is in fact a nexus of notions that "purist" Marxists find a touch worrying. To the Subject should be added Morality and Aesthetics. These make up a triad that has secured for itself a privileged place within post-Marxist theory; but it lies uncomfortably alongside the "scientific" narrative of class warfare. There is a further twist with respect to this idealist triad. Increasingly advanced forms of class exploitation are to dissolve under their own contradictions and to produce (finally) a communist society in which (ironically) Morality and Aesthetics are ubiquitously embodied in a new elevated and creative Subject happily splashing around in a wholly uninhibited and fulfilled manner. On this model, capitalism may well produce its own gravediggers but they remain the faceless agents of class interests, just as they do in Lukács's *History and Class Consciousness*. It is Marx, however, who writes with discernible feeling of the corporeal lives of French socialist workers "Smoking, eating, drinking," of how "Company, association, conversation, which in its turn has society as its goal, is enough for them. The brotherhood of man is not a hollow phrase, it is a reality, and the nobility of man shines forth upon us from their work-worn figures."[13] The only way around this is to claim, like Althusser, that these are the words of Marx before he became a Marxist.

That Marxism is fundamentally normative, as will be argued in the next chapter, is maintained, among others, by Steven Lukes (1987), who makes an astute distinction between Recht (legal, class-based systems of morality designed to preserve existing power relations) and emancipation (the axiomatic notion of liberation implied by classless society). This distinction will be pushed somewhat further, so that two notions of morality are coupled: one, deeper and universalist (Luke's emancipation), and the other more superficial but that may, nonetheless, find expression in the strategies designed to bring about the first. In this sense, the second notion is more than Lukes's Recht. This double morality will resurface below and, in particular, in the last two chapters, as an attempt is made to arrive at credible normative conclusions through narrative arguments. But remaining for the moment with Marxism, it is clear that Lukes is hardly unique in wanting to establish a firm ethical basis that does not contradict the epistemology of the metatheory. Even Perry Anderson is concerned at the apparent lack of a theoretical basis for morality, although he does deplore the influence of its substitute: aesthetics.[14]

One notes here a clear difference between the British and German schools. Turning to aesthetics as a means of securing a normative basis for philosophical argument has been among German intellectuals, at the very least since Kant's *Third Critique,* a standard strategy. And this in its very character violates the spatial and causal relationship between the (Marxist) categories of base and superstructure. Many German Marxist philosophers have been no less influenced by this than German intellectuals in general. Partly as a result, chapter 5 will be structured around the problematic role of aesthetics with respect to both normative values and a narrative grounded in teleology. This is a teleology that, as we will see, Kant employs so that it is exclusively focused on the telos. Furthermore, he will attempt to deduce from it the existence of God. However, of particular importance is the positive notion of the Kantian subject *in* the collective, which at moments recalls the idealistic notion of a communist society in that the harmonious model of the greatest good (Kant's summum bonum) involves no harmful payoff for the individual. In particular, it is instructive that Kant's utopianism comes about through an insistence on teleology that pays little attention (unlike Marxist theory) to the manner in which the goal is to be reached.

However mainstream British Marxist thinking has, at least traditionally, been disinclined to abstract anything so agreeable and determining from aesthetics. There is, for instance, nothing like Ernst Bloch's romanticizing on art and utopianism. Rather, it has been inclined to hold onto the classic causal model and to imprison aesthetics within the sphere of the contingent. To compromise with the priority of economic determinism was to throw overboard the intellectual crown jewels of the theory. Anderson, for instance, looked askance at the decadent "hypertrophy of the aesthetic."[15] But even if we leave aside the vast field of theoretical work aesthetics has spawned, we are still confronted by massive ambivalences among the framers of Marxist philosophy. Certainly, there is no problem hoovering up quotations on aesthetics from Marx and Engels that lie at odds with the classic axioms of base and superstructure.[16]

One consequence of all this is an ironic but understandable reluctance on the part of Anglo-Saxon Marxists who have specialized in literary theory to make big claims for the unmediated insights of their own field. Hardly wanting to appear more concerned with decoration than substance, they willingly insist(ed) on the contingent nature of their own disciplines. Once Terry Eagleton was much concerned to sink morality in hard materialist structures rather than in aesthetics and talked of the "rehabilitation of the 'scientific' Marx."[17] He questioned the importance of alienation—a favorite source for those seeking an ethically rooted notion of human nature in Marx —and with something of a flourish declared: "The morality of *Capital* does not lie in the fine pages of passionate indignation directed against the bestialities of capitalism, it lies…in the laying bare of the mechanisms whereby surplus-value is extracted from labor power."[18] However, his recent work makes of the sensuous character of individual experience a fundamental category. And he now sees alienation as a sensitive and morally revealing phenomenon.[19] For if alienation is permitted, so must the question "alienated from what?" Clearly, there has to be a richer notion of human nature to give it meaning. Yet this is not without problems. If Marx's classless ideal allows a full expression of all individual potential then it would also allow the full expression of any negative characteristics also in play. Therefore, Eagleton asks rhetorically: "Is it the aim of historical struggle to balance my capacity to torture in symmetrical, proportionate relation to my capacity to love?"[20] Given that Marx's answer (and Eagleton's) would be "no," clearly some notion of the "good" in respect of (nonalienated) human nature is inescapable. Eagleton's further pursuit of this theme will be a matter for the next chapter, but he has clearly moved onto an intellectual terrain that demands a profound reconciliation between the subject and the collective.

Even so, the problem of the subject remains intractable. There is perhaps no problem with the Hegelian World Historical Individual who butchers his way to empire and thereby grandly serves the interests of the World Spirit, but when economics and class are the key historical factors the collective takes precedence over the singular hero and difficulties follow. True, as Lukács did not initially seem to realize to the chagrin of the Leninists, exceptional leaders will be necessary but only in so far as they facilitate predetermined historical development and with it the psychic liberation of the masses. And, ironically, it will be the extent to which those subjects singly (but still placed in the mass) develop their suppressed potential and attain a higher level of self-expression, that will validate the metatheory. Engels writes to Heinz Starkenburg in 1894 that "men make their history themselves" and suggests that in the future they will do so "with a collective will."[21] Clearly, it can only be those "men" who vindicate the theory in its most overt utopian form. And it is exactly here that the dialectic struggle between the individual and structures, between nature and narrative, becomes most acute and, ultimately, most bloody. The theoretical status and the actual "character" of the subject, of the unique individual ego, remains a battleground, though one hopes it will no longer be so murderously replete a killing field as during the Stalinist purges and beyond.

However, talk of the ego implies a theory of human nature so focused on the individual that the polarity made up of the subject and the collective must shift in the direction of the former. And psychology, axiomatically subject focused, has proved to be the most influential explanatory model of human nature customarily, but by no means always, opposed to Marxism.

Given that he spent some time in Vienna and got to know the "Freudians," it is hardly to be wondered at that Trotsky was interested in psychoanalysis. Moreover, as the Soviet triumph required the self-confident assertion that new people were being created, some interest in the creation of the ego was inevitable. If—to put the matter at its most naive—mental problems that existed elsewhere were to disappear, and Soviet Man evolve free from the psychoses of the capitalist world, then someone as intellectually sophisticated as Trotsky was likely to be fascinated by the originality and explanatory power of Freudian thought. Even so it may seem a little odd that in *Literature and Revolution* he should have preferred psychoanalysis to "native" Russian behaviorism, given that Freudianism elevates the past over the future and has deep *irresolvable* psychic struggles as its fundamental explanatory axioms. In fact, it remains *that* theory which most trenchantly questions optimistic narratives. It is a dystopia whose telos paradoxically lies in the earliest years of the subject's life and, yet further back, in a violent tribal prehistory that in no way posits, or permits, a utopian ideal. Clearly, this is why the perverse retrospective "telos" is so easily dissected, dismantled, and reassembled in accordance with the arbitrary wishes of its inventor/discoverer and his disciples. Nevertheless, despite all the exposés of its inconsistencies and swindles, Freudianism remains a powerful alternative to optimistic teleologies, not least because its pessimism has, all too often, been proved right. Furthermore, as a narrative explanation it suffers—although this is part of its seductive power—from a singularity in its linear storytelling. For these reasons it is the subject of chapter 4. It might, however, be remarked here that Freudianism does take full advantage of an axiom intrinsic to its structure: being right may well be the ultimate narrative reward of all pessimists. Certainly its own history in the Soviet Union was not a happy one.

By the time of the First Congress of Soviet Writers (1934) there had, presumably, been ample opportunity for the revolution to have effected its mysteries in the lives of its children/citizens. In the public sphere, dominant ideology made it radiantly clear that everything was going according to plan. All writers, according to Louis Fischer, were "ordered, in the middle of the 1930s, to treat the present as though it did not exist and the future as though it had already arrived."[22] To simply propose a Five-Year Plan was to guarantee its completion. Meanwhile, writers were "engineers of the human soul," at least according to Stalin, who had chosen "socialist realism as the path for Soviet literature and art."[23] Perhaps one might see the Terror as a measure of how disappointed Stalin was in his people— people who had failed to take advantage of the opportunities he had given them. Obedience was now underpinned by the crudest form of behaviorism and an unreal world of fiction and ceremony assumed precedence over material reality in the psychic life of the nation. Stalinism is not only the triumph of terror, but also of the extraordinary ideology whose potency seems to have grown the more unreal it became. Logically there emerges a macabre similarity between the suffering of the Soviet collective, trapped in what Jeffrey Brooks calls a "performative" culture where gratitude was a perpetual public duty, and the comrade at a show trial sincerely confessing crimes he had not committed and begging for his own destruction as a traitor to leader, party, and history.

Understandably liberals and democratic socialists have reacted to the terrors of Stalinism with a high degree of intellectual timidity. Radical change, anything that smacks of revolution, grand narratives proclaiming deep theoretical premises are terrors too terrible to contemplate. Karl Popper, Isaiah Berlin, Arthur Koestler, Tony Judt, et al., and from a left-wing perspective Jürgen Habermas, all lean to circumspection and incremental change. If you cannot make an omelet without breaking eggs then we shall just have to do without omelets. Not least because, as Berlin says, the omelets never get made anyway.[24] Popper's (1974) horror at the death of communist friends in Vienna 1919, Koestler's (1945) fear of the Jesuitical zeal of the commissar, Isaiah Berlin's (1980) shock at seeing a policeman dragged to his death in Riga, which surely underpins his notion of "negative liberty,"[25] and Tony Judt's disgust at Eric Hobsbawn's continued loyalty to the party,[26] are products of a comfortable capitalist culture where, as Fukuyama "knows," fundamental problems have been resolved and we can concentrate on making sure things do not get out of hand. Neither does this, at the very least, pay adequate respect to the bloody sacrifices of the past on which modern liberties, in all their inequalities, rest, nor does it have much purchase in, as Eagleton once said, the jungles of Guatemala.[27]

Behind all this is the attempt to take violence out of the equation; an option that this book rejects in the final two chapters. Certainly there are those (Marcuse [1972] and Merleau-Ponty [1971] for instance) who resist timidity and pacifism, but the untroubled moral superiority of the present "consensus" makes bloodletting unacceptable... at least at "home." Under these circumstances, any theory of revolution is indefensible. This raises the question of the guilt *in* grand radical theories and in Marxism in particular, and highlights another form of double morality in which standards that are domestically unimpeachable are readily violated through acts of national self-interest in external affairs. We find ourselves in the self-evidently contradictory position of insisting on the eradication of certain types of arbitrary power and overt state violence in "our" domestic lives as long as that does not stop us from rupturing the lives of those who live overseas and who do not seem to be behaving in our best interests, which is to say in the best interests of capitalism, which is to say (more or less) in the best interests of the west, which is to say (in large measure) in the best interests of the United States.

Mind you, if we accept the role of great men in history—of, as it were, Founding Fathers—it would be possible to give some temporal and dramatic explanation for the emergence of what the pacifists and the incrementalists, fearful of revolutionary activity, see as the mutant gene that has done so much damage to the emancipatory core of Marxist thinking. It is however a terminologically closed argument as Marx and Engels—it is assumed—went off the rails when they became Marxists. Some time ago, Peter Demetz was able to give an adept account of this Fall as he marked out the steps by which both men abandoned a youthful dedication to poetry and drama. Had they persisted, they would have become enlightened children of Goethe. Instead, they turned to the murky business of economics, class struggle, and revolution. The result was an alleged moral collapse.[28] Perhaps Auden was right and poetry does indeed make nothing happen, but who would have thought that ditching poetry for economics would have such awesome consequences. And clearly when the mutant gene of revolutionary theory has got into the ideological DNA, everyone becomes a carrier and guilt is more or less generalized. Then dismissive, normatively based historical judgment is a piece of pie. Even so, it is striking that the notion of great revolutionary men, who in this account are compelled to lead us all astray, does not go away. The awkward dialectic of subject and system remains, even here, very much in play.

Now it is axiomatic that all the threads of Stalinism are to be found in Lenin(ism). The System is judged to have triumphed over those individuals hitherto portrayed, even celebrated, as determining the historical narrative. For instance, Dmitry Volkogonov writes passionate revisionist biographies of Soviet leaders exposing the inherent criminality of the system. Yet, ironically he enthusiastically accepts the standard formal pairing kernel to Stalinist propaganda: that is, heroic mentor Lenin and heroic acolyte Stalin. But he does so only to invert its message. They were equally bad; the Stalinist horror being premised on the system created by Lenin. This line of argument soon slips into a common solecism of systems-based, "historical" analysis: either agency disappears or it assumes odd, anthropomorphic forms. The system, we are told, needed a Stalin. And presumably what the system needs, it gets...by simply producing it.

One of the great difficulties in this matter is the "distancing" of the past. The scare quotes are there to remind us that we cannot be sure when past narratives are dead and buried. In fact they never are. Even so, the horrors of recent history have a different status within narratives than those, allegedly, long gone. Quite irrespective of body counts, we cannot write with the same revulsion about Tamerlane as we do about Stalin. One way out of this dilemma is to give recent horrors a didactic patina: "They must never happen again." Another is simply to leave them in the form of memoirs while historians concentrate on the logistic factors that allowed, let us say, the Khmer Rouge to commit genocide. A third, and more epistemologically dangerous practice, is to give the whole historical package a paradigmatic quality, so that didacticism is raised to an absolute category. This has always been the case with standard postwar German accounts of the Third Reich and has been axiomatic for some time now with Stalinism. In fact, both paradigms were thrown competitively together at the time of the Historians Debate. This generated arguments whose pedantry became a little disturbing (which had the higher body count, which employed the more "pure" form of industrial mass-killing etc?) and whose historical insights might be doubted. The deeper problem here, however, is that once the absolute category is attained, the didactic message takes on an essentialist moral quality; it becomes estranged from the process of explanation, of cause and effect, and—above all—of comparison. In short, it ceases to be a historical activity in the normal narrative sense.

This was the dilemma liberal German historians got themselves into in the 1980s when, led by Habermas, they turned their guns on Ernst Nolte. But Nolte's sin was, epistemologically regarded, merely the standard practice of historiography. That is, he made comparisons between the holocaust and other acts of genocide, irrespective of whether they predated or postdated it. This is not only a legitimate historical activity, it is also expressive of an epistemological dichotomy intrinsic to the practice of history. Historical events, no matter how they are temporally framed, take meaning on a continuum whose poles are made up of the absolute unique and the absolute clone. The paradigmatic disposition leans to the former, while extreme relativism and a passion for topographies lead to the latter. But no historical event is unambivalently either. They are all to some degree different in their ontological status and find different places along the continuum and, moreover, being dynamic in respect of both their temporal character (time frames for historical periods are always a matter for argument) and in the meanings that are abstracted from this they can never—or should never—be said to have settled definitively at any one place. Ricoeur, I suggest, is dealing in similar concepts when he remarks that the rejection of a "covering model" (which is close to a paradigm) implies "a return to the conception of an event as unique." He remains, however, well aware of the danger of an absolute notion of the "unique," pointing out that what historians have in mind by this term is "that nothing exists *exactly* like their object of inquiry" and that the historical task remains to search "for those respects in which the events considered and their circumstances differ from those with which it would be natural to group them under one classificatory term."[29] But at the time of the Historians Debate, Left intellectuals, particularly those more inclined to philosophy than history, were determined to hold onto the Third Reich as a paradigm of evil. Convinced that Nolte was somehow writing off the past, they were crippled by the fear that "explanation" might so contextualize the period as to relativize it and thereby undercut its absolute moral authority and, further, compromise the psychic horror on which the liberal postwar German settlement had been successfully built. They may well have been good and genuine moralists, but they were bad historians. The same intellectual absolutism with respect to the Soviet model still produces similar dichotomies.

Working yet further backwards, this procedure also appears to be dubious in the hands of those who otherwise apply it in so blasé a fashion to the collapse of allegedly socialist societies. Retrospectively the world is seen to be explicable; pathbreaking individuals do indeed seem to carry the story forward in a positive sense. Cromwell is an heroic figure, laying down many of the contradictory premises that lead to the modern world, as though he were a progenitor of those structures that are later to constrict the excesses of "great men" such as himself. His crimes, his scarcely bashful employment of terror to defeat "his" counterrevolution, can be forgiven on Hegelian grounds. There is no use in complaining about the brutalities of world historical individuals. Even the peripheral whingeing of the Irish—who might *just* be thought to have cause for complaint—is ignored by liberals, just as that of the Kulaks was once ignored by Soviet apologists. This time the eggs and omelet aphorism is employed approvingly for, after all, the recipe is "now" seventeenth-century, embryonic capitalism. But the closer you get to the present, the more sentiment colors historical analysis and the more that analysis becomes inconsistently judgmental. In general, it appears domestic violence among our own tribe may be tolerated, but only as long as it is so distant as to lose all the customary connotations that close in upon us when we have a sense of its presence.

The various tensions that surround the conflicting—and possibly reconcilable—claims of subject and system have always found a powerful mode of expression in literature. But literature is hardly neutral in the matter. Rather in respect of the individual/collective dichotomy, it is inclined toward the former in that it privileges subject/character. It does not "need" to do so,[30] but given the difficulties of dramatizing large scale structures in a manner that relegates subjects to a secondary determined level, it is not surprising that, to name but one example, even the most unbending forms of socialist realism (celebrating heroic workers and the proletarian class etc.,) have given way to the drama of the individual. This will become a vital consideration when, in chapter 6, realism and Bertolt Brecht are employed to take the general argument into new territory. In the meantime one can readily see that the stage-play, clearly a very straightforward example, puts the subject as character before us in the most corporeal yet deeply ambivalent manner: actor versus role. The novel meanwhile is still the privileged expression for the aspirations of a bourgeoisie for whom life is a complex interactive struggle played out among individuals. In literature, destiny is dramatic, shaped, completed. It does indeed have an End and moreover one that is often happy, if not downright utopian.

But it is literature's stepchild—literary criticism—that has turned out to be one of the most creative areas of investigation into narrative and subject. Put simply, literary criticism has been driven by the conflicting claims of intrinsic and extrinsic epistemologies. Is the study of literary texts a hermeneutic activity contained, as with Northrop Frye (1957), within the parameters of literature itself so that criticism becomes a "pure" activity premised on genre-based concepts (pastoral poem, tragic play etc.,) largely unmediated and uncorrupted by the "alien" considerations of other disciplines? Or does the world outside the text, as all Marxists, Freudians, feminists, et al. claim, turn out to be the only credible topography where literature can find meaning and analysis can sensibly take place? If the second option is to be preferred—and it is—we are confronted by an interesting contradiction: the most radical analytical activities produced by literary criticism seem to have concentrated on texts in a manner more epistemologically pure than that of any traditionalist. Poststructuralism and deconstruction have made texts—and seemingly texts alone—the sole site of meaning. Given that the ' "author" has been, in some cases explicitly, written out of texts it is hardly possible to write about texts in a nonanthropomorphic manner. Texts generate more meanings than intended (by whom?), they axiomatically undercut at all times their own overt agendas, they collapse (as though suffering a psychic dissolution) into multifarious significations, and as chains of signifiers they inevitably link up with other such chains in a riot of propagation whose outcomes we can never predict.

To avoid misunderstandings, it is better to state now that I am highly sympathetic to, in one form or another, these theories, but not when they are unmediated by external considerations. The chief one is *competing* narratives, whose role in these pages cannot be overstated. But remaining with radical literary criticism, we need to return to the creation of subjects to appreciate, in the first instance, the value of critical theory. In placing the subject (in all "his" ambivalences) within the text as a contradictory and plural product *of* the text, modern critical analysis has shown itself able to generate a wide body of striking theoretical material. The problematizing of the subject drawn—above all by Lacan, from psychoanalysis—has been one of its most fruitful accomplishments. However, as it is assumed that texts dissolve in a plethora of self-generated, contradictory signification, a potentially antagonistic relationship is produced between meaning and narrative. The forms of radical interpretation preferred here will be those that in aesthetics hold onto not only the subject, no matter how deconstructed, but also the narrative nature of reality, no matter how overwhelmed by heterogeneity. Jameson has the Lacanian category of the "Symbolic" in mind when he writes that "'character' is that point in the narrative text at which the problem of the insertion of the subject into the Symbolic most acutely arises,"[31] but the general term of reference is to texts as a whole and Jameson, above all with respect to narrative, is taken to be right.

It is argued that no form of aesthetics that sacrifices narrative can be seriously productive when dealing with reality. Consequently, while Brechtian realism is favored in chapter 6, much radical feminist theory is treated as counterproductive in chapter 3. In short, poststructuralism functions here is a theoretical tool. Therefore accepting, for argument's sake, the Derridean axiom that there is nothing outside the text, the manner in which texts are flooded with "alien" signification is seen as producing a plurality. And this plurality is constitutive of multiple competing narratives. At this point, some illustration of narrative plurality in the wider historical context is desirable. The following remarks and the examples they give rise to are appropriately wide-ranging and, inevitably, arbitrarily chosen.

Things invariably happen noticeably slower or faster than anticipated. The moment of collapse, the sudden change of direction takes us by surprise. Thick concrete walls protected by armed guards in watchtowers

invariably look impregnable until we suddenly see the people they are supposed to intimidate dancing on top of them and spraying each other, and
the guards, with bubbly. Afterwards, we are illuminating at explaining
why it all had to happen at that point, how certain subterranean forces
came together to break the dam, compelling oligarchies to make shifts
hitherto regarded as axiomatically beyond them. And then, if we have still
not convinced ourselves, we can speculate on the role of "chance."

Chance would indeed be a fine thing. But too often the historian's task
seems, at least to him, to explain everything so that an interwoven pattern
is produced in which the whole explanatory fabric would unravel if a single
thread came loose. The empirical power of what incontestably *did* happen
makes speculation as to what otherwise might have happened (something
that will later crop up as "subjunctive action") merely a matter for intellectual play. Furthermore, the power of the explanation is measured in part
by just this ability to "explain what actually happened in all its concrete
details,"[32] so that the result is utterly coherent and no "anomalies" are left.
And when seduced by the power of seamless totality, the historian can
resemble another powerful thinker obsessed with the past. Freud's revela-
tory method was designed to explain everything, to make each piece in the
puzzle fit so neatly that the reader of his complex but *very singular* narratives
would take aesthetic pleasure from the illuminating manner in which the
overall picture emerged from the initial, confused collection of symbols,
words, and dreams. In this, Freud is a special case in respect of the continuum mentioned above in that he effects a remarkable synthesis between
its two poles: the paradigm and the clone. He, brilliantly, but fraudulently,
conflates both terms so that the absolutely unique individual history he
constructs for the patient is a perfect reflection of the grand collective paradigm in respect of all of *its* elements. The continuum becomes a circle.

There is a further consideration, already touched upon in the remarks
on historical paradigms, that takes us a step closer to plurality. The past
seldom sets us free. If we return to death again, we might consider the
nature of grief. Grief, not unreasonably, is assumed to be a type of suffering through which one has to work, so that it gradually diminishes
until it no longer emotionally cripples. Indeed, many sufferers feel uneasy
as they realize that they can forget the deceased for ever longer periods.
Nonetheless, there will always be times when the pain returns, and sometimes it comes back in a surprisingly fierce manner. History—as a grand
memory game—plays the same tricks on us but in a much more potent
and tenacious manner. The past may indeed be another country and no
doubt they do/did things differently there, but to what extent is it past?

When Germans talk about *working* through the past, their terminology is similar to when they talk about grief. They are well aware that the

naive notion, popular immediately after the end of the Third Reich, that all you needed to do was to put your head down, get to work, establish a manifestly successful law-abiding democratic state, simply did not/does not deliver in the manner hoped. Even over several generations, the connotations of the past do not gradually fade and then dissolve. Instead, periodically they return like an old rash in a new and virulent form. It is no accident that German intellectuals constantly turn to the notion of the "presence" of the past.

Above all, they have an odd relationship with their history. The crimes of the Third Reich have been deliberately fetishized so as to become a perverse moral paradigm employed to vindicate the virtues of the contemporary state. Therefore, Germans cannot escape in the manner of other peoples. Far from rejecting something such as Daniel Goldhagen's 1996 book that generalizes wildly and asks banally: "How could the Germans have been so cruel to those poor Jews?", many felt obliged to welcome both it and him. And while this is not the place to speculate on an Amfortas complex (i.e., the masochistic appeal of regular bleeding), it is appropriate to remark that German intellectuals treat William Faulkner's aphorism from *Requiem for a Nun*—"The past is never dead. It's not even the past"—as an axiom.[33]

The German case also indicates the dangers of allowing one narrative to monopolize the field. For in reality we live trapped in a multitude of stories. They predate us, form us, and generate the possibilities of our future(s). Reality is not something out there with which narrative, the necessary godchild of death, deals, or encounters or, even, shapes. Narrative is constitutive of reality, just as death in all its teleological absolutism, is constitutive of narrative. The world we inherit is in its pure ontological character a construct of dynamic competing stories. We do not simply enter those stories and do our best to comprehend and control them (but we do that too); rather we are the product of them, and every active moment of our lives is shaped by the failures and successes of this dynamic. Moreover, the stories we selectively attempt to foreground are forever skewered by demands and reinterpretations that we imagined had long since lost any immediate purchase.

In this context the two notions of morality mentioned above are pertinent. For instance, the superficial moral narrative, which is formed of strategies designed to realize deep-seated ethical principles, is often exposed as inadequate by the persistent presence of exactly those principles in the national ideology. Consider the history of black Americans. The Declaration of Independence trumpets principles as to "self-evident" truths that the Constitution with respect to "persons held to service or labor," violates. The 1863 emancipation and the thirteenth and fourteenth

amendments might then be seen as the victory of the former over the latter. Yet when one considers post Civil War history, it is clear that the self-
evident truths have not been adequately realized and the past has certainly
not gone away. Interestingly, it could be argued that the so-called original
sin of the American republic was not necessary, in that the Framers might
have refused to enable slavery ("bondage") in the Constitution, although
that would have been an extremely difficult option. However, the so-called
three-fifths clause and the explicit guarantee that the African slave trade
would continue until 1808 (at least), suggest that the alternative was an
implicit consideration.

A second example centers on a fundamental principle that was never
honored nor was it ever intended that it should be. It, too, involves the dominant narrative of a sovereign state and will give us some idea of how subtle
and varied the strategies of rewriting and narrative invention can be.

New Zealanders used to be brought up to believe that, despite all
the superficial anomalies between Maori and white New Zealanders
("Pakeha"), one country made up of one people had evolved. And indeed,
it once seemed that little spin-doctoring was needed to make something
unique out of their society. For while the statistics on education, health,
life expectancy, and so forth, showed discrepancies (to the detriment of
Maori), they were minor in respect of those societies with similar colonial
histories. However, it was exactly the naivete and vanity of the dominant
story that led to its deconstruction.

New Zealand history had always celebrated a founding document that
marked the moment it became part of the British Empire in 1840. This,
the Treaty of Waitangi, made grand, ambivalent, and highly simplistic
promises to the Maori. Had these promises been kept, colonization would
have been impossible. But throughout New Zealand history the text (dangerously curt) had been celebrated and read in the schoolroom. This had
always been an uncomfortable activity in that, while its unequaled high
ideological status was never in question, the fact that its three articles had
been literally ignored had to be admitted. The whole matter was abstracted
into the realm of symbolism, probably to avoid a serious encounter with
discrepancies so plainly extant. Nonetheless, given its high status it was
difficult to resist acknowledging the Treaty of Waitangi as a legally binding text. When this was finally done, the deeper ethical narrative could no
longer be avoided. It immediately shattered the popular ideology that the
facts of New Zealand's history had hitherto unproblematically—or so it
was believed—produced.

The elevation of the Treaty of Waitangi (now usually and tellingly
called just "The Treaty") into a legally binding and secular object with
the religious aura of something such as the Turin Shroud (a grand copy is

displayed in this fashion in New Zealand's national museum) has enabled a thorough unpicking and retelling of the New Zealand story. The sudden rending of the dominant *singular* narrative has not only forced most white New Zealanders to acknowledge the lies and delusions of the past, but also to call into question their own narratively formed notion of who they are. Furthermore, they find themselves trapped in a new and unpleasant story pejoratively called "The Treaty Industry," which has come about as restitution is made. But the matter is messy. There is, for instance, little evidence that the sudden transfer of large sums to Maori organizations (the Maori of course cannot have their country back) is having the intended result. New Zealanders may now be two peoples (if other Polynesians and recent Asian immigrants are left out of the equation) whether they like it or not, but the discrepancies in the figures for life expectancy, health, and so forth, have increased between many subgroups in the bicultural paradigm. Today the cry from growing numbers of both Maori and Pakeha is for "closure." They want this new and disruptive narrative brought under control. Above all they insist upon telos. The matter must have an end.

Elevating the Treaty of Waitangi to the sublime has had other instructive consequences. An indigenous narrative opposed to that of European colonization is now necessary. But it turns out that this has to be, largely, invented. If Maori are to claim that the fact of colonization was a disaster and to make normative inferences as a result, they are forced to fabricate a pre-European society as a superior, prelapsarian model of the sort that was, ironically, once popular among romantic European artists, as well as twentieth-century anthropologists of the Margaret Mead school. The Polynesian world and the noble savage (the adjective always makes something attractive out of the noun) would have (once again) to deliver the necessary normative underpinning. But for this to work the Maori apologist would have to account for the treatment of women in pre-European society, tribal warfare, slavery, and cannibalism...to say nothing of pre-Christian belief systems that Maori have long rejected. Above all, Maori find themselves caught in a dilemma in that they have no unmediated access to their own alleged heritage simply because they are themselves no longer Maori in the sense their ancestors were. For instance many, probably most, would not be able to talk to their ancestors should it be possible for them to meet. In this, the epistemological development between the past and the present is more radical for Maori than for Pakeha, who are not confronted by a violent shift from one narrative structure into an anachronistically alien Other. Thus, the Maori is painfully trapped in that he asserts a form of seemingly unimpeachable authenticity (he is, after all, the *first* New Zealander), but is unable to express that authenticity without corrupting it with the cultural values of the potent, contemporary world. And this occurs not simply because he lives in and understands that contemporary world, but also because his knowledge of the other world is weak and thus heavily dependent on fantasy.

As a result, many Maori activists find themselves inventing cultural identities that, paradoxically but logically, conform to the European notion of what such a pre-European society should culturally signify. The inventive strategies—some explicitly, and many implicitly, dishonest—employed to get around the narratively inherent problems are, at the very least, remarkable in their epistemological freedom. For instance, it is striking how useful kitsch has turned out to be. By trivializing New Zealand history, by reducing it to a mixture of fact and colorful fantasy (notably Maori myths), numerous intellectual elisions that erase fundamental dichotomies are possible. In this, the contradictions within both competing narratives (traditional and radical) are betrayed by a recourse to imaginative fiction that explicitly violates all empirical verities. And this now can be "enjoyed" in the country's national museum: "Te Papa."

If New Zealanders have had to give up the beneficent unambiguous story of their islands, this does not mean that dominant narratives are abandoned simply because they are infantile. The propaganda worth of such stories is often embedded in the delusions of peoples who have long and, they imagine, glorious histories. When during the Falklands War, Margaret Thatcher took to talking of "Our Island's Story" the schoolboy language alone made it clear that she was remarketing a singular retelling of history. Victory in the south Atlantic enabled a vulgar reductionism in national discourse and facilitated a great deal of ideological trash. On the other hand, serious efforts can be made to erase a narrative so radically that a whole people is written out of history. After all, the Palestinians were told by Golda Meir in 1969 that there were no such people but, if there were, she was one. Relevant here is the dreadful success of Israeli propaganda in this matter, at least in the West.

A last example will illustrate how malleable narrative is, no matter that propagandists want to make out of it an unambiguous interpretative tool. It concerns a successful rewrite born of a collective desire to hold on to a kitsch myth. Moreover, it was taken so far as to evoke a fake, lost utopia. It occurred in 1997 when Princess Diana died.

The crowds that gathered over several days for the funeral were trapped by both a deep sense of grief (loss) and a sense of shame. Doubtless they were not, for the most part, aware of the latter, which they probably subsumed into the former. However, it was implicit in their hatred of the press. Clearly the very masses that mourned the dead princess were the same masses that bought the tabloids and had followed in lascivious and vicarious detail the drama of her life, her love affairs, her private telephone conversations, and the state of her thighs. Above all, they had been preprogramed to enjoy the coming tragedies. They could, and did, look forward eagerly to a soap opera stamped by health problems, broken relationships and, if they got really lucky, drug abuse, and more suicide attempts.

Although the public's collusion in the matter was hypocritical, it had good grounds for deluding itself. The princess's television appearances, her tearful mini-collapses, had created a bond, which millions were convinced was entirely authentic. Her future suffering would be something they could take to heart while shaking their heads sadly. Diana's extravagant and arbitrary choice of a title ("Queen of Hearts") made it clear how well aware of this bonding she was. Surely no one else could have had recourse to such sentimental kitsch without becoming an immediate subject of mockery.

Whereas the end result of this drama was, inevitably, death, it was assumed to be a long way off. The shock of the actual death—out of narrative synch— must have evoked the most tremendous feelings of guilt. The processes of sublimation and displacement that followed bordered on the psychotic. The national crisis expressed in banks of flowers, grim silences, public weeping, attacks on Camilla Parker Bowles, above all the mammoth queuing in order to pour one's heart out at astonishing length in books of condolence, expressed a potent emotional indulgence that hid what must have been obvious to some but suppressed by most: namely they had colluded in the culture and praxis that had facilitated the fatal accident. In turning on the press and violating other, if lesser, taboos (e.g. attacking the royal family), they showed just how stunned by the early death they were and how unable, as a result, to face its implications.

The funeral was a remarkable event in that a mass act of self-delusion was engineered. The utopian moment of the fairy-tale wedding in 1981 was recovered, but this time as tragedy. The years in between were tolerated solely to give space to that tragedy. All of the negative facts and fantasies associated with the princess were blocked out and guilt feelings were repressed. This was largely accomplished by rewinding so that, in effect, the princess buried was the virginal icon of 16 years earlier (Elton John's "England's Rose") and when taken to her grave her hearse was drenched in flowers as though one were bidding farewell to an unsullied, teenage martyr/saint.

It may well be that this remarkable rewriting and rewinding to recover a benign story took added effect from modern media technology. Audiences today are skilled in handling multiple narratives because they are more au fait in playing with videos and tapes, and editing their own recordings. Narrative mixing of temporality that springs Ricoeur's model, together with the whole "back to the future" business, and so forth, is easily processed by them. I recall reading of a preview-showing of a Hollywood action movie in front of a young Californian audience who cried out "Fast forward! Fast forward!" during the love scenes. It reminds one of Ricoeur's misplaced fear that narrative in general is dying and that one can only hope that new forms will emerge. He allows himself a wistful sigh ("And yet...and yet"[34]). But this is much too defeatist. The fecundity of narrative forms and their epistemological necessity is not to be gainsaid. One is more likely to convince oneself of narrative's exhausted nature by inventing elaborate taxonomies of forms, or "covering models," or succumbing to grand theories of circularity, and then sorrowfully observing how they all do not, ultimately, measure up. But what has failed here is the forensic activity, not historical reality. The analysis of narrative as form(s) is, as with history, always caught in the solecism of employing structures to explain dynamics. It is the destiny of all topologies, no matter how elaborate, to fail. In this they also reflect an axiom of literary criticism. Creative artists will always break the taxonomic/genre rules sooner or later and in such a manner that the rules qua rules are shown to be debilitating. All models of history, which are formal and thus inevitably compelled to shift the narrative dynamic into the alien epistemology of diverse structures and patterns—quite possibly explained as grand cycles whose coming stories are thereby predictable—are caught in the same dilemma and end in a parallel failure. One can hardly infer from that that history does not happen, or that it will go away.

Nonetheless, there are powerful theories that either do not deal adequately with narrative or reject it, even though narrative theory can be produced from out of their contradictions. Postmodernism is an interesting case in that it maintains an odd relationship with narrative, playing with it when convenient and dispensing with it at will. Jean-François Lyotard is much concerned with the character of narrative games in opposition to scientific models, but the matter is kept within firm limits. He declares: "I define postmodern as incredulity toward meta-narratives."[35] Plurality is certainly being foregrounded by Lyotard, but only to undercut knowledge and meaning by flooding them with alternatives. Furthermore, given that plurality is a virtue in itself, no single alternative is invested with any more meaning, let alone truth claim, than any other. However, postmodernism now covers such a wide variety of disparate cultural discourses that to seek in it a coherent analytical basis is probably senseless. There is however one rich intellectual and theoretical seam that maintains a complex and shifting relationship with storytelling: feminism. And while this is the subject of chapter 3, it is sufficiently important to say something about it now.

There is a strong strand of hostility toward narrative as an explanatory category among feminists, in particular the leading French feminists of the 1970s and 1980s. Narrative is phallocentric, and in being written it privileges the male upstanding first "person" pronoun. It is claimed that: "Language does not merely name male superiority: it produces it."[36] The Woman—she really does need a capital "W" here—must not allow herself to be placed in such a discourse, for if she does she sacrifices ipso facto her deeper identity. *She* exists in an ontology of cycles, of seasons, and of moons. This is so sex and gender specific that the male is guilty of the grossest of solecisms if he thinks he can talk about it. Furthermore being essentialist, biologism cannot be avoided. And this produces the odd result that although feminists have been exceptionally skilled and original at unpicking the strategies whereby the woman is placed in, and distorted by, masculine discourse, the ontological distinction is so absolute and unbridgeable that the body—as, ironically, a Freudian first principle—remains the site of first (and last) authentication. Motherhood and "gynocritics" are productive of deeper levels of meaning than (inherently corrupted) phallocentrism. Even a feminist thinker as remarkable as Julia Kristeva, who distrusts the notion of an intrinsically "l'écriture féminine" ("nothing in women's past or present publications seems to allow us to affirm that there is a feminine writing"[37]), cannot avoid succumbing, in part, to the determining power of biology. Women's Time is formed by "cycles" and is "cosmic" in character, and one discerns "the eternal recurrence of a biological rhythm which conforms to that of nature."[38] However, it is striking and extremely pertinent to the argument of this book that Kristeva herself violates these "cosmic" parameters when she immediately afterward acknowledges what is always there but which notions of cycles and rhythms would like to dismiss as inconsequential. Women's time "rests on its own stumbling block, which is the stumbling block of death."[39]

Yet if the "pure" feminist position seems to demand—at least to narratively thrusting men possessed of what Irigaray calls a "violating penis"[40]—a type of mysterious exclusivity, this does not mean that dynamic language is impermissible. But it must be of a type that expresses the woman's experience of reality, which is to say the language of immediate excess. For Luce Irigaray, its expansive and erotic character could not be clearer given that: "Woman touches herself all the time, and moreover no one can forbid her to do so, for her genitals are formed of two lips in continuous contact."[41] Thus, the body necessarily becomes the site of ebullient signification at the expense of traditional discourse. Hélène Cixous claims that: "A woman's body with its thousand and one thresholds of ardor...will make the old single-grooved mother tongue reverberate with more than one language."[42] Thus, with the entry into the Lacanian Symbolic, texts will be generated that utterly reject the standard, that is to say male, language. And when the woman escapes from masculine discourse, identity, language, and body are collectively suffused. Then the "Woman" will "overflow" for she has "felt so full of luminous torrents that [she] could burst."[43] Moreover, her libido is "cosmic" (again) and "her unconscious is world-wide" and she is "spacious singing flesh."[44]

The use of the female singular in the above brief account is deliberate because it evokes a peculiar characteristic of the essentialist position. Women writers who foreground the Woman are inadvertently playing a phallocentric game. Men—especially male artists—are happy with the notion that the difficulties of gender identity and sexual life can be got round by turning women into a collective but homogeneous signifier. In this they are assisted by those feminist theorists who move easily from a celebration of knowledge sited in their *own* bodies to an unconditional understanding of sex and gender in general. The simplification of: "In woman, personal history blends together with the history of all women, as well as national and world history"[45] is highly attractive, both to those who are included in the definition and, perhaps more importantly, those who are not. This unproblematic notion of the Woman may be readily exploited by men who can define it according to the changing and wholly arbitrary requirements of their own self-interests. The Woman is then a diva, an odalisque, an idiot, and a whore. "She" functions rather nicely as Symbol. And is this not, at least in great part, the result of dispensing with narrative? If there are no stories where destiny is worked out, if multifarious dynamic reality is ditched, then what is there to play with but cycles and forms that sublimely reproduce, under their own internal dynamic, their own intrinsic self-evident axioms? Narrative reality then finds its enfeebled expression in the nebulous gush of a jejune notion of flux. The Woman is awash with signification, but heaven forbid that anyone should channel it into noncelebratory action external to the body or question the manner in which women attain a sublime unproblematic Singular that has about it the whiff of Stalinist megalomania, "she will bring about a mutation in human relations...in all praxis."[46]

Were I to characterize the last few paragraphs as partial, I would be guilty of mightily understating the case. The topography of the field today is so wide and varied that even a workable generalization is impossible except perhaps along the hardly useful lines of Maggie Humm's conclusion that "the cultural and political alignments and agendas...are far more plural and open...than any we have ever known."[47] But we should at least acknowledge the presence of those feminists who understood the determining role of material power. As Toril Moi notes, American feminists were never indifferent to the strategies of power, no matter how simplistic or "reflectionist" writers such as Kate Millett may seem today. More significantly we should not forget the degree to which Simone de Beauvoir unwaveringly tackled the material oppression of women. It is not surprising that in an interview in 1972, she says she is not impressed by the idea "that woman has special ties to the earth, the rhythm of the moon, to tides etc., that she has more soul... if there is something true in all that, it is not in terms of our nature, but of the conditions of our life." And "it is ridiculous and absurd... to think that the feminine body gives you a new vision of the world... it would be like constructing a counter-penis."[48] But she must be forgiven these observations—especially the latter—given that she had not (yet) read Irigaray.

But it is to discourse that we must return, not least because it is women's literature and its ambivalent relationship with narrative that is the chief interest of this polemic. The very notion of women's writing is contentious. Toril Moi, for instance, sees a danger that the terms "masculine" and "feminine" "themselves imprison us within a binary logic"[49] and Nina Baym asserts that "this powerful language is ours as much as it is men's."[50] Even the allegedly determining significance of the body and motherhood is open to doubt. Judith Kegan Gardiner is unhappy with a literature (she has Doris Lessing in mind) in which men fulfill their linear, goal oriented, and adventurous agenda (as always) and women "peddle along their natural cycles." And when she observes that: "According to this theory, empathy belongs to women, history to men," she returns us to the categories that are important here.[51] At which point we can postpone this topic until chapter 3.

Although there are forms that are antagonistically placed in respect of narrative, there are others that are suffused by it; none more so than sport. And this is the case whether we are talking about a participatory activity or something "passively" enjoyed. In fact I will attempt to show in chapter 6 that this "passivity" is false and that sport amounts to a highly complex narrative interaction. That it has a problematic but unusually fruitful relationship with narratives will be seen as kernel to its character. And, moreover, that relationship will be best appreciated when sport is coupled with aesthetics. This, in turn, will produce a clearer notion of realism. Above all, the confluence of terminology—the manner in which narrative, truth, history, aesthetics, and realism, spill over into each other—will mark out the messy terrain on which whatever normative conclusions subsequently produced will stand or sink.

In all of this there is a dichotomy that one might find, prime facie, troubling. It is the apparent discrepancy between narrative pluralism and telos. Although self-evidently focused and singular, telos is held to be essential. But, having a utopian character, it rarely attains empirical expression of itself. Nevertheless, narrative epistemologies are forced to posit a telos in order to vindicate both their hermeneutics and their, if any, interventionist programs. It is clear that Utopia is not likely to step fully costumed on to the stage. It is enough that the normative values it embodies be used as a yardstick by which to measure the success or otherwise of specific and conditional empirical actions. And this is to say that telos, despite its singularity, is paradoxically generative of a plurality of strategic actions designed to realize normative values embodied in the teleological paradigm. The success and failure of those strategic actions is the determining question. They must be subjected to time frames and judgment based on empirical reality and short term definable goals. In chapter 7, this will become a critical consideration. But in general, the manner in which normative values can be abstracted from telos is a matter for, above all, the last half of this book.

Therefore, all of what follows is an attempt to invest narrative with matters that, at first sight, seem alien to its nature. Death shapes it and vindicates both universalism and telos, which are in turn employed in a Kantian fashion to establish a common good (summum bonum) and infer a possible morality. Aesthetics, meanwhile, will turn out to be the extrinsic glue that binds these elements together. In fact, it is hoped it will turn out to be more than this. For even if it does not logically establish the desired values, it will, at the very least, heavily imply them.

If now we turn to Marxism it is, in part, to illustrate several of the binary pairings critical to the above: individual/collective, superficial morality/ deep-seated principles, dominant metahistory/narrative plurality, bloody insurrectionist action/utopian telos. However, Marxist humanism is not foregrounded to circumvent Marxism's abuses, but to underpin its core utopian element and, therefore, to underline its betrayal. Marxist humanism remains the most optimistic and subtle attempt to create a beneficent metanarrative. It is, moreover, one whose loss may be more than we can bear unless something similarly effective can be found to replace it. So if the past is not dead, Marxist humanism may yet have to attain its full normative form, and thereby to fully express its implied challenge to the present. Given that it evokes the grandest possible narrative in a context that throws together all the necessary antinomies that might explode it, it becomes the first step in tackling Narrative and Truth.

Chapter 2

Marxist Humanism
Hegel, Marx, Lukács, Eagleton, Habermas

Tackling the problem that arises in Marxism due to the (apparently) conflicting claims of the individual subject and the grand metatheory, Fredric Jameson writes: "The solution can only lie, it seems to me, in the renewal of Utopian thinking, of creative speculation as to the place of the subject at the other end of historical time, in a social order that has put behind it class organization...alienated labor and the implacable determinism of a historical logic beyond the control of humanity."[1] The categories and concepts evoked by this—individual and group, utopian idealism, grand historical parameters in which the subject is not reduced to a plaything, alienated and thus by implication nonalienated life—are the bread and salt of what is here called Marxist humanism. What follows is, in part, an attempt to establish Marxist humanism as a beneficial, superior, and ethically loaded expression of narrative understanding.

It may be unfortunate that the collapse of Marxism—premised on the collapse of the Soviet Imperial system—has instigated a new structuralism, but it is hardly inappropriate. In fact, it may well be more apposite than even the apologists of the present capitalist triumphalism appreciate.

The disreputable contemporary status of Marxism rests on a double critique: One, that it was immoral; and, two, that history has proved it false. Naturally, these two positions are usually maintained simultaneously and often so subsumed into each other that any distinction appears to dissolve. Furthermore, many people would be uncomfortable with the implied proposition that it is possible to be immoral and, within the broadest historical parameters, to be proved right, although that possibility is taken here as conceptually tenable. Nevertheless, in returning to Marxism it is clear that although morality and failure are not interdependent, let alone synonyms, Marxism's moral turpitude is invariably part of the argument, if not of the equation, when the nature of its historical failure, as manifest in the collapse and in many cases disintegration of the states that made up the Soviet bloc, are discussed.

However this double attack on Marxism produces a contradiction. The historical failure, premised on the notion of simply losing out, of succumbing to the incontrovertible judgment of history (a judgment that a Marxist more than anyone is obliged to accept), has bred a form of structuralist thinking, which presupposes that a socioeconomic system has now developed that has, as it were, not only seen into the soul of history—just as Marxism was thought to have once done—but has, moreover, transcended it as a category. It is not merely that capitalist democracy has solved the riddle of history and knows itself to be that solution, but that history itself has been drained of its customary content and significance. As a result the triumphant system is, unlike Marxism, not dependent on Narrative as a self-explanatory tool, with the proviso that it celebrates a privileged story that has led to the meaningful Fall, which is to say to the incontrovertible and dramatic defeat of its rival. Moreover, it makes no great epistemological claims for itself, aside from a single, necessary, and modest given (which is, appropriately, oceanic in its significance): that although the victorious system is by no means perfect and never will be, it is far and away the best option there is or ever will be. In economic terms, this means that while the gap between the poor and the rich gets bigger (which is to say injustices are by definition increasing) the poor are nevertheless getting less poor. It is a measure of the admirable honesty of its apologists, that this principle is called "trickle down": a term redolent with what once would have been called injustices. Indeed, the shift in "egalitarian" language is striking. This is particularly the case with once nominally socialist parties that feel compelled to redefine their identities as they adjust to the new hegemony. Watching young men looting designer clothes and laptops in August 2011 in Britain, one wondered if they, too, were not Tony Blair's "stakeholders." Unfairness is now essential, a point of purchase on which the system turns. Spin doctors duly make it electorally presentable by—what else?—calling it fair. It is now a synonym for "choice" and thus, under false colors, is incorporated into the humane language of conventional political discourse. Self-evidently this is a fairness denied to a substantial section of the population. Some time ago, New Labor in Britain based both its propaganda and its social policy, notably in respect of health care and education, on exactly such a conflation of the terms "fairness" and "choice."

Furthermore, the system is mysterious. Although it has taken on a lot of water since the banking crisis of 2008, the manner of its survival remains remarkable. We are told with undiluted confidence that there is no alternative. Once indeed we were encouraged to infer it was blessed with a consciousness, although George Soros now says bluntly: "That paradigm has proven to be false."[2] Nevertheless, there has been "a shift from an era in which the...national governments......sought to seize and exercise control over their economies to an era in which the ideas of competition, openness, privatization, and deregulation have captured world economic thinking."[3] Our task is to understand the market, lubricate it with tax cuts, and only use subsidies and tariffs when we want to screw Third World competitors who can produce food more cheaply than our own domestic farmers. This is an example of a general contradiction that will find other expressions in these pages: the normative values of internal democracy— such as they are—are knowingly violated in external affairs. Nevertheless, market apologists are keen to show that Marxism has been disproved by history—which is to say by the demonstrable failure of its own narrative— only to celebrate as victor a *system* that lies at odds with the very notion of history.

What is absent in this celebration of a system that now simply *is*, is a necessary role for morality. The normative category of truth has become, in the first instance, a perverse expression of history in that the victorious narrative is morally vindicated as right per se. In other words, it is Panglossian. Truth is nothing but a synonym for the victorious narrative itself. It brings nothing to it that it does not already possess. Thereafter the model is gradually unburdened of its narrative roots until it is declared a self-evident fact. To use language we will return to in chapter 6, it becomes naturalistic (as opposed to realist), in that it allegedly requires no dynamic validation. Only the given victory need be acknowledged as a self-evident virtue, implying, in the best determinist fashion, that history is not only axiomatically right but ipso facto impeccable. Therefore, if we are dealing with a sublime, structuralist market we have nothing further to worry about and quite possibly nothing fundamental to think about.

Ironically, under these conditions attacks on the wickedness of an extinct Marxism seem polemically inappropriate, an alien element smuggled into the debate by capitalist apologists simply to make us feel good about the way everything has turned out. That is, not only have we won, but the other lot were a pack of bastards *anyway*. Yet it is not the moral turpitude of the losers that in the last instance tells, or should tell: merely the losing and the winning. The celebration of the structuralist victory makes it clear that moral considerations are at best window dressing. In this manner we enjoy a triumph free from ethically based contemplation of the future (we will simply obey free-market principles in dealing with each "necessary" and thus healthy difficulty as it arises), while also remaining free to judge and condemn the past to whatever degree is convenient for us.

To what extent, then, is the end of history—which is packaged as history now explained to as great a degree as possible—the end of morality? It is axiomatic to the argument here that if discredited Marxism is to be revitalized, it can only be done if a moral core, loaded with real consequences for the conduct of events, can be established. This question leads us back to the most remarkable aspect of Marxism. This is not, as is customarily assumed, the iron laws of history and the riddle of social change "finally" explained, but an absolutely necessary core: namely a fundamental assumption as to the moral worth of the individual and the importance of his struggle to realize the full expression of all his talents.

This was not something that Marx and Engels got from Hegel. For notwithstanding all its abstractions, the Hegelian explanation of the metanarrative is mechanistic and breathtakingly free of moral conundrums—though not of inherent contradictions. In fact the new capitalist structuralism, for all its ahistorical character, has far more in common with Hegelian objectivity than does Marxism. It is exactly Hegelian rationality, that readiness to celebrate the empirically real by virtue of a grand idealist interpretation of history through which the "real" is made manifest, that capitalist triumphalism so closely mirrors. That Hegel is explicitly teleological hardly seems to matter. Surely it is not more fanciful to claim that the Prussian State is the highest manifestation of the Historic Spirit than to see in free-market capitalism all the great dichotomies of socioeconomic life reconciled. Both solve the riddle of history because both know that history is hell-bent on solutions and both are disposed to treat whatever happens as rational and thus desirable. And this is a disposition that is hardly likely to be diluted when it transpires that the judgment of history seems to be working in the interests of your state, or tribe, or stock exchange. The real intellectual challenge crops up when history has gone against you and you are not in so cowardly a frame of mind as to rationalize it away as though it were a faithless lover whom, if the truth were told, you never really cared for anyway. It is this task that now faces Marxists still holding onto the moral core of the philosophy—a core that their own "scientific" comrades, far more than any supposed enemies, renounced and betrayed in both theory and praxis.

True, it should be pointed out that Marx explicitly and even enthusiastically adopted the Hegelian notion of historical rationality. Moreover, he developed it into a more sophisticated explanatory tool by virtue, in the first instance, of upturning the causal link between materialism and idealism. After all, Marxist rationality neatly incorporates consciousness and culture as determined categories within the new materialist-historical parameters and happily promulgates further and more exact mechanistic laws, which manifest the rationality of the metasystem. How nice it is—and how *rational*—that societies only set themselves those problems they can solve, and that the ruling ideas of any time are the ideas of the ruling class. The only trouble with these formulations is that they are by no means true in the overweening positivist form in which they were first declared. Meanwhile, the desire to hold on to them has frequently generated jejune analyses of the social systems they purported to elucidate. And this leaves Marxists the task of picking up the pieces of a theory that has been invalidated by incontrovertible historical reality.

However, no matter how confident early Marxism may have sounded as it explained history to (at that time) an unequaled degree, it never (even in its earliest stages) lost contact with the ethical qualities and utopian core enshrined in the model of primitive communism and extant in the (romantic) image of proletarian nobility. Now, it may be argued that this is simply to misrepresent the development of the theory; that the ethical and utopian values of the early texts are merely a sentimental residue that was later dispatched by more rigorous and enlightened, or more narrow-minded and doctrinaire, thinking. For instance, as noted in chapter 1, Louis Althusser takes the former position and Peter Demetz the latter. I suggest a different interpretation. Rather than seeing the moral/utopian core fading and losing ground as the theory becomes more sophisticated and securely rooted in materialist thinking (or for that matter more wrong-headed and determinist), it is better to see it becoming a more potent, if usually implicit, reference point as the mechanistic explanations fail to deliver. Certainly it is clear that for many Marxists to resort to the early texts (although it must not be forgotten that the *1844 Manuscripts* were published late and the *Theses on Feuerbach* were found by Engels in an old notebook) is tantamount to an admission of failure. Instead, the problems thrown up by history were to be painfully shoehorned into what had become the standard, fully matured interpretation. But every time there was a major shift and a more sophisticated explanation of the interaction between social apparatuses was developed, whether it was Gramsci's use of common sense or Althusser's account of ideological overdetermination, the feel for the humanist values expressed in terms of a subject who is not simply a puppet of grand forces and whose longings are not merely reflex actions or the product of false consciousness, became ever a tad stronger. Better to assert that if Marxism is to recover itself and to function in the most modern form possible, it will have to return to first principles. And it is this moral and utopian root, and not the inversion whereby the deepest causal level is shown to be materialist and not idealist, that, surprisingly, most distinguishes the "Young-Hegelian" Marx from Hegel.

This link between the first paradigmatic Marxist model and a utopian/ narrative epistemology was touched on in chapter 1. However, the quote by Jameson at the beginning of this chapter reminds us of the paradigm at the end of the story—a paradigm that is supposed to initiate a richer history liberated from class warfare. The earlier paradigm of primitive communism reminds us how value-loaded the narrative we in fact experience as actors actually is. That paradigm has the character of a fable, a religious Eden, from which we morally fall, or from which we are banished when we discover that knowledge is bound up with private property and its expropriation. It is hardly surprising that so many Marxists pretended it did not exist, or that it was an expression of intellectual infantilism. And both paradigms have—as paradigms inevitably do—a static ahistorical quality. Thus, given Marxism's claim to be nothing less than *the* Theory of history, it is rather odd to be confronted by them. And if that were not bad enough, they are in their utopian dress so saturated with benign connotations that the whole notion of dialectical struggle seems foreign. It may be that the traditional discomfort they elicit has as much to do with the way they "feel," as with their alien epistemological status. They are so unpleasantly soft and warm. How *can* they be placed in the context of dialectical materialism, which feeds on exploitation and has confidently revealed the pitiless iron laws of social evolution? Certainly the benign picture of the historical subject they present seems far removed from Hegel.

From him we learn that man is not "free by nature" but only becomes so by the evolving manifestations of the utterly rational Objective Spirit. An assumed "state of nature...in which man is imagined in possession of his natural rights and the unlimited exercise and enjoyment of his freedom..." is "...not a historical fact." "Freedom as the *ideal* of the original state of nature does not *exist* as original and natural" and where "Primitive conditions can be found...they are marked by brute passions and acts of violence."[4]

Hegel is not in the Rousseauesque (and Marxist) camp. He is, at least in part, Hobbesian. And, as we will see in chapter 4, the Freudian narrative proceeds from much the same pessimistic premise. In fact Hegel anticipates the Freudian causal link between repression, or "suppression," and the creation of "thought," "knowledge," and "art and religion."[5] The fascist narrative is similar, although it not only proceeds from Hobbesian (or Hegelian) premises; it does not want to escape them. Struggle and battle remain ennobling constants until most of humanity has been turned into slaves at the service of the *Übermenschen*. Marxism, however, cannot escape its optimistic teleology, not because of the iron laws of material history based on the mysterious wonder of the dialectic—these are merely hopeful, albeit brilliantly formulated, second level explanatory structures—but because it is grounded in a notion of the human individual morally refulgent and, moreover, pregnant with further potential; potential, which while materially productive, is fundamentally normative in character. And in the end Marxism will return us collectively, greatly enriched, to the first unproblematic paradigm. For fully developed Communism "...equals humanism...it is the *genuine* resolution of the conflict between men and nature and between men and men."[6]

A further consideration, which encourages us to see Marxism as ethical in nature, is the manner in which, in comparison to Hegel, the individual is treated. Marxism cannot dismiss the individual, even when he is intellectually imprisoned by false consciousness—a catchall that blithely explains away the actions of *any* member of the class of history who has not cottoned on to where he in fact stands in the general run of events. Marx knows that everyone can be saved, that a dialectical development can give sight to the blind, and turn every man into an artist, and bring us all to the point where the divisions between any kind of work and every kind of creativity no longer exist. As we will see in chapter 6, there is an important expression of this in Brecht's Teaching Plays, not least because Brecht does not avoid its revolutionary and violent premise.

All of this implies that everyone strives— in the first instance without knowing it—toward the famous apotheosis in *The German Ideology*. This is surely a nineteenth-century version of renaissance man made universal in that specialization is transcended. It foregrounds the ethical, whole man, as opposed to the piecework laborer. For, in a "...communist society nobody has one exclusive sphere of activity but each can become accomplished in any branch he wishes ...."[7] As one commentator remarks, this is taken to mean that, because we will all paint, "...the status of 'painter' is not assumed even from time to time."[8] Here is the moral core again, but now explicitly defined in terms of the subject of history as an individual "developing in an all-round fashion,"[9] namely someone who works (i.e., creates), which is to say he hunts in the morning, fishes in the afternoon and then, having reared cattle in the evening, does criticism *after dinner*...well, there have to be priorities.[10] Perhaps in passing it is worthwhile acknowledging that this poetic image of the complete Marxist man has inevitably evoked, directly or otherwise, a good deal of irony. My own favorite is from the Boulting Brothers' 1959 film *I'm all right Jack* where Peter Sellers, as the pro-Soviet obstructionist trade union secretary Fred Kite is asked by Ian Carmichael's upper class twit, Stanley Windrush, whether he has in fact ever been to the Soviet Union. Sellers's answer is something like: "No I haven't lad. But it must be bloody wonderful... cutting the grain in the day and the ballet in the evening."

However, we are not limited to taking the piss when it comes to the flagrant romanticism of this formulation of the communist ideal. If we triumph over the naivete of the portrait painted for us in *The German Ideology*, we might readily see that something like this paradigm is necessary if any positive, as opposed to fascist, moral core whatsoever is to be posited, irrespective of how the language employed might date. It need not be seen as lying outside the parameters of rigorous philosophical thought either. Kant's moral law, the categorical imperative that asserts the fundamental maxim that one may only will that which can be willed universally, leads to similar values. Thomas Auxter, who takes a less hardwired approach than is customary to Kant's apparently ateleological notion of duty or obligation, sees this as unavoidable. Establishing that Kant in fact possessed a "moral teleology" (not least because Kant himself says so in *The Critique of Judgement*[11]), he shows that the deontological principle—the axiom that duty places the emphasis on intentions rather than on consequences—is obliged nonetheless to take into account outcomes to the degree that a model of an ideal community inevitably comes into play. That is, Kant's argument is saturated by the consequences of a "moral teleology," so that the question of what that telos *is* can only be circumvented by a deontology so "rigorous" that it makes nonsense of the Kantian argument itself. This is chiefly because in Kant's *moral teleology* both terms are so intertwined that neither can be independently sacrificed. Likewise determining, in respect to the question of what kind of morally grounded society Kant has in mind, are the linked categories of universalism and the rational: "Insofar as humans are rational they will the same universal order in which the absolute value of every rational being is recognized,"[12] which is to say that the universalist principle means that the communal ideal must be a harmonious one.[13]

Although the consequences of Kant's teleology, above all with respect to aesthetics as a normative category, are dealt with in chapter 5, one notes here the germ of an ontology that in celebrating rationality, an innate drive toward universalism, and the collective interconnectedness of human beings, later finds expression in intersubjectivity and Habermasian discourse ethics. This is not the place to pursue this theme—Habermas will crop up later in this chapter—but it should be acknowledged now that the romantic *ideal* of Marxist humanism is not foreign to Kant's rigorous critique of the utilitarian values of Reason and Judgment. In particular, one notes his definition of essential ends as "the ends which are at the same time duties" in that they are "one's own perfection and the happiness of others."[14] This leads Auxter, who is not explicitly pursuing a Marxist agenda, to a parallel definition that recalls the communist paradigm of *The German Ideology*. It is an interwoven community "... in which each side of the personality is valued and brought into accord with the others."[15] Hegel, however, doesn't bother with anything as benign as this nor is Hegel's chief historical agent the most populous class working out its own higher con- sciousness as a means of liberating us all. It is arguably the World Historical Individuals pushing forward the Absolute Spirit by the bloody sacrifice of unimportant men and women, whose seemingly legitimate complaints as they fall under the chariot wheels of history are in fact inadmissible. The World Historical Individuals "stand outside of morality" and the "litany of the private virtues of modesty, humility, love, and charity must not be raised against them." In fact "world history (if it wanted to) could *on prin- ciple* altogether ignore the sphere of morality..."[16] The irony lies in that Marxism, while mechanistically based on class and driven by a dialectic dependent on the exploitation of groups of men and women, accords every- one *moral* worth, offers salvation to every man because—to use language that would appall a scientific Marxist—anthropomorphic History, if not God, loves him and longs to set him free.

And it is this dichotomy between the moral status of the subject and the explanatory, dynamic function of class struggle that has generated so much debate. "Scientific" Marxists have striven to preserve the objective, uncon- taminated character of the metanarrative, its closed explanatory "total- ity." Dowling may call it a "providential fable"[17] but it is exactly this that scientific Marxists reject. For history "...does not have a Subject...but a *motor*...the class struggle."[18] Meanwhile even the most subtle Marxist cultural critics feel the need to proclaim their echt, materialist credentials. One can always find, as was noted in chapter 1, flourishes to the effect that the notion of alienation, attractive to Marxist moralists, and danger- ous to Marxist positivists because it is meaningless unless there is a subject who has a nature from which he can be alienated, is as nothing when put alongside the *mechanisms* whereby surplus value is "extracted" from labor power.

It is striking how great the fear of the subject is. As soon as he is allowed into the equation on his own terms, the explanatory structure collapses and with it the intellectual credibility of the thinker who has, allegedly, moved beyond humanism (and subjectivity) to objectivity. All so-called scientific thinking in the *social* sciences shares, in one form or another, this desire to land on the firm terrain of explicable objectivity, along with an attendant fear of slipping back into the sump of subject-based sentimental- ity. Althusser is very alive to this danger. Marx became a "scientist" after 1845 whereupon "...man as the 'subject' of history disappears." Moreover: "Society is not composed of individuals."[19] His determination in the matter is palpable: "I'm sorry: I will not give way on this point."[20] He is not the only one. An odd example is Georg Lukács.

Lukács's initial, highly theorized attempt to avoid the dangers of the subject and ground the grand narrative in inescapable iron laws was among the most striking partly because, while utterly dialectic, it was the least materialist. For him the system is all, it is well-nigh sublime, and its key characteristic is Hegelian "totality." Engels asserts that history takes place in the "actual struggles in the brains of the combatants,"[21] but for Lukács, this is a collective proletarian brain. He invents a metadevelopment forcing a particular class, by virtue of the dialectic drive, to an unprecedented level of wisdom and therewith to the salvation of the world. And this cannot be dismissed as a nonmechanistic process simply because it accords priority to the development of consciousness and not economics. For Marx did not give Hegel "a materialist twist" as it were, rather it is: "The category of totality, the all-pervasive supremacy of the whole over the parts [which] is the essence of the method which Marx took over from Hegel and brilliantly transformed into the foundations of a new *science.*"[22] What is striking in the Lukácsian account is that it dogs classic materialist Marxism, giving an idealist twist to every step: "When the Communist Manifesto makes the point that the bourgeoisie produces its own gravediggers this is valid ideologically as well as economically."[23]

Although it is true that the complicated explanatory process of reification that Lukács employs allows for human agency, it is a crude, even misleading, notion of agency. It has nothing to do with the individual, while the proletarian collective that stands in its place as the agent of everything positive has a purely evolutionary function and a determinist character. Whereas Lenin in *What is to be Done?* had insisted repeatedly that it is the duty of the intellectual to improve the theoretical understanding of the proletariat (for the intellectual to do *his* job), in Lukács the proletariat is the predestined tool of history and does not need extrinsic Leninist instruction. Moreover, the development of its covert collective understanding—conscious understanding only comes at the end of the historical process—is placed within a dialectical model, which is at least as mechanistically based as the materialist account that it so carefully apes. In this Lukács, just like today's triumphant capitalists, realizes the Hegelian observation noted above, that one could *on principle* talk about history without morality. Above all, one notes that when Lukács explains how greater economic production deepens the process of reification (a process that affects both bourgeoisie and proletariat but from which only the proletariat can learn) he employs the classic terminology of the scientific Marxist. Thus, it is the *motor* of class interests that ultimately cripples the bourgeoisie while sublimely driving the proletariat, partly through welcome setbacks and further exploitation, to a level of consciousness that will allow it to become the universalizing subject of history.

Among the dilemmas that Lukács's intervention into Marxism and history generates—the Leninists were so angry he returned to Marxism and literature—is the hoary chestnut of the role of the bourgeois intellectual. *History and Class Consciousness* may well, in effect, declare this dichotomy to be a chimera, but it cannot explain how it is that the bourgeois intellectual Lukács not only understands this, but *knows* he understands it. There is no dilemma with Marx, Engels, and Lenin, who are fully at home in the role of pedagogues. But Lukács should have had a problem teaching the working class something that it, and not he, was actually learning day by day. Ironically, it is his brilliance as an intellectual that leads us inexorably to the conclusion that as an intellectual he is utterly redundant. Put another way, one notices that his indifference, even hostility, to the subject forces him to "solve" the tensions between the binary pair of subject and collective by dissolving the former entirely into the latter. But there is a double irony here. Lukács factors himself, as subject, out of the idealist historical narrative, and then reverse somersaults when he returns to literature, praising stories that foreground unique ("flesh and blood") individuals.

It is only now, following the collapse of nominally Marxist states, that we can best appreciate what was lost when the humanist ideal was sacrificed to various forms of scientism. How dialectically appropriate it is that in the rubble of the empirical failure, the rust of the noncompetitive factories and all the rest, the normative core has not only survived but has seldom seemed more relevant. Moreover, in contradistinction to the messy materialist terrain, it survives impeccably partly because, as the ontological antithesis of materialism, it feeds off the categorical difference between the two, and partly because ethical values are exceptionally difficult to sustain in an argument unless they can be taken to assert (Kantian) universal axioms. Thus, the notion of a Marxist society implying an optimistic ideal of human nature and resting upon the model of the self-fulfilled individual is the paradoxical but potent residue of the failure of Marxist regimes to reach exactly that goal by liberating their citizens through the public appropriation of the means of production. This has happened in part because liberal capitalism's (ahistorical) celebration of its (historical) victory has left a gap. For in its purest form capitalism does not generate deep-seated ethical arguments because it does not need to. After all it has no goal, it is not going anywhere that is not a quantitative rather than a qualitative extension of present productivity and the attendant inequitable distribution of wealth. It does not imagine any substantive intrinsic moral improvement among the citizenry and, in any case, needs a notion of benevolent greed/competitiveness to engineer growth. A morally virtuous model of the human being would be the death of capitalism. It is just as indifferent to the sufferings of the spear-carriers of history as Hegel, although it is probably only at extreme times (hurricane Katrina, say) when this becomes apparent domestically. Even so, such disasters can be window dressed so as to fudge their greater significance for the wider society. As a result, moral probity does not need to be inferred or projected forward. Rather it is blatantly extant in present societies. The necessary laws, mechanisms, duties are imagined to be, to all intents and purposes, already set on the deepest level that it is rational for capitalism to bother with. The problems that arise are secondary and technical, and are to be solved with fine-tuning. Therefore, it is hardly surprising that in exploiting as effectively as possible the gap produced by capitalism's moral indifference, (reconstructed) Marxists might well choose to "regress" to that notion of an idealized ethical core that scientific Marxism exposed as essentialist and redundant.

Terry Eagleton, who is deeply concerned with the contemporary validity of Marxism (his latest book [2011] is *Why Marx Was Right*), no longer tells us that its greatest revelations are to be found in the economic or "scientific" texts. The appropriation of the surplus value of labor now gives way to the *1844 Manuscripts*. Early texts, once dismissed as immature steps on the road to a substantive theory of economic and social life, which itself would transcend those early texts, are now dominant because they embody—and they most certainly *do* embody—respect for the sensuous reality of the lives of men and women. Moreover, Eagleton wants to go as far as possible and put what is essentially a religious norm—hitherto treated with contempt by every dialectical materialist keen to put as much clear water as possible between himself and metaphysics—back into the heart of the theory. We are dealing now with spiritual values. So where once "non-scientific," or humanist Marxists found the moral core in aesthetics, they are now to find it in the hardly unrelated notion of spiritual fulfillment, in "flourishing" (a key word in *After Theory* [2003] and one that recalls the paradigm of the self-fulfilled individual found in the *German Ideology*), in Aristotle's *Nicomachean Ethics* and in the *Book of Isaiah*. Universal values, grand narratives, essentialism, God are back on the agenda. The book's title, moreover, is adroitly ambivalent in that we may be "after" theory in that we have moved beyond it. Or perhaps we are still in pursuit of it. If the former interpretation suggests a general sense of frustration with the profligate history of "Theory" during the last decades, the latter implies the recapture of the spiritual values that we should not have let get away. The Marxist materialist purist (the connotations of the terminology are joyfully messy) must be appalled. What on earth is leftover of the grand theory?

Probably nothing, or little, in respect of Marxist scientism. That need not matter. After all, was not the trouble with Marxists that they always wanted to *be* Marxists? They were crusaders armed with an explanatory model that delivered on every level from the most trivial and contingently ideological to the allegedly all-determining materialist. Marxism gave you the lot. Moreover—and more importantly—in being a theory of causation and thus able to guide action and foresee consequences, it was also able to defend its status as a comprehensive and discrete metatheory. In short, it was in possession of intellectual crown jewels that placed every other theory of history under its explanatory umbrella. And if pressed even the Marxist humanist had, at the last, to talk of class struggle, the surplus value of labor, productivity, and the contingent nature of the ideological, if he did not want to come across as just another well-meaning new world mystic. If these were given up or—worse—shown to be so corrupted as to be no longer tenable, then baby and bathwater both were down the plughole of history. In this context, the return to the Paris Manuscripts looks like a shift designed to change the material of Marxism while allowing one to keep the title with all its many-sided connotations; although, they are now connotations for which one is no longer prepared to go to the wall.

Perhaps these are trivial considerations; mere questions of style. Perhaps they are to be enjoyed merely for the irony whereby the famous camera obscura that Marx used to get Hegel the right way up has now to be employed by Marxist humanists to set Marx back on his feet. Although it should be acknowledged that in putting the slide the other way up in the projector one is not returning to the amoralism found in Hegel's *Reason in History*. Instead one is returning to what *seems* like a form of idealism in order to get moral questions back into the heart of things. It is capitalism's present structuralist reification, which is the true expression of (ahistorical) amoralism.

Still, however tolerantly we may dismiss the charge of intellectual inconsistency when Marxism's failure is accommodated by turning the theory around to hold onto it—most of the criticism is probably only a form of tarted up *Schadenfreude* in any case—it is worthwhile posing the question of how things got to this state. For we are not talking chiefly about the collapse of the Soviet Empire, although it is a little disturbing just how many Marxists, who were *never* passionate Soviet apologists, saw in its disintegration proof positive that the game was up. It is something of a puzzle that left-wing theorists, who were adept at shifting the parameters of their theoretical work to accommodate whatever surfaced and who, by and large, dismissed as simplistic the Popperian criticism that they were always avoiding any criteria that might prove them wrong, should so dramatically bottle out at the collapse of the Soviet system. Perhaps here there is a further irony. The dialectical materialists proved themselves wholly materialist after all. Such a colossal event—although the Soviet Union had long since ceased to have any theoretical relevance for them—was so powerful that it somehow flooded back into the sphere of intellectual struggle and overwhelmed it. It simply could not be ignored and if there was to be a reaction, it would have to be correspondingly seismic. Was this particular narrative so potent that Western Communist parties were forced to fold up their tents and sneak away in the night, leaving a note behind saying that after all nobody's perfect and we all make mistakes? Certainly the subsequent capitulation paradoxically enabled the disintegration of theory in general in that it sank under the unconstrained theoretical profligacy that followed. As a result Grand Theories have become intellectually discredited; the bête noire of postmodernists.

However, there was a time when left-wing theory, at its broadest, was going somewhere. Moreover, the teleology of everything that Marx and Engels had set in motion gradually became clearer and more striking in intellectual—that is to say, theoretical—terms largely because the actual histories of Western capitalist societies increasingly failed to confirm everything the teleology implied. Indeed, it became one of the functions of the theoreticians to somehow explain that dichotomy while not letting go of the crown jewels. Althusser, giving us a "scientific" explanation for the power of (false) ideology as a function of apparatuses and Gramsci doing much the same with hegemony, were not only original and insightful, but they also had the status of high-class rationalists accounting for what had happened but should not have... and vice versa. Yet despite—or perhaps because of—their brilliance, they inevitably left themselves open to the Popperian charge that they had moved the goalposts to avoid a proper scientific test of Marxism's intellectual probity.

Nonetheless, theory motored on. The continual supply of books and essays trumpeted its advance. Each generation was dealing with the aporias thrown up by the previous one. The very terminology, the historically arrogant—worse, complacent—use of the term modernism and then the prefix "post" implying the "next" step, declared that progress was what it was all about. It was not just history that was "Whig"; the theory itself was getting better and going further. It is the collapse of this that is most striking and, not surprisingly, most worrying to someone such as Terry Eagleton who does not see the need to move on as tantamount to moving out of the broader Marxist theoretical framework. And has not the plethora of publications together with the determination to progress ever onwards led to a mentality that is terrified of not keeping up, of being left behind? Ultimately this breeds a belief that going *anywhere new* is better than staying put—a belief, and fear, that lies behind a great deal of postmodernism. But whatever Eagleton's criticisms of the plethora and disintegration of theory amount to, they do not constitute an argument that theory itself can be ditched. Far from it. He declares that it remains "indispensable."

The collapse and disintegration of left-wing theory has been more the result of its uncontrolled fecundity than its intellectual shortcomings. It has been impossible to hold onto a set of fundamental axioms that would have allowed a coherent and consistent left-wing analysis. Cultural Studies degrees once attempted to integrate a range of concepts. The goal was to synthesize, not disintegrate. Now they are like supermarkets. The students shop among the shelves and pop into their trolleys whatever takes their fancy; and "fancy" is what intellectual imagination has now degenerated into. Deep-seated first principles, bold syntheses are off the menu. Essentialism, privileged explanation, moral judgments are all now arrogant forms of domination. The supermarket or the shopping mall is assuredly the symbolic library of the postmodernist, and naturally only an elitist would look down his nose at this.

There is a further, wholly fitting, characteristic of postmodernism that seems to escape many of its apologists: it perfectly embodies the degeneracy it supposedly attacks. As a theoretical position it is a mess. Its willful character, its ability to spill over into anything and everything, its wholly arbitrary and unstable collection of bits and pieces, make dubious the proposition that there is something called postmodernism about which—as here—it is sensible to talk. It is no more coherent to talk about postmodernism within its own parameters than it is to claim that the term "shopping" means that on principle everyone arrives at the checkout with the same selection of articles, irrespective of what, in fact, is in their trolleys. In its chaotic practices and in its taste for changing fashion, it celebrates as a "theory" the collapse of coherent theory. It is the amorphous and unstable progeny of theory gone wild, and it is driven by its own vanity into an infinite *reductio ad absurdum* as the validity of any subjective interest shifts unproblematically into the validity of any other. The very notion of a grand explanatory story is anathema. Instead we are told to "...maximize as much as possible the multiplication of small narratives."[24] There is a clear parallel in contemporary fine arts, where any artist who calls himself a "postmodernist" can throw together an arbitrary collection of objects (usually personal detritus) and call it an "installation." Both terms (postmodernism and installation) function as fig leaves allegedly giving intellectual weight to otherwise theoretically void and nakedly unmediated subjective propositions.

Reacting to this dismissively—as here—gives good cause to return to the resuscitated notion of Marxist spirituality as found in the early texts.

Moreover, there is a further vital consideration; one that will couple that spirituality with something unambiguously corporeal. Some paragraphs back, in the context of the early Marxist texts I wrote of "what *seems* like a form of idealism." That was not entirely fair. The "seems" was a rhetorical swindle. Although Marx took the notion of alienation from Hegel,[25] it assumes a clear *materialist* form in the *Economic and Philosophic Manuscripts of 1844*. For instance, the worker is alienated from his tools and from the objects he produces, as well as from himself and, most tellingly, from his comrades. The two latter examples might imply a type of idealism. To be alienated from oneself and from others sounds like a classic expression of emotional and psychic dislocation. However, there is one consideration that that gives the lie to this and takes us back unambiguously to a self-evident materialist category: the body.

The early texts are saturated by the sensuous. Whatever their Hegelian origins they are fundamentally "material" in tone and character. Certainly the use of "sensuousness" is bold and violates strict parameters, but its grounding in the body is not open to doubt. And if we can accept (as we should) an elision between the categories of the senses and of human essentialism so that each dissolves into the other, we will find ourselves obliged to consider a synthesis between the spiritual and the sensual. Marx writes that "... not only the five senses but also *the so-called* mental senses—the practical senses (will, love etc.)—in a word, human sense—the humanness of the senses—comes to me by virtue... of humanized nature .... [and therefore the]... forming of the five senses is a labor of the entire history of the world down to the present..."[26] Here is a way of thinking that liberates the historically contingent, materialist and idealist positions so that each can take full advantage of the mediating power of the other.

Love and everything else explicitly proclaimed in these early texts of Marx are the fundamentals of Marxism humanism. Foolish they may be to some, arguably mere incipient first stumblings to others, but they are hardly unorthodox in the context of the grand theory. Moreover, it will take fierce and bloody surgery to get rid of them, as Althusser, wielding the cleaver and insisting that he would not be deflected, clearly realized. Yet more disturbing, if that surgery is accomplished in as much as it is *deemed* a success, it will have handed—unintentionally—a colossal rationalization for butchery on the mass level. The triumph of scientific determinism provides the theoretical underpinning for the unambiguous evaluation of the sins of individuals who have neglected to do their historic duty by failing to rise to the necessary level of class-based consciousness and obedience. And as much as this book is, in part, an argument for a privileged form of Marxist humanism, it may seem reasonable to regret that those Marxists concerned with normative values did not suggest somewhat earlier that it might be the economic determinists and "scientific" dialectical materialists who have thrown out the baby with the bathwater.

At this point it should be noted that the celebration of the body in the early Marxist texts is not paralleled by the corporeal essentialism of the feminist position mentioned in the first chapter. Marxism is theoretically richer than that particular polemic, which moves from the woman's unmediated experience of her own body as an unrestrained oceanic trope, to the claim that meaning (largely framed in terms of physical pleasure or "jouissance") can be directly inferred from this exclusive fount. For instance, in many of the feminist essentialist texts, there is no historical framework for the female body qua body. It is nature's beneficent gift unmediated by the changing social and political roles of women, however important they may otherwise be regarded, nor does it really need to be theorized. It is basically there to be enjoyed. But Marx turns to the body and sensuousness to engage with evolution, with change, and this finds expression in the notion of the spiritual nature of man as a *social* animal. Irigaray and Cixous however, are often so fixated on the flesh that they transcend it in a surprisingly ethereal manner. It (the singular female body) can hardly be grounded anywhere, and as it assumes an absolute category by virtue of being universal to women, the polemic in its praise starts to read, paradoxically, like a form of idealism. However much the individual may "sing" of her own subjective polymorphous pleasures, she defines herself—and them—in universalist nonsubjective terms. This much shapeless physicality cannot be contained intellectually within the form from which it supposedly takes meaning. It is so undifferentiated that it attains the status of the meaningless, of the unreal, and uncouples itself as Idea from the purely empirical, corporeal material that gave it birth. As a result, it can only take on the character of its dialectical opposite. The body celebrated by Cixous and Irigaray is a pure category, an abstract platonic Ideal.

Returning to the social, one notes that the sensuality Marx foregrounds in the early texts is seldom restricted to the individual. A crude materialist approach, one that unambiguously began with first principles, might well begin with the body as the singular subject, but such a subject would, in the Marxist context, soon emerge as banal, going nowhere. In passing we should note that, alongside various feminists, it will be Freud who will seem to take us back to the body in essentialist terms, but that he too will feel, ultimately, compelled to make the most far-reaching social/species claims for the individual—claims that precede, with unlimited consequences, the moment of birth. Like Freud, Marx has much to say about "species being," and it is the unambiguous argument of the early texts that the notion of sensuous life can only find meaningful expression in the community. The social is then treated as a category that, by definition, transcends any initial subjectively based essentialism. To return to a passage already partly quoted: Communism is "the real appropriation of the human essence by and for man . . . [is] therefore . . . the complete return of man to himself as a social (i.e. human) being—a return become conscious, and accomplished within the entire wealth of previous development." And this is explicitly what Marx means when he declares that "communism equals humanism."[27] Alienation/estrangement is thus transcended as man becomes "human," which is to say he becomes "social." The two terms are buckled together unambiguously in the *1844 Manuscripts*.

However, if we are determined that the dual concepts (subject and social) are not to be uncoupled but must retain their dialectical interdependence, we are likely to find ourselves on difficult terrain when we consider these would-be unproblematic resolutions in the historical and narrative terms evoked by Marxist humanism. The place of the subject is certainly in the social, but the status of the latter is wholly expressed in the enriched (social) life enjoyed by the former who does not in any way lose his individual identity. He remains the *ultimate* (utopian) site on which the emancipatory theory has to deliver in praxis. Thus to sacrifice, on the basis of moral arguments, the individual must be to wager a great deal of the moral credit of Marxist humanist theory itself. It is this problem, which overtly evokes and colors all the most pressing and intractable dilemmas of (social) human existence, that, for instance Brecht, tackled on a highly sophisticated level in the Teaching Plays and which, ironically, gave his critics opportunity to denounce him as a Stalinist apologist. And it is the dilemma elicited by the same problem that has led many former left-wing thinkers to desert Marxist revolutionary praxis for a form of nervous incrementalism in respect of both "utopian" thinking and social change, on the grounds that the sacrifice of the individual leads too readily to the sacrifice of the mass and thus the burden of revolutionary action is not to be borne.

But while we might claim for argument's sake that "ideally" there is no tension between the subject and the social and that they exist happily blended into each other under the rubric of Marxist philosophy, they surely lead to inherently contradictory notions of theory and praxis. For these key categories evoke a utopian goal that is, in all its manifold untroubled reconciliations, unattainable in commonsense terms. Does anyone believe that the Eden enshrined in *The German Ideology* is a reachable goal, even within the most generous time frame? But while the function of this "goal" is clearly normative, its context is narrative. This uncomfortable state of affairs shifts the balance from goal to methods. And it is this that encourages Marxists—as the Popperians claim—to perpetrate all too realizable, brutal short-term measures ostensibly to reach unattainable long-term ends. The Marxist humanist must, on the other hand, maintain that as he never loses sight of the paradigmatic goal, he can legitimately practice a form of radical, that is to say on occasions bloody, action, which the incrementalist, in his turn, cannot entertain and which the capitalist, in his, cannot desire, at least not in the domestic context. In short, the normative value in the theory, no matter that it appears sensuously and socially grounded, remains not only extrinsic in utopian terms but dubious in the context of practical politics in that it posits an allegedly material category that remains perfect by virtue of its projected but nevertheless unrealizable character. Paradigm and practicality simply cannot be dissolved so unproblematically into each other.

Thus, Marxists are faced with the awkward task of employing an *impeccable* ideal to unpick the contingent ideals ruling classes employ to delude and manipulate their subjects. Further, the impeccable ideal (which for all its "sensuousness" and collective character is certainly an ideological category) is by definition invulnerable to the debunking process, which historically contingent ideologies cannot escape. A division, parallel to the moral division made by Steven Lukes mentioned in the first chapter, is then mandatory between one ideological category (the superficial ideologies serving the interests of the power elite) and an atemporal, discrete ideological category enshrining normative values used to interpret and expose the former. The self-evidently inconsistent nature of this— to put the matter mildly—may well be an unavoidable product of thinking dialectically *and* ethically about history, but the inherent conflicting elements are hardly likely to lead to unproblematic conclusions as to what political, which is to say bloody, actions are desirable.

And surely the Marxist revolutionary cannot argue that the *immediate* effects of revolutions, however evil the overthrown oligarchies, are inevitably going to be, in all cases, positive. To be naive enough to make a mistake of that sort you would have to think as crassly as the American administration, which sincerely believed that the direct consequences of battlefield victory in Iraq would be peace, stability, and improvements in the general quality of life. And, moreover, that the loss of life caused by invasion (measured, one hopes, as much in Iraqi dead as in American) would emerge as morally tenable. However, if commonsense terms are to be applied to the messy terrain of history just as freely as they are to be applied to the utopian ideal of Marxism, then all those involved in bloody action, whether capitalists or Marxists, are confronted by a praxis that in no way permits a simple, ever-onward, ever-upward Whig interpretation, although theological boy scouts in both camps will continue to believe that it does. This leaves Marxists unavoidably stuck with the burden of having to fit a sublime, final, and "unmessy" goal within a practice that in its "messy" epistemological character cannot express that goal. Furthermore, unlike the capitalist or the oligarch, Marxism is bound by its notion of progress. To take action that cannot deliver in the short term and which, as a necessary dialectical axiom, may conceivably go awry in the long term, is a contingent aspect of Marxist theory that, far from being circumvented by Marxist humanism, is underlined by it. The dialectic cuts both ways and anyone who thinks that synthesis as the antithesis of the antithesis comes about as a result of some untroubled act of molecularlike reproduction in the field of sociology has clearly no serious interest in human history.

So it is hardly surprising that there has been a loss of courage. But there is little comfort to be found among the apologists for bourgeois libertarianism. They certainly exhibit elevated "moral" values, but entertain, at best, hopelessly castrated political action on the ground. No one, for instance, applying the theories of Karl Popper or Isaiah Berlin to the history of the Palestinian people over the last 50 years could possibly have much serious interest in ameliorating suffering or emancipating the oppressed. One should, therefore, be thankful if the radical resists this temptation. It is a trap that Eagleton nicely captures when he talks of, "...the contradiction of all utopianism, that its very images of harmony threaten to hijack the radical impulses they hope to promote."[28]

The foregoing discussion of Terry Eagleton's recent work in respect of what I have called Marxist humanism can be fruitfully placed alongside one highly creative figure from a different intellectual tradition: Jürgen Habermas. Such a comparison should give rise to a deeper appreciation of the theoretical richness, practical application, and—above all—moral weight of the humanist position. Appropriately, Habermas will mirror the same concern for the spiritual and the corporeal.

Language, as a category that does not so much interpret the world as effectively create both it and the subject, has been radical theory's principal object of study during the last decades. Moreover, the innovatory development of language-based theory has not been confined to that plethora of ideas associated with poststructuralism and deconstruction, which underpins a good deal of radical French thought. A parallel but very different development has taken place in Germany. There the philosophers who developed communication theory and, in many cases, made strenuous efforts to embed ethics within it, have argued that the category of language forms the basis of a practical philosophy that escapes the academy and is applicable to social practices as a whole, in that it intrinsically empowers, in principle, all citizens equally in problem-solving, rule-based and—potentially—ethically grounded communal activity. Further, Jürgen Habermas has argued that discourse theory also tackles on a deeper and more innovatory level the classic antinomy of German academic and idealist philosophy: namely the seemingly irreconcilable claims of subject and object; the individual and (his perception of) the empirical world. Objective truth, normative justification as a social category, and the authenticity of the subject are seen, by him, as interwoven and "shown to best advantage by discourse theory in that it introduces categories which classical philosophy lacks..."[29]

But if language is self-evidently the means by which we are placed, unavoidably, in relation to each other (which would be the quality stressed in practical German discourse theory), it is, however, also the means by which radical theorists elsewhere have most thoroughly shattered the unity of the subject and the authority of the empirical world. The sensuous and attractive paradigm of nonestranged individuals making up the social that we have hitherto entertained under the rubric of Marxist humanism starts to look very naive when placed alongside the chaotic nexus of theories generated by the gaps and incoherences allegedly intrinsic to language: the notion of lack, of the eternal deferral of meaning, of the uncontrollable shifting of signifieds beneath chains of language signifiers, and—above all—the model of a subject forever confronted by the dislocation and instability of his own subjectivity.

Nonetheless, a couple of general points should be made in defense of communication theory when seen as an applied philosophy. In turning to the notion of language it takes on a special character. It muddies the waters of classic (German) ontology-based philosophy in that it introduces a third term into the binary subject/object opposition. The subject's perception of the world, the strategies by which knowledge of the world is deduced or inferred, all the metaphysical questions that flow from attempts to ground morality in a philosophical system, that is to say what Habermas calls "the-one sided construction of European philosophy on the world of Being,"[30] are thrown by communication ethics into a radically different framework. The assertion that language is a mechanism that places us in *intersubjective* relationships that are themselves generative of knowledge, of decision-making, and of notions of respect and justice (which is to say ethics) is, seemingly, to liberate that philosophy from a range of dichotomies that have been its defining issues since, at the very least, Kant. If Habermas and the philosophers of discourse/communication ethics can keep metaphysics out of the practice without sacrificing its fundamental ethical axioms, a very great change will have been effected. However, it is by no means clear that that can be done. Karl-Otto Apel, one of discourse ethics founding figures, has argued that the normative values of justice, and equality, and so forth, cannot be deduced from the theory itself, but must be to some extent dependent on extrinsic transcendental values.[31]

There is a another characteristic of discourse ethics, which should be touched on here. There is a tendency, above all in the work of Habermas, to shift the epistemological goalposts, or at the very least to change emphasis rather too freely. A student of the Frankfurt School of Social Research, he has been accused of moving, when it suits him, too readily between the identities of philosopher and sociologist. Wolfgang Kuhlmann, taking up a position similar to Apel's, points out: "It is in fact the case that [Habermas's] *The Theory of Communicative Action* does not claim to be solely descriptive in character. It is also normative."[32] That is, it *implies* extrinsic transcendental values that Habermas will not, or does not want to, entertain openly. Furthermore it "is not simply one materialist (sociological) theory among others. Rather it is much more concerned with a project which marks out the conceptual and methodological parameters for other particular, empirical undertakings."[33] As such Habermas must accept that "transcendental philosophy" cannot be shown in its best light when treated as a form of sociology. Habermas has, allegedly, played fast and loose with both categories and has failed to take into account that (transcendental) philosophy stands "opposite" to and "on a different level" from the (social) sciences.[34]

However, perhaps communication ethics' respect for the Other as formed by language can be a slightly richer and more corporeal field than its doubters imagine. Eagleton, for instance, criticizes in Habermas exactly that lack of sensuousness and shared experience that he (Eagleton) wants to put at the center of a theory that is "After Theory." Claiming that a liberal model of society merely "wants individuals to flourish in their own space, without mutual interference" and that "the political space in question…is really there to wedge people apart" he makes a pejorative link with Habermas's ideal of a public sphere where "each person is free to express herself as she wishes; but there is little recognition of the way in which social interaction itself can become the vital medium of individual self-expression at its best. Nobody here—to put the point in a different theoretical idiom—seems to receive themselves back as a subject from the Other, as opposed to attending with due sensitivity to what the other has to say."[35] However a later (apparent) broadening in Habermas's position may go further in the direction that Eagleton has in mind.

Habermas now suggests that a renewed respect for religious feeling and the refusal to succumb to an overweening scientism, will amount to an enrichment of both our daily lives and our philosophy. Moreover it is implicit in his essay *Faith and Knowledge* (*Glauben und Wissen*)[36] that this respect for religion is not indifferent to the sensuousness of shared life. Indeed it is precisely because of an issue utterly, if paradoxically, suffused by the notion of the body that Habermas has turned to the postsecular argument—namely the consequences of recent and radical advances in gene technology.[37]

Of course Habermas is not going soft on fundamentalism, whether Christian or Muslim. After all he and Derrida—hardly an intellectual blood brother—mounted a mutual campaign against it and the abuses of the "war on terrorism" in the German press.[38] Rather, he is struck by the shortcomings of a purely scientific and instrumental attempt at human understanding that, turning to Max Weber, he sees as factoring out of our lives our feeling for "the magic of the world" (16). Scientific knowledge that clinically describes the individual, no matter how exhaustively, as a discrete ego, comes up short. In daily life, on the other hand, the important category of "common-sense" functions as "a third party" that finds its "own way" between religion and science (13). This leads us to take up an intimate relation with others, to express through intersubjectivity—itself developed through the dynamic of "normatively regulated interaction" (19)—a given tolerance. One finds here, although in different language, the same awareness of humanist values that motivates Eagleton. Yet, it is clear that the religious sensibility that Habermas wishes to underline is placed within the post-Kantian premises of tolerance and secularity, and it is also clear that the place he allows for faith can only be occupied when faith has gutted itself of its absolute, all-powerful elements; that is of exclusive authority as to the will of God, along with revealed knowledge as to the certainty of damnation or salvation. This might well seem like a religion robbed of its own crown jewels. For instance, Habermas is quite clear that it must submit "to the premises of the constitutionally established state, founded on profane (worldly) morality" (14). But in turning to what we at first might assume to be the other side of the equation, he argues that it is the task of the worldly "neutral state" to remain open to the arguments and appeals of both knowledge and faith. But this, I suggest, puts a notion of the state, which by definition remains secular and enlightened, in the position of a false arbiter. It is seen as an objective conceptual umbrella under which the two rival categories are equally sheltered. But that umbrella is an inevitable result of the historical victory of the Enlightenment whereby the claims of religion gave ground to and, in their best Habermasian manifestation, absorbed the secularity of empirical knowledge and reason. Nonetheless, Habermas maintains, in what reads like a strategy that allows him an expansive embrace of religion while not sacrificing a tad of his secular philosophy/sociology, that the secular state must permit a degree of pluralism because it maintains an "equal distance" between both faith and knowledge. Furthermore, the nondoctrinaire, secular state is able to learn because "without sacrificing its own independence, it remains, osmosis-like, open to both sides" (15).

Clearly, the notion of religion here is not one that would be recognized by a fundamentalist hell-bent on privileging the chosen and dispatching the damned. That, however, need hardly trouble us. But it does remain a notion of faith, albeit uncoupled from extreme essentialism, that transcends the daily, mundane lives of men and women. What Habermas desires is the entry of the religious sensibility into *exactly* that mundane realm. Thus, the value of the religious sensibility is discerned wholly within the parameters of intersubjectivity and discourse ethics, which is to say in the here and now and in respect of practical worldly problems. Habermas underlines the shortcomings of pure secular thinking, which turns "sin into guilt" and the violation of "God's commandments into the breaking of human laws." In opposition to this, he finds in the religious disposition a "desire for forgiveness" and a genuine wish to somehow undo the suffering of others, as though the narratives of misfortune could be rewound and made good. In fact, "our lost hope of a resurrection leaves a discernible emptiness" (24). Reason, meanwhile, has found itself overtaxed, unable to carry through its absolute program, and "has despaired of itself." So, Habermas turns to the paradoxical formulations of Adorno and Horkheimer who are driven to assert the necessity of that which is axiomatically denied: one knows that there is no God, but one "believes in Him nonetheless" (27). But even as Habermas, in terms as strong as these, evokes our need for the religious sensibility, the feeling does not entirely dissipate that this postsecular appeal to faith merely amounts to the old secularity differently packaged. Is it an appeal to a religion that can find a place for God only by virtue of playful dialectical formulations? Well, Habermas does turn to God and in a manner that is not without the ambiguities one might expect of this awkward marriage between a secularity that does not give up fundamental principles and a religion that must do exactly that, if it is to fulfill the "religious" function now desired of it.

When the biblical God is explicitly thrown into the mix (the reference is to Genesis 1: 27) it is done so in a manner that surely amounts to a good deal more than either playful irony or a clever polemical strategy. God, we are reminded, "created man in His own image, in the image of God created He him." To this Habermas couples the axiom that God is love. This he asserts in a grammatical construction, which allows us, if we must, to doubt that God, in fact, created Adam and Eve in his own image, but not, paradoxically, that God is love (30).[39] Immediately thereafter the signifiers "love" and "in the same image" are dissolved into each other, and it is stated that it is clear to everyone what is meant by love. That is, love is impossible without the recognition of the Other, just as freedom without the same recognition is likewise impossible. The Other, created just as we have been, is thus for us a further manifestation of God, and the values of love and freedom, which enshrine the worth and place of the individual, are thereby also linked with the fundamentals of intersubjectivity in that they can have no meaning without the Other. Moreover, both values have been placed unambiguously in a religious framework in that the former (the subject) is made in the image of God and the later (intersubjectivity — which can now be seen as a humanist collective) is a necessary expression of God's love. Although there may be a certain syntactical sleight of hand in Habermas's construction, it is nevertheless as good an expression as one can imagine of what Peter Dews calls the "paradoxical achievement of intersubjectivity."[40]

It is this strategy that allows Habermas to address a scientific problem (gene-technology, cloning etc., are clearly on his mind following the row with Sloterdijk[41]) in a manner that takes full advantage of religious sensibility while not ditching the secular values of discourse ethics. In warning of the dangers of cloning, he reminds us that we are locked simultaneously into two categories: individuation and the social. Furthermore, he points out that while we are created in the image of God, that does not place us in the position of God, although it does remind us of the love and respect we are obliged to show others. Certainly he does not take advantage of the ambivalent formulation whereby we are and are not a divine simulacrum, an individual and a (mirror) image. One can imagine what riches a poststructuralist would find here and what fun he would have. But the centrality of, the obsession with, the unstable and split ego is exactly what Habermas does *not* share with the French poststructuralists. And although he has nothing explicit to say concerning the sensuousness of collective life, and he is hardly likely to evoke Marx's image of the nineteenth-century French proletariat that so impressed Eagleton, [42] it may seem that in turning to religion and employing it in his own fashion, Habermas is freed from Eagleton's criticism that in Habermasian philosophy no one "seems to receive themselves back as a subject from the Other."

In general, the tensions between the potentially competing categories of the subject and the collective have, throughout this chapter, molded the argument on a variety of levels. They can be seen as fundamental ontological categories in which Being itself is defined in terms, in the first case, of a struggle centered on the subject or, in the second case, by a notion of language that generates the phenomenon of intersubjectivity as the fundamental category of existence. The latter can then be put in opposition to the obsessively subject-centered theory of the (chiefly) French school. Both positions, however, do not free themselves from normative values. Even Derrida in his final years was not trying to strip philosophy of ethical values. On the other hand, the strenuous analytical efforts of discourse theorists to somehow ground normative values within the theory's own parameters while maintaining both a nonmetaphysical epistemology and the impeccably liberal maxim that one is, after all, "fallible,"[43] are here treated as significant because such an effort is made and such values are thereby deemed necessary.

Of greater significance is the degree to which discourse ethics is focused on the here and now and, consequently, on practical problem-solving. Clearly important is the manner in which the rights of individual entry into, and participation in, the speech community are enshrined so that the fundamental category of "Us" is able to do its work. However, I believe this is a mechanism predisposed, if not to no action, at least to action on the most timid scale. Profoundly influenced by the work of Karl Popper, German culture remains terrified of bold steps and, for all its liberal associations, it embodies a fundamentally conservative mind-set. The agony the Social Democrat Party of Germany (SPD)/Green government had to go through before it could take even the most curtailed belligerent action in Kosovo was astonishing. Moreover, there was general amazement that Habermas, and Apel, were prepared to even consider it.

But the argument for Marxist humanism laid out here goes beyond incrementalism and consequently rejects Popperian quibbles. Above all, two ingredients, which the libertarian would see as poisonous, have been added to the dish. They are, however, simply unavoidable if we are not to castrate ourselves intellectually or cripple ourselves as political actors. The first is the intellectually discredited and idealist notion of utopia; the second, which is dependent on the first, is the question of the ethical basis for engaging in real and potentially violent struggles. The legitimacy of the timid position is dependent on a stable and relatively compassionate social settlement being already in situ. But such a settlement seldom, if ever, gets there in the first place by methods that enshrine the values allegedly embodied in the model. Berlin's "negative liberty" can never, by definition, emancipate a slave. And Popper's belief that all we can really do is to try "to make life a little less terrible and a little less unjust in every generation"[44] presupposes that one is working within an already established benign but slow apparatus, which at best delivers constricted piecemeal progress. Even if we put aside the fact that this is manifestly not the case over most of the globe and concentrate only on the triumphant democracies, we soon see that the relations that hold those democracies in the international sphere— and never have their leaders insisted more passionately that we live in a "global" world—make it clear that the wider reality is exactly of the sort that does *not* allow the modest Weltanschauung colored by a fear of radical change and a distrust of utopian thinking because, as Berlin confidently generalizes, it "only ends in bitterness and frustration."[45] If globalization is of any conceptual value, it is chiefly because it makes it impossible to overlook how much of our wealth and security is the product of crimes committed outside the borders not only of our common rooms but also of our nations, crimes which cause pressing suffering in the lives of individuals who do not have time for the luxury of progress in its gradualist form. They need the immediate ministrations of the radical and the gun.

It is readily admitted that the values thrown together in this chapter form a self-evidently contradictory collection of forcibly coupled opposites: idealism and empiricism, the ethical and the pragmatic, the collective and the subject, the corporeal and the religious, teleology as an incentive to realizable actions and a utopian telos whose function is essentially paradigmatic. If I believe we cannot forgo all the ingredients that have been thrown together here under the umbrella of Marxist humanism, it is not because we can avoid the more unpleasant consequences by virtue of the nasty tastes being overwhelmed by the agreeable ones. Oddly we should take our cue from the incremental pessimists. Isaiah Berlin, for instance, could scarcely write anything or give an interview without quoting Kant's aphorism that we are made from "crooked timber." But we flunk the narrative nature of our lives and the grander story of the world if we use our axiomatic status as sinners as a rationalization for pulling in our horns and not taking risks. A clear-sighted view of the world around us unmistakably shows that we do not have that option if we are to believe in progress, even of a shrunken sort. The messy terrain of history now clear to everyone who still thinks narratively—that is, not just to disappointed Marxists—Is not merely a feature of the external world. It is constitutive of us as well, no matter if we emphasize our status as subjects (whether unstable or coherent) or alternatively prefer a model in which we are bound and connected to each other in potentially caring collectives. It is unlikely that we will make true sense of our place, our story, our desires, and our duties if we attempt to avoid any of these elements, irrespective of how unpalatable they may be.

One turns now to women's writing, both in respect of feminist theory and women's fiction, because there the problematic of narrative is unusually clear in that women have either been written out of dominant narratives or have been accorded an inferior place in both its stories and its discourse/language. As such women theorists and women novelists have been compelled to engage with narrative in a more skeptical and sophisticated manner than men. The result has been a rich—but by no means a homogeneous—body of theoretical work. Nonetheless, its place here is highly polemical. As this book makes the most ambitious, normative, and explanatory claims for narrative, it takes issue with that strand of feminist literary theory that has rejected it as axiomatically corrupted. Consequently, the following chapter is both highly instrumental and highly partial in the use it makes of women's writing.

Chapter 3

Women and Writing
Women Theorists, Women Novelists, Jane Austen, Charlotte Brontë

Andrea Nye, paraphrasing Hélène Cixous, writes that "a woman's text is like an egg, it is not closed but endless."[1] This proposition is particularly apposite in the wider context of radical feminist theory in that it links a literary category (the text) with an explicitly biological and female category (the egg), and it thereby produces a definition of women's writing exactly at odds with the categories that shape and drive this book. Nonetheless, Nye's explicitly nonnarrative, telos free, position follows—despite the unavoidable nebulousness of its terminology—stringently on from the notion that identity/subjectivity is created in language, and that language is formed by phallocentrism. It has therefore become an intractable and unavoidable structure from which escape seems improbable. The question then surfaces: How is the feminist to respond to this incontrovertible but hostile given? Luce Irigaray is addressing this challenge and her own attempt at an escape when she says of her doctoral thesis: "Strictly speaking *Speculum* has no beginning or end. The architectonics of the text, or texts, confounds the linearity of an outline, the teleology of discourse, within which there is no possible place for the 'feminine,' except the traditional place of the repressed, the censured."[2]

Both formulations (Nye's and Irigaray's) express an ambitious feminist shift that wants to break free but which, in its uncompromising alternative epistemology, pays *formal* respect to the overwhelming nature of the prison in which women are held by phallocentrism. That is, it is compelled to reflect the absolute nature of the paradigm, in that any compromise with it would lead at best to degrees of self-inflicted mutilation. For were one to accept the masculine (contaminated) category of language on its own terms (and many feminists such as Cixous and Irigaray talk up the enemy in a manner that brings them perilously close to a point where there is no *coherent* option but to capitulate), a logical reaction might be that women have no choice but to grin and bear it. That is, given the biological implications of phallocentrism, you could no more change the fundamentals of the master language than you could shed your body.

This is hardly an attractive proposition. It is, however, based on a dichotomy that by definition curtails the apparently limitless claims of phallocentrism. The feminist critique, even in its far-reaching rejectionist form, requires at the very least a sense (biologically and linguistically expressed) of what has been excluded by phallocentrism. Without such a sense, the category would become so absolute as to drive radical feminists to a conclusion that some of them actually seem to welcome: namely that language is, after all, an unproblematic homogeneous category. However merely to *think* the alternative undercuts the megalomania of phallocentrism as a biological and linguistic given. If women were trapped unambivalently within its parameters, the best that could follow would be an inferior, underdeveloped form of the same thing. Phallocentrism's triumph would then be expressed by, and measured in terms of, the "self-evidently" inferior female phallus (clitoris). And it is this rather perverse form of biologism that seems to be, in effect, practiced by Lacan.

There is a certain chutzpah in this. It is as though Lacan is mocking Freud's description of the woman as a dark continent that leaves the male analyst bemused as to what women "want." The discoverer of "penis envy" is here shamelessly outbid by an uninhibited disciple who, having changed the determining categories of Freudian thinking by foregrounding discourse, redefines what women want in terms of what they are—and are not—able to say. This he does by defining the dual categories of discourse and biology so that each is determining for the other. Irigaray notes a suitably audacious passage of Lacan's that encapsulates just this: "There is no woman who is not excluded by the nature of things, which is the nature of words, and it must be said that, if there is something they complain a lot about at the moment, that is what it is—except that they don't know what they are saying, that's the whole difference between them and me."[3]

Lacan, not surprisingly, produced a countereffect among his female doctoral students expressed in terms that are, however fanciful, as ontologically fundamental and biological as his own. Here is the real triumph, no matter that gender priority is upended, of Freud's axiom that ultimately everything is biology. And it is equally unsurprising that the clitoris is rejected by feminists in favor of the ever touching, erotically meaningful and *speaking* lips of the vagina.[4] Thereby language and biology remain just as indissoluble in the radical reaction as they are in the initial, inimical theory. The result can seem like a formal victory over a supposedly defeated enemy who, nevertheless, still seems to be calling the shots—although the target has been turned around. For this particular feminist alternative is essentially one half of a binary pair of which the phallocentric "vanquished" is the *essential* other. Nonetheless, it does give women the choice between the contaminated given, and the richer radical antithesis. But even this might be a poisoned chalice in that the radical feminist option seems to forgo power. Victory is enshrined in semantics and female "jouissance." Have radical feminists happily dispensed with teleology, with power, with history, because the oceanic cycles they have discovered are so much richer? Or is it simply that the latter will not allow, coherently, of the former?

As has already been illustrated in chapter 1, the style of this new liberated writing intrinsically expresses the character of the radical break in that it is awash with the riches open to the women who dare to make that break. Indeed style—as an allegedly unmediated expression-cum-manifestation of the body—*becomes* the substance of the argument. And although it begins with biology, some kind of metamorphosis occurs that allows both (body and writing) to shatter all limitations and take wing. Irigaray, for instance, rhapsodizes: "Our horizon will never stop expanding: we are always open. Stretching out, never ceasing to unfold ourselves, we have so many voices to invent in order to express all of us everywhere…,"[5] and so on. What all this might mean for writing is made "clear" by Cixous: "Write! and your self-seeking text will know itself better than flesh and blood, rising, insurrectionary dough kneading itself, with sonorous, perfumed ingredients, a lively combination of flying colors, leaves, and rivers plunging into the sea we feed."[6]

This is an astonishing and an attractive proposition for those, unlike me, who are in a position to see whether it can be realized in its own terms, which—to make the point yet again—are terms that allow no compromise, based as they are on both an ontology and an epistemology utterly sex specific. That is, the male can neither "be" nor "know" what is at issue here. It is perforce a hermetically closed polemic. But although it is not permissible to claim that this kind of writing does not do what it claims to do, it is entirely proper to be clear about what it does not do that it never claimed it would. In this, male ignorance is no obstacle. Moreover, if the categories it rejects (above all narrative) are instructive with respect to women in society (which is a heterogeneous structure), and if they are productive of meaning (of both resolution and further conflict), then the ambivalent relationship between creative women writers, and narrative, and female subjectivity is of great significance. It is to this significance, particularly as it is expressed in the novels of women writers, that the rest of this chapter is devoted. It will take as its principal examples Jane Austen and Charlotte Brontë. Furthermore, in examining these two novelists, women theorists will, and should have, pride of place.

Analyzing the manner in which the female experience has been marginalized or inscribed in codes, feminist critics who have never sacrificed their right to allegedly masculine language have, understandably, paid a great deal of attention to sexuality. But it has been a sexuality broadly enough defined as to include, alongside socially impermissible "dark passions," the rage and imprisonment felt by the woman author. This is a rage often expressed by a marginalized female character who stands in opposition to the virtuous heroine. Such a figure is dangerous because she represents passions and truths that the author cannot (or, for reasons of taste, is not allowed to) handle truthfully. But let such a character into the story and she will cause havoc. The logical solution is to declare her mad and to lock her away. And there is indeed a great deal still to be said for what was the classic argument of *The Madwoman in the Attic* in 1979.[7] On this basis, we might see Bertha Mason in *Jane Eyre* as having a structural and semantic identity similar to that of Caliban in the *Tempest*—at least as it is brilliantly dramatized by W. H. Auden. That is, she is "the one creature... [the author] cannot... admit,"[8] or, to return to *Jane Eyre*, she is that figure whose anarchic potential may explode the whole aesthetic because in her violent passions and wild hunted nature she is "Jane's dark double."[9]

But if we look at the "madwoman" as a source of truths otherwise repressed, we will see that her deeper significance lies in what she *does* rather than solely in what she represents. It is not her potential for disorder, or her dark symbolic role, that is most important, but her *narrative* function within a literary form of which she is productive exactly because of that potential. And this includes her implicit "presence" in the culminating closure from which she is physically banished but which, in merely taking place, encapsulates how indispensable she has been. Her determining role is perfectly, if paradoxically, blatant in the manner in which she is discarded by whatever fictional device (death is clearly the simplest) that takes the author's fancy. Therefore, the "disorder" she embodies is not best expressed by the cell in which she is chained (i.e., as the incarcerated dark "alter ego" that "symbolizes the passionate and sexual side of Jane's personality," as Elaine Showalter has it,[10]) but as a propulsive, generative force. Paradoxically, that significance is best inferred from an aesthetic form that culminates in happy lovers who, having overcome all obstacles, head for the altar and the implied utopia that must follow it. And here we might put aside the madwoman for a moment to look at the question of closure in terms that are not limited to the Gothic, which is otherwise her natural milieu.

The classic (blissful) closure parallels, in fanciful form, the Marxist teleological goal in that it also opens out the topography on which "real history" (or true abiding romance) will subsequently flourish in terms that are atemporal. However, being devoid of tension and dialectics, the realist novelist is in no position to know or describe it without violating it, although I daresay we may assume that there too the grain will be happily cut during the day and the ballet enjoyed in the evening. Furthermore, any observation that muddies the paradigm, no matter how seemingly slight or passing, will be correspondingly seismic in implication. Yet it is perfectly understandable if the perspicacious novelist, unhappy about reducing a long labor to the level of the fairy story, has difficulty in holding her tongue at this point. Perhaps the most obvious examples are the tart observations of Jane Austen as she hurries her stories, once all the misunderstandings have been cleared up, to their peremptory happy endings.

Having willingly trapped herself within the strictures of rural communities, Austen emerges as socially precise and clear-sighted. Thus, for her the happy endings, despite their makeshift character, have a more integrated place in the overall fictional Weltanschauung. For instance, it is exceptionally clear that it is the responsibility of women to make as good a *socially* appropriate marriage as possible. After all, Emma's biggest mistake is to forget who might be an appropriate mate for Harriet Smith with respect to class and background. This encourages both women to overestimate Harriet's chances and this in turn threatens the well-being of the highly defined, interwoven world of Highbury. And marriage is so important a social event (as it is not, for instance in Charlotte Brontë novels where egotistical and sexual passion is not only present but occasionally near unrestrained) that it is notable how far she will go to get even her foolish or deplorable single women husbands. This is often neatly integrated into the story in that the man who has been misjudged by the brilliant heroine can prove his worth by sorting out the difficulties into which the misguided women—often relations of the heroine—have got themselves. Male characters going off to London, or wherever, to do the right thing are particularly useful in this respect in that they leave the geography of the novel, sort out a problem, and do not require that the novelist follow them—a couple of letters with London or Antigua postmarks addressed to the worried ladies in the country will suffice.

However, the idea of community and all the bitchiness, generosity, manipulation, and wit that make it work, mean that the closure, although unmistakably a narrative gesture designed to satisfy the reader as to the blissful life awaiting the privileged women when wed, cannot be sealed off from the society in which it takes place. The ideological and narrative bind in the Austen novel is that the journey that gets us to the solution profoundly problematizes that solution. As her subject is marriage and money and all the ramifications that follow, she is compelled to contaminate her closure as a prerequisite for reaching it. Certainly we are rewarded with a superficially sublime ending, but the course of the book makes it clear to us that marriage is not only to be arrived at in a messy way, but that it is itself a difficult even messy business as soon as the newly wedded husband and wife dutifully reenter social life. Consequently, she cannot allow us the notion that the happy couple will (as with Brontë's Jane Eyre and Edward Rochester) preserve their blissful state by living outside of the community. In short, being such a sharp-eyed (and at times sharp-tongued) social writer, Austen is trapped by the exactness and complexity of her own creation. She can no more imagine a utopian existence that escapes her social world than she can follow her male characters to London or Antigua. No doubt she flatters us in not, entirely, hiding her ironic awareness of the jerry-built character of her happy endings, but she is forced, nonetheless, to pay homage at the last to the genre. No wonder then that, having cobbled the thing together, she is eager to hurry from the room for fear that if she stays, she will be compelled to watch as the whole thing falls to pieces like a poorly constructed bookshelf.

However, should the novel celebrate unashamedly the epistemological shift and happily deliver to the reader the perfect ending and the implied unwritable utopian future, it can attempt to preclude all doubts by the paradoxical device of flagrantly trumpeting the idealized nature and alien epistemological status of it all. For is not the closure merely an "event" to which the novel has been driving? Clearly closure has never, in itself, been the source of the novel's pleasures. In this context, for the critics to make a fuss about closure-as-happy-ending is just as "foolish" as all that speculative energy devoted to arguing why King Lear does what he does at the beginning of Shakespeare's play. The bluff commonsense answer is that if he did not blunder the partition of the kingdom, there would not be a play. Moreover, the happy ending in the novel may be seen as even less problematic, in that being immaculate it may not even belong stylistically in the narrative. Sometimes, for instance, the final aesthetic enthronement stands beyond the parameters of what the novel troubles to tell the reader, in that the text comes to an end before the wedding is described. Furthermore, no attempt is made to hide the impossible fit between the synthetic character of that closure and the realist, even commonsense, qualities that have up to then been in play. Thus, a form that engages in a fresh way with "real" and complex social life may solve, at the close, its aesthetic problems by violating the realist axioms that have been driving it. In these circumstances, the still relatively inexperienced author may be "forced" to acknowledge the artificiality in a manner so shameless as to earn the reader's admiration.

Consider, for instance, the manner in which Jane Austen in *Sense and Sensibility* marries Marianne off to Colonel Brandon (there being no other candidate) chiefly because, in this case, one suspects she feels compelled to do so by the aesthetic structure. This is a marriage that makes nonsense of Marianne's narrative/polemical role in the novel hitherto. Austen will find more subtle and sophisticated ways of dealing with these sorts of difficulties, but here she simply invites the reader, in effect, to do her best to believe it. No credible explanation is offered but for the incontrovertible fact that life is sometimes a puzzle. No doubt stranger things happen at sea. After all, Colonel Brandon "still sought the constitutional safeguard of a flannel waistcoat!" That exclamation mark is an ironic exaggeration designed to preclude further discussion. What follows is the bare: "But so it was." We see that the crucial thing was to *arrive* at this point, come hell or high water.

So, in returning to the madwoman we will do *her* more justice if we stress that, although her terrible presence may be heard only as eerie noises in the night, she is a highly effective motor of the plot. She will be exceptionally fruitful in generating lurid obstacles, in order that the improbably perfect closure is reached. It is, for instance, appropriate that it is Bertha's function (although she cannot be present in the church) to scupper the premature wedding attempted by Jane and Mr. Rochester (Chapter 26). In fact, the clichéd melodrama in the church allows Brontë to go beyond the customary sublime signifier of a wedding at the end (Chapter 38). In pushing the novel narratively beyond the true wedding, without succumbing to any notion of prosaic realism, she pursues an agenda that has always been saturated with, and focused on, an idealized model of romantic atemporal bliss uncontaminated by any conscious textual irony. Furthermore, in not being a social novelist in the manner of Jane Austen, she is carrying less complicated ideological baggage and can paint a married utopia for us without stepping outside the parameters of romance. So the "real" wedding is easily done with. Only the absolutely essential players are there. It is definitely not a social event with implications for a community. Therefore, we should not let the famous "Reader, I married him" underplay what follows: "A quiet wedding we had." This is essential if we are to appreciate the asocial character of Jane's immaculate description: so asocial in fact, and so rhapsodically insisted upon, that the word "society" shrinks in its term of reference. For she tells us that she is "extraordinarily blest...blest beyond what language can express; because I am my husband's life as fully as he is mine. No woman was ever nearer to her mate than I am: ever more absolutely bone of his bone and flesh of his flesh. I know no weariness of my Edward's society: he knows none of mine, any more than we each do of the pulsation of the heart that beats in our separate bosoms."

However, this does not mean problems have not had to be solved for this to work. Above all, the closure has to resolve the chief dramatic tension in the novel and its most abrasive ideological conundrum that, to get down to brass tacks, is Jane's lack of power vis-à-vis Rochester: the man she showered with "sirs" when they were reunited in Chapter 37 and now tells us is "my Edward." The solution is appropriately grotesque. In blinding the dominant male so that he will forever be dependent on—in effect the property of—his devoted helpmate, Brontë skillfully marries the Gothic atmosphere of the narrative with an extrinsic soft-focused future in which Jane will never have cause to imagine that her husband will be out of *her* sight for a moment: an apposite irony that may strike the reader but can hardly be voiced by the narrator. In this, she is in debt to the dark double who kicked the plot back into life by starting the fire that killed her and emasculated the alpha male in that he will never again be fit for action in a male adventure. Any future narration could not take the form of this male going off to fight Napoleon while occasionally dreaming of his wife at home before the hearth knitting booties for his kiddies. And he will certainly never return to the Caribbean to import another dark, dangerous, and alien woman.

Jane is victorious because Rochester is rewritten in an entirely feminine manner in that he becomes the feminine creation of a feminine text, despite that text initially celebrating his disruptive masculine character. And at the very end, in what a reader prepared to speculate on the unconscious motives of the author might well see as an act of textual sadism, this ideal is toyed with as a cat might toy with a mouse. Rochester is rewarded, after two years of what we know to have been good behavior, with a little bit of sight in one eye. But this is kept carefully within limits—after all, there is no practical reason why he should not be accorded fictional 20/20 vision. However, that is hardly the author's purpose. All she does is put him in a position where he does not need 24-hour care. Was Jane getting just a little peeved at being a full-time nurse? Well, she could hardly admit of it: "never did I weary of conducting him where he wished to go." Whatever the case, the new and final authorial beneficence is not unconditional. Rochester may be able to get around on his own now, but his singular eyesight is so limited that, if no longer crippled, he is at least hamstrung. If he wanders off, Jane can put her book down, her feet up, and close her two good eyes in the knowledge that *her* Edward is not going anywhere. And, in case we might imagine that he is trying to muscle his way back into the novel as narrative, which is to say to assert himself in the *text* in the customary masculine manner, it is made (unconsciously on the author's part?) clear to us that this is something we need not fear. The ocular improvement "does not permit him to read and write very well." The poor dear.

And all this is really down to Bertha. Does Jane have any idea how much she owes her antithetical sister? Certainly had the first wedding not been aborted, if Bertha had never existed, Jane would never have enjoyed the triumph over her beloved that follows the second wedding. And Bertha's "sacrifice" is complete. Not content with starting the fire that castrates the heroic male, the practical pyromaniac hurls herself from the roof of Thornfield, so that her departure is as undoubted as possible. As with the vampire, it is best to extinguish the otherworldly monster in a variety of ways if you want to sleep soundly in your bed certain there is no chance of her popping suddenly out of the wardrobe yet again.

Thus, the madwoman provides the purchase, the tension, that is necessary if things are not only to be, but to happen. Ultimately, she will be replaced by less feverish sisters, free of Gothic trappings. And should the Gothic survive, it can be mocked as in *Northanger Abbey*, or it can be played with and then exposed as bogus by rational argument, which is, ultimately, the agenda of *Villette*. Meanwhile, the willful, the malicious, the easily deluded, the simply wrongheaded women will take over the narrative function the madwoman previously fulfilled and, in the context of more complex but mundane social relationships, instigate the incidents and accidents, the slights, the setbacks and misunderstandings that will drive the story.

At this point a near equation between two terms that have already been thrown together should be acknowledged: realism and narration. More will be said about a privileged definition of realism below and in chapter 6, but for the moment it is treated as an expression of narration. That is, narration might exist without earning the epithet realist, but no text defined here as realist can be anything other than profoundly narrative in character. Up to now that narrative impulse has, in the context of female novelists, been focused on the individual female character, although it has been explicitly asserted that both the grand guignol Gothic female and the foolish gossip or snob et al. should be seen in the context of the virtuous heroines whose structural antipodes they seemingly are. And if now, to remain within the orbit of female novelists, we return to Jane Austen, we will discover that she proves no less illuminating in this matter than in so many others.

There is in Jane Austen's novels a structural tension between the claims of action on the one hand, and feminine intelligence and virtue on the other. The principal aesthetic dilemma she has to solve is how to make the novels run when, as a clear reflection of the position of women, her privileged characters are not allowed to do much and her particularly virtuous women are allowed to do less. Virtue is, unlike its manifestation in the masculine novel of adventure, largely a passive quality, even when the women are intelligent. It is their brothers who go to sea, and win renown and moral kudos by defeating Napoleon, although of course we are never allowed to witness any of this for if we were to, the women would lose all but the most clichéd fictional identities and be swept from the board merely to be picked up later as rewards portioned off to heroic returning males. Furthermore, Austen is in this as sharp-eyed as she is in so much else to do with her society. We are allowed to sense that she is well aware that the masculine worlds of action and business are, in fact, far from heroic or unambivalent and that it would throw everything into disorder were we to become better informed as to what the men get up to after they have galloped off elsewhere.

When Sir Thomas Bertram is dispatched to Antigua in order that matters may get a little out of hand at Mansfield Park, his ostensible motivations are the financial problems on his slave-run estates. In choosing such an option, Austen gives excellent reason why she should not wish us to accompany him. It would push the novel entirely off its moral kilter. But she does allow us the sense that the matter involves something terrible and makes it clear that the implications of leaving the rural communities can be oceanic. In this manner, Austen foregrounds her chosen world that, being domestic in form and driven by female desire in narrative, cedes to the feminine ideal in the rural community a freedom from *ostensibly* great sins. This leaves the novelist the task of finding finer gradations of good and bad in a world where action is far removed from running slave plantations or fighting sea battles (which, as Captain Wentworth makes clear in *Persuasion*, can also be a very effective moneymaking undertaking). It is a measure of her success that she is able to invest her own imaginative world with a moral significance that possesses the, at the very least, same range and richness as the masculine world of action and dirty money. But that still leaves the seemingly intractable problem of what is to be made out of the morally admirable women, for, if they are to shape the agenda, they are in danger of writing themselves out of the narratives. And if not so, there is the additional danger that we will end up with little other than pious tracts on good behavior.

Austen's most pleasurable response to this problem is wit. Hers is a form of wit that leans not to grand and supposedly shocking Shavian paradoxes, but to something that could, and on occasions does, produce the petty put-down. Given the aesthetic form in play, her wit has little option but to feed on exactly perceived imperfections and hypocrisies as they surface in social intercourse. That is, it is not an erudite category. But this type of wit does become a conduit whereby out of what at first seems unusually constricted material, brilliant and finely graduated social portrayals emerge; portrayals that we find perspicacious with respect to human folly (a far more illuminating category than human sagacity) despite there being areas of experience—sexuality, great evil, unrestrained passion, radical political ideas (all to be found in Charlotte Brontë)—that are largely excluded. But although wit is a fruitful move stylistically (the danger of excessive piety is thereby avoided) and it is certainly a source of pleasure for the reader, it is not in itself enough of a solution.

Although it is true that the positive female characters may make telling remarks and carry off fine conversations that show they are percipient commentators on the mores of their curtailed worlds, and although it is equally clear that intelligent and worthy men should be attracted to them, when it comes to the doing they are always to some degree hamstrung, even to the extent of having to watch in near despair as those very men fail to appreciate their virtues and seem perilously close to falling into the inappropriate hands of the likes of Mary Crawford in *Mansfield Park*. And in some cases, the virtuous females are well-nigh crippled because Austen is prone, perhaps as a counterweight to her more tartly-tongued heroines, to the attractions of exceptionally passive, morally centered women such as Jane Bennet, and Fanny Price, and Anne Elliot who, as a sign of their goodness (which itself is often a sign of their exceptional financial dependency), largely forgo the raillery of their more willful sisters. This only aggravates the aesthetic problems the author faces. How is she to center such characters narratively? Being passive, they are not as useful for the plot as sharp-tongued but nonetheless virtuous ladies such as Elizabeth Bennet, or Elinor Dashwood, or Emma Woodhouse, to say nothing of the silly gals prone to run off with rogues, and the dangerous busybodies, snobs, and seductresses who are certainly going to make things go, but quite possibly go awry.

It is this that leads to the "pairing" of female characters. But this is not a glib or systematic literary device. Austen attempts a highly inventive range of solutions—*Emma*, for instance can be seen as a novel in which the title figure is in herself an embodiment, and an attempted resolution, of a dialectical struggle that began with *Sense and Sensibility* (Marianne and Elinor) and *Pride and Prejudice* (Jane and Elizabeth). But all these attempts worry over the problem of finding forms that permit female characters to colonize narrative action and thereby attain power. And, moreover, this shift into narration need not require that the essentialist notion of the feminine be stripped of its particular moral status. Women will retain that claim on virtue which is the perverse reward the novel of action usually affords the good lady who, normally, is pure because she is still. In a fine swindle, women in Austen's case may cash in on both sides of the equation, so that the critical antagonism between virtue/intelligence and action is resolved in that neither claim is unambiguously abandoned in favor of the other. It is, therefore, important to do some justice to the subtlety with which Austen stakes out a moral and narrative topology considerably more expansive than one would have thought possible on first encountering the parameters of her aesthetic.

Folly, in particular, is a vital factor in Austen's narrative aesthetic. But it is folly most effectively manifested by the heroines, rather than by the obvious fools. We learn that "Marianne Dashwood was born to an extraordinary fate. She was born to discover the falsehood of her own opinions, and to counteract, by her conduct, her most favorite maxims." Meanwhile, Elizabeth Bennet and Emma are both shown to be wrong, the former chiefly in respect of Mr. Darcy and the latter in respect of everything. Yet, both are narratively vindicated in that they attain at the end their desired destinies, no matter how ignorant they may have hitherto been of those desires.

However, the narrative focus on virtue rewarded can involve acts of repression against which the character may rebel, as Jane in Chapter 12 of *Jane Eyre*, raging against her fate as woman, famously does. These signals—especially when, as here, they rupture the text and shock Virginia Woolf—suggest that the author is a good deal more ambivalent than good literary manners permit, and that she thereby (unconsciously) encourages the reader to a more ambivalent attitude toward characters and plotlines. It is not that here is a form of women's writing as a distinct epistemological discourse—that is to say the women's text qua text with which this chapter began—but that there is a distinct *women's narrative* that is expressed in the nineteenth-century novel by an obedience to values that one might see (or subconsciously feel) as inimical but which, nonetheless, are, at the last, forced upon the plot so that it, in turn, can vindicate them. And it is doubts as to these, often highly artificial, master narratives that lead to the opening out of the repressed plurality of irreconcilable alternative stories that the master narratives are designed to repress. At the end of *Sense and Sensibility* we sense, rightly, that great violence is done to Marianne because she is shoehorned so mercilessly and clumsily into her "master" destiny. We cannot *but* see the injustice of it.

In this manner the woman's text, when it deals with the destinies of women, is forever throwing up by implication more liberating alternatives more deeply inscribed within the debilitating but (finally) oh-so-blissful narratives that *do* happen. Nevertheless, this is not a purist poststructuralist position: it does not exclude the author, nor does it foreground texts saturated by limitless significations in such a way that qualitative, let alone normative, distinctions are impermissible. Be that as it may, it is suggested that women writers will axiomatically produce—not women's discourse as such—but women's narratives. What they repress are the destinies (a favorite word in women's novels of the nineteenth century) of women characters, and it is these narrative repressions that lead to the outbursts which attract radical critics. But those frustrations express histories that cannot be told, or cannot be told fairly, so that the range of reconciliations at the end of the novels *imply*, with varying degrees of disguise, possibilities that are, we are to believe, not to be countenanced. In other words, it would be more theoretically productive if poststructuralism were used as a means of narrative deconstruction and not as a device for the production of limitless games of word association. What are, after all, the *chains* of signifiers poststructuralists talk of if not narratives?

If poststructuralism is entertained in this constricted form, it exposes the limitations of an aesthetic that privileges the debilitating but adroit skills of the novelist. Thus Virginia Woolf, who can hardly be blamed for not resorting to poststructuralist theory, is nonetheless unwise to complain that Jane Eyre's fury fractures the aesthetic bounds of the text: "That is an awkward break, I thought."[11] Furthermore, her objection to (but fascination with) Charlotte Brontë's "force" ("the more tremendous for being constricted"[12]) is also based on a misplaced fear of aesthetic bad manners. Rather it should be welcomed as it spills out over the page and liberates the text, just as Bertha Mason liberates the story. It is the rupture that floods the novel with the meanings and *jouissance* that conventional literary values keep in check.

Austen, meanwhile, is determined on finding forms that castrate the dangerous, if clearly less melodramatic, possibilities that her stories throw up. Nonetheless she is, on poststructural principle, no more able than Charlotte Brontë to control the plurality of meaning that is the inevitable result of the act of writing, or shackle her chains of signifiers to signifieds so unproblematically that the latter never escape their given, unambiguous signs. But her attempt is remarkable for its sophistication. Moreover, she is more likely to be *superficially* successful in that her material, being carefully restricted, is more resilient to violent invasion and more able to circumvent the rupture of the repressed.

Pride and Prejudice employs polarities in a much more subtle manner than *Sense and Sensibility*. The title qualities are not, of course, opposed. What is opposed are the relative follies of good and bad characters and how the former triumph over theirs and the latter endure punishments appropriate to their indiscretions. But given that the plot is driven by the errors of the two principal lovers, the alternative pair comes across as very pale. If Mr. Bingley gets more room for maneuver than Jane Bennet, that is "merely" an expression of his sex.

The principal dynamic of *Pride and Prejudice* is produced by the two leading lovers, abrasively driving each other on. Darcy is particularly interesting. Marriageable heroes in Jane Austen are naturally enough solid fellows. They may on occasions show signs of falling under the influence of morally dubious women, but in the end they are dependable. If there is a certain amount of sparring between the couple who are destined to wed—as between Knightley and Emma—it is resolved in the superficial triumph of the male to whom the female submits. Emma, for instance, tells Mr. Knightley that she will never be able to call him George. But Darcy and Elizabeth are engaged in equal combat, which is rather odd given that the match Elizabeth is going to make (Pemberley and the whole quasi-aristocratic job lot) is far and away grander than that attained by any of her sisters in the Austen canon. But Darcy's wealth gives him more room for willful behavior than his fictional brother heroes. If his virtue is partly enshrined in his wealth, his intelligence is the means by which he will overcome prejudice and snobbery. After the wedding, money and privilege are just there to be enjoyed and we are back to postclosure happy families. But the novel as a story tells us of the freedom—the psychological, even willful, freedom—that an income guarantees.

Emma has an income—a good one. For her, the problem of marriage *and* money does not exist. It is this that led Ellen Moers to expose, brilliantly and crisply, the solecism at the heart of Lionel Trilling's praise. Trilling pronounces that Emma has a "moral life" as a man does. Moers sees immediately that this is "merely" to say that she has money enough to control her own destiny.[13] But we should note the cost of that independence, which is to address the problematic manner by which it is fruitfully manipulated authorially so that it drives the action, delivers surprising twists and turns, and teaches us the need for socially responsible behavior. For although Emma is not under the customary financial pressure to find the appropriate husband, she has unusual responsibilities in the community. Her duties and her failures here are the logical, fictional results of her exceptional freedoms. In short, Emma's punishment/reward is that she gets everything wrong but in doing so makes the narrative work. Resolving in her own character active intervention with intelligence and virtue, she has a "life"—and certainly one she can afford—that none of her sisters can aspire to. Furthermore, she synthesizes in herself the structural and dynamic dilemmas to which *all* the female characters in the Austen books are vulnerable. One notes that in a series of novels about women hers is the only name to appear, finally, in a title. She is sovereign, the apparent mistress—as character and signifier—of everything she surveys. It is as if she has taken the pen in hand and is writing the story as authoritatively as the omniscient third person author. And the narrative reward—the inevitable payoff—is that she is utterly, even dangerously, wrong. Of course, being a highly intelligent and virtuous heroine she not only sees her folly but also torments herself with it. "With insufferable vanity had she believed herself in the secret of every body's feelings; with unpardonable arrogance proposed to arrange every body's destiny. She was proved to have been *universally* mistaken." (Chapter 11, my emphasis.) Could her punishment and her humiliation be greater? And yet somehow it is all bogus. In her manipulation of folly, how far Austen has traveled since Marianne

For after the shocking realization, Emma does not have to wait long before she is rewarded with what, had she known it, she had always wanted. After this, the remaining matters are tied up with the customary brisk rationalizations that right every wrong and pair off those who are to be paired off, and the reader can take them as seriously as she pleases. All that matters is that she understands no harm has been done. Among the problems that remain however, is the key question of Emma's status after she has bowed down before the male who will—in effect—now own her. And Austen is quite explicit on the ownership question: there is not going to be anything here such as the "My Edward" stuff in *Jane Eyre*. Her Mr. Knightley will always be addressed by the chivalric title inscribed in his surname. The former employee Jane Eyre forgoes "sir" literally, while Emma adopts it metaphorically.

However, this superficial capitulation elucidates a variety of contradictions. Given that she was an unintentional mischief-maker who, in inventing the novel, has given us a lot of pleasure, and also given that she finds happiness, we feel the satisfaction that comes from the attractions of the fully realized character. Happy endings would be poor things if they did not, at least superficially, make us happy too. But the narrative contradiction remains pungent. Emma is far and away the most narratively determining figure Austen creates. She has no life outside of events, no symbolic function that is not an expression of her intelligence and her deeds. Unlike her sister in folly, Marianne Dashwood who also sees that she has been mistaken in everything, Emma is not representative of an idea or a Weltanschauung that has purchase beyond the parameters of her community—unless it is the very idea of activity, of doing things, as reason itself for being. That is, the sharpness of her mind and tongue is expressed in actions, and this of itself is a considerable aesthetic achievement when we remember that the character is so unusually intelligent and, in the literal sense at least, thoughtful.

Nevertheless, although one can understand why certain readers and critics find an element of tragedy in her final comeuppance, they are surely troubling themselves unnecessarily. Gilbert and Gubar are being simplistic when they argue that Emma: "finds that she has all along been manipulated as a character in someone else's fiction." This is to accord the book's climax an aesthetic identity it transcends. After all, the telos of the happy ending has always been trite. We all know the story goes on. But in this case, we can confidently speculate how Emma will use her high position to further meddle and manipulate for the common good—and her own amusement. The deeper paradox of her folly is that it is a (temporally uncurtailed) guarantee of her status as storyteller. The formal conclusion qua conclusion is small and—worse—irrelevant beer in respect of the text. It is not a reconciliation of antithetical qualities (Emma alone possesses all the Austen qualities), nor is it a reward for being a good girl (Emma is rewarded for being a bad one). Certainly it is generally true that formal closures degenerate easily into feel-good gestures external to the adventures from which the plot has been woven. Does Cervantes not give back Don Quixote his reason shortly before killing him? But this is not the case here. We can see that if being active is Emma's raison d'être *for* being, that will not change.

This intense concentration of qualities within the singular figure is also productive with respect to social values. They take on a parallel intense form in which questions of communal responsibility focus on the heroine in an unusually integrated manner. No Austen heroine, no matter how rich and independent, will escape society as the necessary tribunal in which her moral worth is evaluated. But in *Emma*, that construct is potent in that the heroine is free enough to do more, which is also to do more harm, and is thereby more vulnerable to legitimate criticism. When Knightley turns on her as they wait for their carriages on Box Hill (Chapter 7) there is nothing preachy about his attack just as there is nothing mild in his language. Her behavior has been unforgivable, she has been "insolent" to Miss Bates, and if we perhaps have enjoyed the style with which Miss Bates was put down then we, too, may have to reconsider our own judgment. Both encounters—that with Miss Bates where Emma says too much and that with Mr. Knightley when, finally, she cannot bring herself to say anything at all—work because the title figure, of herself, covers all the relevant moral and narrative territory. No extrinsic commentary is required to make the matter clear. The aesthetic seems at this moment to seamlessly produce, under its own dynamic, both the desired problem and its perfect resolution—which is the temporary and merited humiliation of the heroine. Character, plot, personal moral standing, one's obligations within the community, all come together in an apparently coherent fashion on this single outing. The world shifts on its axis on Box Hill. It shifts and we feel the ground move under our feet.

And all this is the outcome of a trivial joke told to, and at the expense of, a spinster who should have been protected against just such an impertinence. And it should be noted, it is not the joke in itself that is the affront but that it is wrongly targeted. Knightley would have been more than happy had it been aimed at a foolish and *rich* woman. But Miss Bates is poor. Moreover, she looks after her ailing mother—who else would if she did not?—and in being Emma's undoubted social inferior and in honoring Emma, she deserves better. Moreover, Miss Bates has no comeback. She does not enter the discourse equally because she is socially unequal. Even had she the wit to reply in kind, she could not have done so. Instead, she moves a little away with Knightley and, mortified, talks of nothing else but how *appropriate* and deserved the jibe has been—once that is, she has worked it out. It is clear that Emma's failure is not merely one of taste, it is much more a dereliction of duty—although we know that she is relatively scrupulous about fulfilling her duty to the poor of Highbury. In this instance Austen, the famous painter of small scenes on constricted canvases, the moralist of the mundane, cashes in big.

The rich narrative status of Emma seems all the more remarkable when we consider the two passive ladies (Fanny Price and Anne Elliot) who, we are told, precede and follow her. Inevitably they set Austen different problems in reconciling narrative and virtue.

It is clear that many of the difficulties contingent upon the passive heroine are solved in *Mansfield Park* by surrounding her with characters who act inappropriately. Moreover, the isolation of Fanny Price is uncompromised in that throughout the bulk of the novel we are to entertain the possibility that the "good" man (Edmund Bertram) will be led astray by the morally dubious intruders (the terminology is well-nigh tautological): Mary and Henry Crawford. That is to say, the only (potentially) worthy male is himself compromised. However, Fanny becomes the silent point without which the plot would, paradoxically, have no substantive function and no normative terms of reference. The other actors (and many are to become "actors" in the literal sense) may be ill-informed with respect to the prosaic difficulties of her life (do they know she is not permitted a fire in her room?), but they need her and duly exploit her. "Fanny being always a very courteous listener, and often the only listener at hand, came in for the complaints and the distresses of most of them." (Chapter 18) In this way, the passive heroine is structurally and narratively centered. And when Sir Thomas Bertram is thrown back into the novel at the end of Chapter 18, this reaches a high point of inventiveness, which is almost to be compared to the manner in which plot, character, and social obligation come together on Box Hill.

Austen's chief device here is to compromise her heroine at the very moment when it might seem she would come, at last, into her wholly unblemished own. This is something Austen's critics might care to recall when they complain that she is a Miss Goody Two Shoes or, to quote C. S. Lewis in *The Screwtape Letter*, an insufferable prig. In fact, Austen plays a very acutely judged trick just before Julia rushes in with the dramatic and—even at this period—quaint cry: "My father is come!"

Just before the return Fanny has been talked into taking part in "Lovers' Vows" because Dr. Grant is ill and Mrs. Grant cannot attend rehearsal. Indeed, as we approach the theatrical climax, we see how Fanny's seduction has been gradual. It begins with needlework for the costumes and continues as Mary Crawford seeks her out in her cold room to rehearse her love scene, only for the two to be disturbed by Edmund who wishes to use Fanny for the same purpose—an act of erotic vicarious game-playing unusual in Austen. However, in the billiard room Fanny is not dragooned into actually rehearsing on the stage, but is merely called upon to read. Nevertheless, in being inveigled into the business she has lost her immaculate status. True, in respect of what later happens, this hardly matters. Her instinctual sense of what is right and proper while the master is away, to say nothing of the damage the others have done the billiard room, puts her in a category that seals her off from the criticism to which they are now vulnerable, as Edmund makes clear to his father in Chapter 20. And "we" had always known that, although she had "derived innocent enjoyment from the play," (Chapter 18) her eyes had been open even when her mouth was shut. Yet, we are once again conscious—as we are, for instance, when Emma visits the poor—of how subtle and contradictory Austen's normative values are. Hardly any action or anybody—not even Fanny Price—is underpinned by motives that are unambiguously pure, no matter how hard they try to behave well. As always, Austen is able to invest the apparent banalities of her plots with weighty moral matters. And this understandably upsets those who see in exactly these constrictions and apparent banalities the evidence of her moral and intellectual shortcomings. Nonetheless, in the case of *Mansfield Park* the hostile argument can be unusually perspicacious.

The problem centers on Antigua and slavery. It is one thing for Austen to unambiguously exclude large areas of "life" from her novels. If, however, the exclusion is (as here) drawn to our attention and, moreover, if the author shows us just how she has manipulated the matter, then in being upfront she is paradoxically vulnerable to the charge of playing fast and loose. And this is the guts of Edward Said's criticism. Further, it is interesting that his is an essentially narratively based attack. Although grounding his analysis on the notion of "space," of the invasion of foreign territory into the novel, he does not emphasize the link between the "darkness" of the alien and sexual threat, or fully exploit its deconstructionist potential, or even heavily stress the threatening Other. Rather he addresses directly the simple question of the (lack of) narrative weight given to what is marginalized. A discerning reader of Austen, he lays out his analysis within what seem parameters legitimate to the novel's intellectual and normative territory. We might put this another way and ask: If propriety is to maintain its lofty place in the hierarchy, how then can it be that the slaves in Antigua, on whose miserable lives the civilized pleasures of Mansfield Park are dependent, have in the novel no purchase on impropriety at all? And, we might note, that "impropriety" is the word repeatedly used in Chapter 20, although only (and is this a conscious irony?) in the context of the amateur theatricals. Meanwhile, Said's language lays particular stress on narrative weight with respect to the rival claims of both places (Antigua and Mansfield Park), and he sounds almost puzzled when he observes that "Austen is so summary in one context, so provocatively rich in the other."[14]

The short response is to deny there are rival claims. It has simply been a mistake to permit into the narrative an element whose moral implications are unquestionably outside Austen's ability to control, and which later take on a historical significance of which at the time of writing she could have had no inkling. But that is glib. In allowing us a glimpse of the world outside in that she uses Antigua *by choice* as the narrative escape route for Sir Bertram, she sets her own "so provocatively rich," world in the context of another that she cannot deal with, but whose more dreadful contradictions flow back to compromise her own otherwise impervious, if limited, communities in a manner that bursts their boundaries as *she* has set them up. She may not have followed Bertram to Antigua but she has allowed him to bring it back with him, not least because he comes back so altered—thinner and kindlier. No doubt she sent him so far away to make as believable as possible the radical change in his character. After all, the new benevolent Sir Thomas is the mechanism by which Fanny's position in the family is upgraded. However, whatever the initial cause, she does not shirk the fact of the slave trade, shows in Chapter 21 that it has been a thwarted topic of conversation, and thereby unmistakably, however summarily, lets the matter in. Much the same intrusion occurs in *Persuasion* when she allows us to learn how Captain Wentworth profited from warfare and how this colors the memory of his ship the "Laconia": "How fast I made money in her" (Chapter 8). There are here parallels, too far-reaching in their social implications to be properly developed, but too important to be ignored. Unlike Virginia Woolf's Mrs. Ramsay, whose quasi-mystical knowledge in *To The Lighthouse* is largely instinctual in that she knows Englishmen rule India but she does not have any conception as to how, Austen *does* understand...and, if given the opportunity, her heroines would as well.

Nonetheless, because it cannot be dealt with properly it is somewhat unsettling that she lets us see that her constricted rural societies are not abstracted from a greater world: a world whose sins involve more than an occasional unwise elopement. In what might seem more a sleight of hand than a refutation of an argument, we could claim that Said's criticism does Austen credit in that she, quite unnecessarily (after all, why not send Sir Thomas off to tend an ill relative in Ireland?), permits the matter of slavery to be mentioned at all. What the disturbing and thereby welcome parallel shows is that both the world within the confines of Mansfield Park and the one outside of them (no matter how far away) are marked by imperfections whose abrasive qualities provide the energy that makes both turn and run—which is to say turn and run in respect of the grand category of history (which "reads" as though it were outside the novel), and in respect of its contained expression in fictional narrative. Just as with Jane's outburst in *Jane Eyre*, the "imperfection" proves illuminating.

There is, however, an implicit contradiction here. On the one hand, Box Hill is praised for its seamlessness, while disruptive themes in *Mansfield Park* and *Persuasion* are praised for being just that: disruptive. However, I see no reason why this should be troubling. The exotic riches of the latter are utterly relevant to the domestic social world Austen has contrived and if they disturb us, then so much the better for us. In any case, the argument for seamlessness is itself dependent on delusion. It is a matter of technical adroitness and not of extrinsic reality, although we want to believe that when skillfully done, it manifests the latter. But in fact all seamless artifacts can be unpicked. If, as in an old "Morecambe and Wise" sketch, we claim "you can't see the joins" (in this case of Ernie Wise's toupee) that only confirms that they are there nonetheless and that we will find them if we look carefully enough. The same conclusion can be drawn from Roland Barthes's piece on the new Citroen. Its seams are likewise disguised.[15] But in praxis, there is no inherent reason for claiming the superiority of texts that disguise their constructs vis-à-vis those that do not...or vice versa. Which is to say that the Brechtian model celebrating the work of art as artifact is (as Brecht well knew) equally unable to establish an intrinsic *ahistorical* superiority over the products of traditional aesthetics.

Furthermore, as the celebration of traditional aesthetics rests on a series of unstable values as to good writing, too often we find ourselves criticizing authors for violating their "own" rules without considering whether those rules have been projected back in an utterly ex post facto manner. And once the author is in the canon, the critic is understandably reluctant to throw her out again. Consequently there is recourse to the "flawed masterpiece" argument. But being an argument compelled to foreground the "flaws," it may unwittingly undermine the assumptions of the aesthetic. As we have seen, a critic as percipient as Virginia Woolf finds herself conceding, if only by implication, that the flaws create the masterpiece in that they are the source of its greatest, if aesthetically and morally dubious, pleasures. After all, every discourse will say more than its author intends, while all great novels are likely to say far more than is good for the author's reputation as a conventional writer.

With *Persuasion* we may have the initial impression that very little is being said. Its heroine—Anne Elliot—is astonishingly inactive, feels, following the reappearance of Captain Wentworth whose proposal of marriage she had rejected before "our" novel began, hopelessly trapped and, while being both intelligent and virtuous, is given no privileged place, morally or narratively, but that which follows from our knowledge that she is the heroine. However if *her* tongue is unusually restrained, Austen's is not and she duly compensates for Anne's exceptional reserve. At times she is just plain cruel. From Chapter 6: "The Musgroves had had the ill fortune of a very troublesome, hopeless son; and the good fortune to lose him before he reached his twentieth year... he had been sent to sea because he was stupid and unmanageable on shore...he had been very little cared for at any time by his family, though quite as much as he deserved; seldom heard of, and scarcely at all regretted, when the intelligence of his death abroad had worked its way to Uppercross." This may not be Brontë's rage and rupture, but some may still find it "deformed and twisted" enough.[16] Certainly, the novel thrives on the tension between several remarkably nasty figures on the one hand and the exquisite values implied in the title figure on the other. She has made her mistake and must now bear the consequences. And Anne knows full well that she is written out. She is even compelled to collude in it. As the novel reaches its climax, there is an exchange with Captain Harville in which she observes, in a manner rich with irony for the reader, that: "Men have had every advantage of us in telling their own story. Education has been theirs in so much higher a degree; the pen has been in their hands. I will not allow books to prove anything." (Chapter 23)

However, Anne's isolation (it can be argued that "her" novel is the first romance and it is over before "ours" begins) allows Austen to go for the social jugular. No wonder that we spend more and more time in Bath. Happily for narrative purposes, people there are not susceptible to the civilizing restraints found in the rural communities. In fact some of them, such as Mrs. Clay and Mr. Elliot, are, in rough contemporary language, just plain assholes. And yet even as she sees this, Anne would not do anything very bold: "It was so humiliating to reflect on the constant deception practiced on her father and Elizabeth." (Chapter 22). Yet the most she can do is speak to Lady Russell.

But the narrative tension of *Persuasion* is not merely a product of seeing how someone as abstracted as Anne can, painful step by painful step, overcome the folly of the past and the inevitable resentment that Wentworth must feel. Ellen Moers observes that it is: "Austen's heart-rending final fantasy of the second chance."[17] In other words, we are maneuvered between two stories, one that is "past" but is always there by implication, and the other that is extant and by which that first story is retold and put to rights. It is essentially a rewrite that struggles to make its own beneficent ending credible despite having to live with the consequences of the previous narrative, which, in turn, it must kick back into life. *Persuasion* is, like all second chance stories, implicitly rooted in a triumph over the ultimate closure—death. As such its modest story realizes narrative on the most significant level.

It is not until Chapter 23 when she discusses with Captain Harville (knowing that Wentworth is near enough to overhear) the relative affections and sensibilities of men and women, that Anne says anything of real interest. Overwrought because her remarks are meant for Wentworth, she allows herself a light touch of irony: "'Your feelings may be the strongest,' replied Anne, 'but the same spirit of analogy will authorize me to assert that ours are the most tender. Man is more robust than woman, but he is not longer lived; which exactly explains my view of the nature of their attachments. Nay, it would be too hard upon you, if it were otherwise. You have difficulties, and privations, and dangers enough to struggle with. You are always laboring and toiling, exposed to every risk and hardship. Your home, country, friends, all quitted. Neither time, nor health, nor life, to be called your own. It would be hard, indeed' (with a faltering voice), 'if woman's feelings were to be added to all this.'"

This is a grand piece of writing and it would be a hard reader who did not feel that the *written* declaration of love it elicits is well deserved. But its fine sensibility is almost alien to the novel as a fictional construct, which is manifestly in hock to the intrigues of the malevolent characters. The finer things, the moral agenda of an Austen novel, are here, paradoxically, both central and peripheral to the story in that it is the author's task to manipulate the other characters to reach a closure in which the principal figure gets to rewrite history without taking part in it, which is to say without taking up her pen. It is Wentworth who is writing (a letter) as Anne makes her pertinent speech. If *Persuasion* is so grand as to evoke the Orpheus myth and all those stories that triumph over death and thereby violate the Hemingway quote with which this book began, it is not surprising that the omniscient author must blatantly bestow on her the benevolent destiny. How could such a heroine realize anything so grand herself...without recourse to the Gothic?

And if we now return to Charlotte Brontë, we return also to those fictional elements that the morally centered "mundane" novel has, in the eyes of its supporters (usually male), transcended. Nonetheless, the feverish world of Brontë is not lacking advocates and it is extremely significant that most of them are women.

Villette has always attracted the most penetrating of women critics: notably Virginia Woolf, Ellen Moers, and Mary Jacobus. And looking at the impassioned manner in which it uses grand guignol elements to dramatize women's desires and repression, one can see why. It is true that at the end all the fantastic elements are exposed as illusory, and the mundane duly triumphs, but that only underlines where the bulk of the novel's pleasure lie. Moreover, this celebration of the Gothic seals the novel off from what will turn out in *Shirley* to be a more powerful expression of female oppression partly because, unlike *Villette*, it forgoes the bizarre. If *Shirley* and *Villette* both illustrate Juliet Mitchell's contention that: "The woman novelist must be an hysteric. Hysteria...is simultaneously what a woman can do both to be feminine and to refuse femininity within patriarchal discourse,"[18] the brilliant and ferocious battle at the end of the former, which drives both hero and heroine to the brink of mental collapse, is to be preferred to what, in the latter, is a series of overheated inventions that make up something that is often little more than a dark fairy tale.

Perhaps this would not be so debilitating if, in narrative terms, we were not invited to take both Lucy Snowe's feverish delusions and then their commonsense resolutions equally seriously. For to privilege the former allows us to talk of what is repressed in the female psyche but only when uncoupled from reality. That in itself might be taken as achievement enough in that it suggests just how great the repression is. But to abandon the fantastic means that the novel's "feminist" message, as far as we have experienced it, is likewise abandoned. There is also the danger that the Gothic will accomplish what unqualified poststructuralism accomplishes across the board: namely the death of narrative as a category simply by virtue of such an excess that distinctions are at worst meaningless and at best arbitrary playthings. Nonetheless, when *Villette* ditches the Gothic it castrates its own agenda. And although that agenda, castrated or not, is impressive enough, it is also likely to lead us to underestimate what Charlotte Brontë can in fact achieve.

Still, it is hardly surprising that Mary Jacobus is fascinated by its deconstructive possibilities, which she brilliantly exploits,[19] or that Woolf calls the novel Brontë's "finest".[20] Ellen Moers is of the same opinion and compares it to *Shirley*, which she sees as "brilliant and also seriously flawed."[21] We should agree promptly, but only if we thank God for those flaws. *Shirley* is far too great an encounter with its subject to escape flaws, far too honest to reconcile—to be able to reconcile—the structural, aesthetic, and intellectual contradictions it throws up. Without its flaws, it would be a much lesser thing.

A simple point of entry is that of the titular "dark" heroine herself. She does not make it until Chapter 11 when the book is more than a third through. Up to that point the story has been the provenance of the passive—and fair—Caroline Helstone, who displays in excess all those qualities we have come to admire in her passive sisters. She is better read than any of them, more delicate in her feelings, more tormented by a love she cannot voice and, despite the competition, in a class of her own when it comes to languishing illnesses. This latter allows a highly contained Gothic element to be introduced when Mrs. Pryor (Caroline's mother, although Caroline does not know it) tends her during the delirious climax of her fever. All of this means that when the active woman arrives the ideological and aesthetic field is clear. Caroline can only become her pale, yet discerning "sister." But if Shirley Keeldar has a clear shot at what it means to be an independent woman, endowed with that "moral worth" Lionel Trilling clumsily conferred on Emma, then she, too, will need the means to enjoy it. And indeed she is a heiress; and willful. But she is most definitely not wrong.

As soon as Shirley enters, a massive battle over identity/gender is instigated. It is in the first instance framed in terms of Shirley's status as an ersatz man. An only child, her parents had wanted a boy and would have called him Shirley too. Moreover, she plays with the notion of being a man. She is a landowner, there is the title "Esquire," and when Helstone joins in the bantering conversation, he refers to Shirley as: "this captain of yeomanry, this young squire." (Chapter 11) All this becomes a running "joke."

However, the notion that an independent woman's entry into the nineteenth-century novel must compel her—if she is not to be an hysteric—to adopt an imitative male identity is far too simplistic in the light of what Brontë does this time. We might remember that during the famous outburst in *Jane Eyre*, Jane declares "women feel as men feel" and her cry, as a result, is for equality. But *Shirley* is more ambitious. Above all the dark heroine is a powerful and *different* sexual presence, and this is felt by everyone around her. As a result two of the men make—for radically different reasons—inappropriate marriage proposals. One case (that of the "strong" contained man: Robert Moore) is particularly apposite in that Shirley feels no sexual attraction to him, but has instead regarded him as an equal and a friend. This was difficult for him to grasp and he blundered. Consequently we see that her notion of liberation, the range of her sensibilities, allows her to move more widely within the novel's topography with respect to the relations she might have with the other characters. She is possessed, in short, of an emotional life that none of them—but for, perhaps, Louis Moore, the man she *will* marry—can equal. For the men at least, she is the dangerous Other: something they unwittingly reveal in their attempts to textually sex-change her .

Nonetheless, she is trapped within time and place, which is to say within convention. It is Robert Moore who, in Chapter 30, reports to us that she declared: "you deny me the possession of all I value most. That is to say, that I am a traitor to all my sisters." But then she capitulates in accordance with stereotypes. She responds to his request for forgiveness, with: "I would, if there were not myself to forgive too... but to have mis-led a sagacious man so far, I must have done wrong." It is a remarkable moment. Neither is there escape from the given social roles, even for this woman, nor will the exceptional freedom she wins in the later struggle with Louis free her from these contradictions. But that struggle and what she makes out of it will reset the parameters, morally and ideologically, to a degree unequaled by any of those "sisters" she presumably had in mind when she addressed Robert. In fact, here Brontë will upturn the model of *Jane Eyre*.

The man worthy of Shirley is thrown into the novel later even than Shirley herself. Louis Moore arrives, rather ghostlike, in Chapter 12. He enriches the conflict because in the first instance, although deeply proud, he is socially not Shirley's equal. Better still, he is employed as a tutor, a "governess." In short, he is a male Jane Eyre. Out of this brilliant shift the novel quarries its far-reaching climax; a climax/closure that is defi-nitely not, as in *Villette,* an external gesture detached from the body of the novel.

Clearly there is great tension between the power that Shirley, as Shirley, possesses vis-à-vis Louis, and the power he possess over her not because of who she is, but simply because she is a woman. If she is to marry she will have to be, in all senses, possessed. Both proud combatants will have to humble themselves, not least because each is fully conscious of, and intel-lectually equal to, the challenge of understanding the dilemma in which the other finds herself/himself. Furthermore, in battle, each is both com-passionate and exploitative. That it is a battle is explicit on every level. That Shirley is fit to fight is likewise explicit in the pagan imagery in which she is clothed, chiefly by Louis. She is: "leopardess", "pantheress" and in Chapter 36: "beautiful forest born... wily, tameless, peerless nature!" And this in a novel pickled in curates.

Equality is established in Chapter 28 by virtue of something that allows no *fundamental* distinction between any two people: death. Shirley believes she may have contracted rabies and wants Louis to kill her should she develop the disease. Brontë handles this in customary style, playing off purple descriptive passages against cool, point-scoring dialogue. But the question of *social* (in)equality cannot be unambiguously settled. In the chapter following this, Louis rages "If I must be her slave, I will not lose my freedom for nothing," Although his inferiority is conditional and not gender fixed, there a sense here of Jane's outburst.

However, as we move toward the climatic encounter, we need to know that Shirley understands that she must be the loser in conventional terms. She refuses the socially superior Sir Philip Nunnely because "He is...not my *master.*" (Chapter 31, Brontë's underlining.), and further: "When I promise to obey, it shall be under the conviction that I can keep that promise." We might sense here a qualification that dilutes the humiliation of striving for a goal that, in part, one despises. Her desire is as much intellectual as sexual, for Louis is brilliant and able to spar with her on equal terms. She is no longer *his* pupil. But if her promise can only be made when she knows she can keep it, we might infer that it will be a promise "extracted" from her on her terms. It is not merely love that she wants, or an end to celibacy, though that question will explicitly crop up when she and Louis confront each other. She also wants friendship with an equal which means, in part, that she must compel *him* to be so. There is no suggestion here that Shirley's married life to Louis will correspond to the life Emma *imagines* she will enjoy with Mr. Knightley.

The showdown—and it is a showdown—comes in Chapter 36 and, as with Robert Moore in Chapter 30, it is supposedly told us by the man. It is a fight that moves back and forth under a brittle veneer of politeness and wit. Both struggle for the same goal, which is not only the submission of the other but a submission in terms in which they too can submit. They play, but savagely, with notions of master and mistress. She allows herself to be portrayed as a wild animal while surgically exploiting his own analogy between himself and her dog Tartar. He uses force to stop her leaving the room and she forces him to declare first, which at least earns him the (in part, humiliating) right to ask her directly if she loves him. Her reply is merciless: "A little bit." And then when they capitulate a certain textual equality is engineered. Names—or rather titles/roles—are played with. He, the tutor/governess, calls her "my pupil, my sovereign." True, she had once been his pupil, and in a way it is part of his agenda to make her that again. Naturally she succumbs in formal terms, as she had known she must. But though she is at first unambivalent ("My master") she still cannot let him, as he *begs* for her, forget what the consequences of all this are for her. She asks: are we "equal then, *sir?*" (my emphasis.) It is also her duty to school him, to teach him that his proud fury as to position and money is contemptible. Louis is still learning and so she tells him in plain language that she wants him *also* as a "friend," which is to say as someone who will respect her in accordance with her standards.

True the closure may seem conventional, but the manner in which it has to be fought for, the degree of humiliation it has involved and, above all, the high degree of awareness on the part of the protagonists, give the standard surrender/triumph model a wholly unconventional character. This is underpinned by privileging the man's voice—a device that compromises authorial authority and undercuts the status of the eponymous heroine. Consequently we have a greater feeling for what both combatants sacrifice as well as their uncertainty as to the cost of that sacrifice.

Indeed Brontë has gone further than women theoreticians, emphasizing the intrinsic patriarchal character of language, seem to appreciate. She has, at the very least, played a double game. Apparently colonizing the male voice out of respect for dominant phallocentric power in a situation (possession and marriage) in which the woman is always inferior, she has exposed the utterly *different* nature of female language and narrative goals. She has done this by forcing the exceptionally intelligent male to enter female discourse, even to voice it, and then reveals how he can never irrevocably master it. He certainly has no reason to believe that the narrative he has ostensibly reached is unequivocally fixed. For instance, Shirley *will* seek a postponement of the wedding.

But of course, none of this would persuade the radical feminists with whom this chapter began. That it convinces me can mean nothing in *that* context. Nor can one deny that Brontë's clichés readily provide ammunition for those who see either a capitulation that, when all is said and done, is no different formally from the customary female capitulation, or a flawed attempt at resetting the parameters, which only emerges as significant because it is so unsuccessful. However, if you do not see texts as flawless, but find riches in their complex and, ultimately, unresolved and unresolvable encounters with "reality," then Brontë's "flawed masterpiece" is doing a lot—something we might remember when we read Woolf's caveat as to the jejune nature of her "philosophic view of life."[22]

Here it is necessary to confess a less than unambiguous position with respect to partisan arguments, that is, as to that camp in which I want to place my argument. Frankly, I wish to have it as many ways as possible in order that the category of narrative as it encounters the question of (female) literature and (female) subjectivity maintain its explanatory priority. Nonetheless, the general tendency has been to reject as fruitless a radical feminist position, principally because it is very difficult to establish a category of women's writing qua writing, which is not contaminated by other categories. It has been a feature of the pluralist feminist position (it certainly does not have to be solely a socialist feminist position) that the presence of race, class, ethnicity, and so on, are inevitably going to mix the broth so that to factor them all out to the point that only gender remains is as absurd as it is impossible. What are we to say, for instance, when Maggie Humm, confronted by the proliferating field of women's writing, observes that "African feminist criticism reconceptualises feminist aesthetics by expanding the terrain of literary criticism into a complex politics of gender, race and writing,"[23] other than: But who on earth thought it could be otherwise?

The radical feminist position also trips up on the more fundamental level of subjectivity. Post-Freudian and Lacanian theory and all that they have spawned, may well suggest that the collision between gender and the symbolic order must lead to the conclusion that somewhere in there an intrinsic woman's language must be trying to get out. However, in the face of the teeming fecundity of the id and the emotional lives of individuals, this is to cram the matter into a too narrow pigeonhole. And that, even before other, broader, sociological factors are permitted entry into the discussion. Therefore, one might conclude that literature, to quote Nelly Furman, is "not per se a patriarchal form of discourse."[24] If that is accepted, for the moment, the argument that the woman is forced inevitably into the role of the hysteric loses its weight, and Juliet Mitchell's case in "Gender and Genre," which has seemed so perspicacious in the context of several of the novels discussed here, would likewise collapse.[25]

Furthermore, any privileging of the hysteric is also troubling in that it would logically colonize the whole field of writing by women. This is something that Mary Jacobus seems to have in mind when she points out that were the maxim of the hysteric valid, it would follow that all readings or interpretations by women would be determined normatively by just this category; and this, one assumes, would also include Mitchell's own theoretical work explaining the maxim.[26] In this case, it would be impossible to break out of the circle. But when the critic asserts a noncontradictory model, it always disintegrates in the face of the heterogeneity of creative writing—something that is, in itself, one of the most welcome functions of fiction. Rita Felski is making this point implicitly when she addresses the multifarious body of women's writing in the latter half of the twentieth century, and she is making it explicitly when she pours into the category of writing the cornucopia of social, sexual, semantic, and historical forces from which it takes nourishment. As a result there can be "no legitimate grounds for classifying any particular style of writing as uniquely or specifically feminine."[27]

All of this would seem to free us from doctrinaire positions and it is all neat enough if you accept the premises. But why should we? I would like to have it both ways—to have recourse to a radical position when it is convenient to do so while rejecting a transcendental notion of *l'écriture féminine*. Or, to place the matter in terms of just one theoretician, I accept what Juliet Mitchell rejects (the female voice), while rejecting her over-riding determined category of a particular type of "hysteria" produced by phallocentrism. The key question is then: What is the nature of this "female voice"?

It is a self-evidently "lesser" notion than the concepts employed by radical theoreticians. It is not a definition based on the creation of subjectivity in language because, as already argued, such a definition collapses under a plethora of other considerations. That the acquisition of identity, the socializing of the individual, the impossibly complex interaction between unconscious drives and lived conscious life are decisive issues is not open to doubt, but no single manipulation of them can settle the issue of language, literature, and identity. Therefore, the notion is "lesser" in that it assumes no definitive, or even confident, interpretation of the manner in which language and gender are rooted in the deeper terrain of subjectivity. All it asserts is that the matter will be unstable, heterogeneous, and will shatter the conceptual borders of even the most broadminded generalization.

Interestingly, this position highlights a contradiction. The radical, deep-seated explanation engages with notions of subjectivity and language on the most *complex* terrain in order (as is clear with the French feminists) to arrive at a *singular*, focused, first cause...for instance the "singing" female body. This is then declared valid across the board. But better to prefer a more "superficial" explanation precisely because it gives us some considerable entry into the complexity and fecundity of not only questions of identity but also of culture in the widest sense. For it transpires that the grand theory is, despite its jargon and the difficulty of its concepts, a strategy of simplification. It is a black and white position disposed, as with most acts of reductionism, to produce ideology at best and propaganda at worst.

Returning to the question of the female voice, the lesser definition can now be put in the context of the entry of the subject into narrative. All the novels examined here are concerned with exactly that; all are knowing encounters with the painful efforts of the female to find a worthy place in a world in which she is always the knowing but inferior subject...and all say more than their authors intend. Furthermore, the violent struggle to realize feminine identity within narrative is characterized by a polyvalence that is expressed in the unstable character of the master narrative, even when the author sees that narrative as self-evident and unproblematic. And this raises the critical question of the nature of realism. Morality and narration, struggle and utopia, subject and community, all come together with respect to realism as well. And it is in this contingent context that the radical nature of poststructuralism can now be best employed.

Felski's notion of realism in women's literature is straightforward, Lukáscian and, in its initial form, too simple. It is, "the depiction of a social reality which is not relativized as the product of a subjective consciousness."[28] It is not clear how any form of writing—and certainly not fiction—can avoid being "relativized as the product of a subjective consciousness," although what Felski wants to consider is, in the first instance, nineteenth-century literature that does not play with stream of consciousness or other later, more radical, stylistic techniques. Instead it takes the empirical world to be objective and knowable. However, what is underplayed in the definition is the problematic of narrative, the difficulty of entry into story for *both* the female author and the female character. The most striking characteristic of the novels examined in this chapter is that their ideological claims as they center on the woman do not fit easily into, or find ready expression within, the category of narrative unless the author resorts to the typical strategies of the woman writer: it can be a form of wish-fulfillment-cum-romance that undercuts social realism, it may mock the whole business of the narrative telos by underlining the synthetic jerry-built closures, or it could abandon social reality completely in favor of the fantastic. But in all the novels, the central female figures are in a struggle with the genre itself and, moreover, in a manner that a male hero in a male novel is not. In that sense, standard goal-orientated fiction *is* inherently patriarchal. It sets out exactly those qualities Anne Elliot (talking to Captain Harville so that Wentworth could overhear) declared were the lot of man, as self-evident, which is to say not in need of justification. The woman must, however, find a place, a story for herself (no matter how passive) and must justify it. And even if she takes the place thrust upon her (by social/fictional convention) she must justify that too. Thus, we should regard George Eliot's criticism of Jane for refusing to take on the role of Rochester's mistress as extremely substantive aesthetically—to say nothing of its social implications. *Jane Eyre* becomes, ultimately, a shallow romance because the justification (for the heroine's morally "superior" flight) is not adequate to the theme of woman's freedom and self-realization as the author herself has broached the matter.

There is a further important characteristic of the woman's struggle within narrative; namely it is a matter of deep decision-making, even when, paradoxically, the decision is that one cannot in all conscience do anything. The central female figures of the Austen and Brontë novels constantly consider, and on a level normally closed to male characters in a male novel, what it is they can do and what it is they should do and rail—in one way or another—against the impossibility of reconciling the two. Thus, the duality made up of author and character tackles narrative possibilities in a manner that is quite different from that of the heroic man of action who is not prevented from doing. But the woman's decision-making function is meaningful because it is constricted. It is not merely a question of tactics, of the best manner of attaining self-realization. It is nothing less than the question of finding space for the heroine and opportunity for action *itself* and in such a manner that certain, variable or arbitrary, aesthetic standards are maintained. It is the struggle over the *possibility* (in narrative fiction as in society) of self-realization. No matter how busy the story, whether due to the mundane gossip of a village chatterbox or the overheated fantasies of a sexually repressed Englishwoman in a foreign city, the question as to the place of the heroine within the story is never decisively settled, and on occasion can be abandoned at the close to ridicule or failure. The author/character pairing is never able, within the genre, to establish the genre and its narrative(s) to the degree that it has the probity and weight of the alternative, overtly phallocentric, discourse. The triumvirate of female author, heroine, and reader are in fact continually asking themselves "Is there really a woman in this text?"—a question that would be absurd were it asked about the hero of a novel written by a man.

Therefore, the question does arise with respect to the "lesser" female voice: Is narrative an intrinsic phallocentric category? If this were so, it would suggest that, in this context at least, Juliet Mitchell is right to talk of the woman compelled to "speak 'masculinely' in a phallocentric world." Frankly, I cannot see how narrative can be anything but, *superficially,* a patriarchal category as long as the exercise of power and the ideology of action is gender weighted—which is still, of course, the case however much we imagine we have moved on from the world of the nineteenth-century novel. However, the "superficiality" of this is its most appealing feature, even with respect to the "dated" novels discussed here. That is, if the matter can be problematized in respect of women's novels produced within the confines of a male apparatus, then the argument as to voice and women's writing might have unusual strength simply because recourse to more modern radical models has not been possible.

The major factor that might be used to underpin the claim that it is superficial to see phallocentrism as determining in narrative, is dependent upon the (implicit) variety of narrative in play. The decision-making woman, the tension between passive and active, foreground a narrative praxis that is plural and it is this plurality that undermines a weak notion of realism when realism is seen merely as an encounter with an empirically unproblematized world, even if that world is but the product of early nineteenth-century fiction. Cora Kaplan approaches this point when, stressing the plurality of factors (class, race, etc.,) that go into (feminine) texts, she observes that they are not merely "metaphors for the sexual," rather they should be seen as "reciprocally constituting each other through a kind of narrative invocation, a set of associative terms in a chain of meaning."[29] Although, I suggest, it would be better to talk here of *chains* of meaning.

It is this pluralism that undercuts the deep-seated patriarchal claim. Conflicting narratives are at work and the heroine is positioned within them, either as that figure best placed to understand them (Anne Elliot, Fanny Price, Jane Eyre), or best placed to (unwisely) manipulate them (Elizabeth Bennet, Emma), or best placed to do both (Shirley). And these competing narratives, which here take their power from the ambivalent and combative place of nineteenth-century women in stories, produce a notion of realism that is polyvalent and contradictory. Therefore, it is here that poststructuralism is most helpful. True, deep-seated "realism" in fiction is defined not in terms of a nonproblematic empirical and knowable world in which the novel has been placed (Felski's notion), but as the competing narratives (explicit and implied) that deconstruct each other as those fictional stories are told. However, it is not a pure poststructuralism in that it does not, as noted above, exclude the author and it certainly does not treat the potentially limitless count of narratives thrown up by deconstruction as all equally valid. That is, the struggle over the various narratives that has been followed here in individual novels is, in the first instance, open to control by the author, and, in the second, by us.

All the novels looked at here show how the woman—even when impeccably behaved—undercuts the (phallocentric) genre. Irony bordering on sarcasm, cries of frustration at the debilitating or crippling power of dominant social and fictional structures, even obedience to convention whether social or literary, are redolent with alternatives, with what is repressed and denied. In the end, one sees that the phallocentric narrative is paradoxically the most fruitful category open to the woman. It becomes the site of a feminine unpicking, a poststructuralist deconstruction that tackles the discourse on the level of its deepest assumptions. And even when that discourse is left, apparently, in command of the field—as in *Jane Eyre* or in the peremptory closures—it is as wounded as Rochester. The dominant masculine narrative is always vulnerable to subversion. Whether by Emma imperially "writing" a novel to establish that she is always wrong while, at the same time, positioning herself so that she has a monopoly of the pleasure (and reward) to be got from narrative, or whether it functions on the highly sophisticated level of semantic irony as when Shirley calls Louis her master after she has placed him at her feet as an explicit ersatz signifier for her devoted dog Tartar.

All this would suggest that one might, after all, succumb to the radical feminist position of Irigaray and Cixous et al. if they would forgo eggs, and torrents, and singing flesh and start taking apart the "enemy" in stories,

Eggs may be "endless," novels are not. The Germans say that everything has an end, but for a sausage, which has two. Well, novels certainly have a first and last page, but outbid the sausage with an abundance of implied alternatives. So, the alternatives radical feminists are looking for are there, but not where they are looking.

Telos, utopia, death, and self-realization remain fundamental categories that any group must employ to write the stories that give their lives meaning. And narrative per se is not *intrinsically* privileged except with regard to these qualities. But because the master narrative in European literature is in general phallocentric, there is, paradoxically, a special case to be made for women's writing. It is in a position to deconstruct that master narrative from the polarity that it fears most, and on a terrain that is more fundamental, if generalized, than more superficial questions of class, and ethnicity, and so forth. One characteristic of this "special" status is clear, a least by implication, in a remarkable book written before the high-water mark of feminist theory. Ellen Moers showed many years ago (1978), when she moved freely between authors, characters, and all the various genres (poems, letters, novels etc.,) in which women express themselves, that no matter how much women writers may consciously reject (or adopt) a notion of language as intrinsically encoded by phallocentricism, they will always be writing to and for other women. That is, a shared gender experience resonates throughout women's literature and gives it a unique and enriched quality. It does not, in the final analysis, matter if this is seen as the product of the history of the tribe or as a result of different notions of subjectivity. What matters is that it is crucial. For while men too, are inevitably writing for other men, they do not know it on a profound level, simply because it is too self-evident to require either knowledge or theory. But women do. And in this respect at least, men's writing qua writing is, I would argue, axiomatically inferior.

However, there is no reason to assume that story-based theories will tend inherently to the multivocal as opposed to the singular. The latter option is very attractive largely because the very notion of narrative implies one might crack the historical code and promulgate a metatheory. The master story will always lead the theoretician seductively to the point where he can triumphantly uncover first principles. Moreover, making sense of everything is a prerequisite for dogma, which is itself pointless unless decked out in the oppressive uniform of authority. And authority is hardly prone to the appeal of diverse, let alone contradictory, interpretations.

So we now turn to one such patriarchal figure who, while dealing in apparent heterogeneity, was determined to reduce it to the explanatory category of a single overriding story. However, that story took its narrative power not from a utopian projection, no matter how qualified, but rather from a rewind so that the first cause itself could be excavated, not as a benign paradigm that throws hope and salvation into the world, but as a real event that created both the individual and the community, and created them both as debilitated and irredeemably imprisoned.

Chapter 4

Freud

Science as Narrative, a Perverse and Singular Teleology, Certainty Masquerading as Doubt

Freud is no doubt being disingenuous when he observes that "it still strikes me myself as strange that the case histories I write should read like short stories,"[1] for as soon as he capitulated to the full consequences of his psychological discoveries (as he saw them) he was compelled to forgo any strict, exclusive notion of standard scientific practice. At the beginning of *Der Traumdeutung* (*The Interpretation of Dreams*)—that massive, frequently revised early work covering the period during which he made what he saw as the discoveries that unlocked the unconscious—he observes that it may all read more like the work of a poet, something that he, as a scientific "researcher," finds a little disturbing. The disingenuousness is then clinched as he adds that the poetic element, however "embarrassing" (he is going to use his own dreams as raw material), is unavoidable.[2]

However, this is a poet who, while maintaining the license of free association characteristic of the artist, knows that he is on a mission to bring literary and thereby—in what might be seen as an ironic payoff—scientific sense to the matter. He must create out of the seeming random material—chronologically muddled, mediated through symbols, formed by condensation ("Verdichtung") and displacement ("Verschiebung")—order. And it transpires that there is only one formal trope, which enables that order: he must make a rational story out of the "impossible" material. He will reconstruct the chronological sequence from out the chaos of the symbols and imaginings that he, as analyst/narrator, has evoked. It is then, in a paradox wholly apposite to Freud, the power of the artistic undertaking together with its successful completion, that is used *retrospectively* as proof of his probity as a scientist. Furthermore, in this celebration of hermeneutics there is a clear parallel with (Marxist) dialectics. The love of the contradiction—for its own aesthetic sake—that can be found most notably in Adorno, is also an expression that what one sees superficially is misleading and must be contradicted by a deeper truth. To take anything at face value is to deny dialectics in the case of Marxism and the unconscious in the case of Freudianism.

The completed interpretation, which becomes apparent as each element (or incident) finds its predetermined (albeit at first unknown) place in the chronology, also functions as an ex post facto proof that exactly that interpretation is scientifically kosher. Therefore, although the initial literary fancy implies inventiveness, the final narrative is seen to fit the rigorous demands of "research." And research, we should not forget, is an empirical activity; it is a matter in which facts take precedence over speculation. This sense of completeness defined in chronological terms is always very upfront in the terminology that Freud uses. He talks of "scenes," frequently of missing scenes that he *knows* exist somewhere because he has breaks in the narrative. And this can be frustrating, especially if the analysand will not cooperate. On one occasion, he wrote to Wilhelm Fliess: "My banker...took off at the critical point, just before he was to bring me the last scenes."[3] But once the story is complete, the matter, taken as an interpretative whole, must also be complete. The story then becomes, again by definition, impeccable so that no single part can be removed or questioned without the whole disintegrating. The aesthetic perfection of the interpretation, expressed as a homogeneous unity in which nothing is left hanging, provides the retrospective validation of both the original scientific goal and the final scientific status of the solution. As he says of his interpretation of the Wolf Man's case (surely one of the most imaginative and arbitrary of all his "solutions") either "everything took place just as I have described it..." or it is "...all a piece of nonsense from start to finish." (G p.199)[4] There is no place for anything in between.

This reconciliation of opposed categories (that of the poet with the scientist; fantasy with empirical research) enables the Freudian enterprise to colonize a wide range of epistemological territory. Few grand narratives can rival it, and this is not merely evidence of an eclectic and erudite mind. The territory is mapped because, as Freud is driven to conclude, everything fits and every element axiomatically vindicates all the others. This, further, underlines a feature of Freudianism, which while not unique to it, is exceptionally well developed: namely, a series of encounters with polarities shown to work in tandem. The question then arises as to how the dialectical reconciliations actually pan out, to what extent the "Aufhebungen" deserve the term in that they preserve, in an enhanced synthesized form, the initial opposed tendencies, or to what degree the final axioms merely amount to the sacrifice of one set of values in the interests of another.

Here one sees in structural and epistemological terms the great danger and the great attraction of the Freudian Weltanschauung. One might place this in the context of both Kant's universalism (for Freud allows of nothing outside his intellectual topography) and his teleology. Moving from a "physio-teleology", which "can never disclose to us anything about a *final end* of creation" (although it is clear that a teleology must by definition posit such an end), Kant remarks that a moral theology, also drawn in the first instance from the argument from design, necessitates not only the final telos to which we must be inexorably, however chaotically, heading, but moreover must evoke an equally necessary powerful notion of origin. That is, in driving us inescapably to think of the "given ends of nature...we must afterward look for a final end, and this final end obliges us to seek the principle of the causality of the supreme cause in question."[5] Freud is the great Pope of this supreme cause, which as a tautological necessity must be retrospective. It is he, more than any other social "scientist," who is engaged unbendingly in an archaeological search for origins; ultimately, of course, an all-explanatory single origin, a fons et origo. And he duly finds it. It turns out to be the ur-act of parricide (Vatermord) uncovered in *Totem and Taboo*. And in its very nature, this is an act that explains equally the destiny of the individual and the origin of the species. It is the psychic trauma through which we all must pass. To make an arbitrary comparison with the paradigm of primitive communism, one notes that Freud's paradigm is both negative (it evokes horrors and shame, and bases human culture and individual "health" on monstrous acts of repression) and highly explicit. For Freud, it is not where we are going that matters. In the case of the individual that can be dealt with by the death wish, while in respect of the species he is largely pessimistic—as is clear in *Civilization and Its Discontents*. The future is simply not his brief. What matters is from whence we have come. And *that* is certainly nothing like the Wordsworthian image of the child trailing clouds of glory. But if Freud's teleology is contradictory in that it is a rewind, it is a rewind of unequaled explanatory power and comprehensiveness. Furthermore, it is one he stringently pursues to its logical—and for many people absurd—anthropological end.

Whereas other theoreticians seeing their metatheories unravel in the face of teeming heterogeneous reality, do their best to rescue what they can and, not unreasonably but in a less than stringent manner, take cover behind the assertion that history is a messy terrain, Freud begins with the mess. But only because he is sure that it hides coherence. Moreover, this coherence reconciles two qualities one might normally think of as opposed: individual uniqueness and universal similarity. Logically the Freudian enterprise necessitates a final (which is to say chronologically, a first) explanation remarkably simple in character. And that despite the cornucopia of brilliant, discrete insights that he excavates.

In this context, it is hardly surprising that the standard dichotomy between the individual and the group is unusually pungent in Freud, as is the parallel polarity in which the clone and the incomparably singular stand at extremes to each other. It is indeed remarkable how the analyst begins not merely with the individual analysand, but with that analysand's most private, which is to say most subjectively determining, characteristics. As a rule we are inclined to protect our intimate fantasies and dreams because they clearly represent that which most nakedly shows us as we are, which is to say shows how we differ, or imagine we differ, from others. The resulting analyses—as in the famous five cases—are, in the first instance, overt celebrations of exactly that discrete notion of subjectivity. And yet, partly as a result of a process by which the accumulative analyses of patients generates a general enriching of the analyst's knowledge, inferences of ever increasing range and substance emerge until it is possible to assert a pattern, first mentioned by Freud in a letter to Fliess on October 15, 1897, when he suggests "a *universal* event in early childhood."[6] The development of this "universal" event produces, ultimately, a first cause by virtue of which human society is engendered out of the primal horde. The individual's psychosis may then be stringently analyzed and intellectually mulled over, but chiefly for the greater purpose of extracting from it a confirmation of values that are not in the first (chronological) instance subject-based at all. In the dialectical opposition made up of subjectivity and the collective, the former is increasingly and determinedly sacrificed to the claims of the latter. Freud, after beginning with his own highly subjective dreams, ends up with something, which in the context of Marxist humanism, we have called "species being."

The dichotomy between the clone and the unique event is easily manipulated within the Freudian model. Rather than moving, as the historian does, along a continuum joining both polarities so that comparisons are inevitably employed that relate historical periods to each other while working out what gives each—arbitrarily defined—period its defining uniqueness, the Freudian model allows free, untroubled, movement so that at all times and at all places on the continuum, the supposedly opposed claims of the uniqueness of the subject and the manner in which this uniqueness is expressed in the shared cultural DNA of the species, are simultaneously asserted in absolute terms. Out of the continuum a ring is formed. Thus, one notes in *The Interpretation of Dreams* the flat statement: "It is my experience, for which I have found no exception, that every dream concerns the person of the dreamer. Dreams are absolutely egotistical."[7] But we can then proceed to a passage, added in 1909, in which we learn that the symbols of the dream "do not belong as such to the dream but to the 'unconscious' of the Volk"[8] and then, in a 1919 revision that shifts the matter decisively in the direction of the species while refusing to forgo the importance of the individual, the formulation that while: "Every dream is a regression to the earliest relationships and experiences of the individual child . . . 'behind this childhood' we are given the opportunity to look into the 'phylogenetic childhood, into the development of the human species' of which the individual childhood is merely an abbreviated [abgekürtze] repetition."[9] Here both opposed terms are apparently maintained, but in fact one has been sacrificed to the overriding claims of the other. The analysis of Serge Pankejeff (the Wolf Man) exhibits exactly this procedure and reveals, in particular, how as the deeper (which, once again, with Freud is not merely a spatial but also a temporal notion in that it must take us further back) anthropological material starts to dominate it turns, of necessity, into a universal cultural inheritance passed "phylogenetically" from generation to generation.

Behind these shifts there lies not only the tensions generated by opposed claims rooted in different sorts of knowledge. Put simply, *they* can all be seen as the products of the radically different status of the imaginative artist vis-à-vis that of the "objective" researcher noted above. And in any case, Freud as author (storyteller) knows how to exploit these oppositions in the most adept and satisfying manner. But there is the greater ("deeper") matter of the cultural genetic inheritance of the species, which increasingly dominates the intellectual construct, although it is an axiom lying outside the parameters of conventional science. The individual DNA, to use language Freud knew nothing of, is trumped by a necessary phylogeneticism that is asserted as an empirical fact because without it, his findings simply could not stand. That is to say, it is necessitated by everything that stringently followed from the first awareness of the hidden Hamlet/Oedipus "universal" fantasy mentioned by Freud to Fliess in 1897. However, its validity as a "fact" is not established according to its own epistemological character or within its own terms, but rather inferred according to quite foreign considerations. It is rather like the activity of the astronomer who comes to the conclusion that his model of the planets will not hold unless he finds a further, as yet unknown, astronomical body. But Freud can never empirically establish phylogenetic inheritance, though that will hardly stop him

claiming that it simply *is*. Thus, his notion of a taboo-based, species universal—a collective psychic printout—becomes the umbrella under which
the teeming abundance of lived experience is contextualized. Which is to
say that, despite its apparent brilliance in handling heterogeneous reality,
it is also the triumph of the deeper singular narrative at the expense of the
plethora of individual stories that initially Freud garnered from his patients
and which, ironically, first inspired the whole enterprise. So if we are to
appreciate just how this wide-reaching, reverse teleology, focused on a first
cause, remorselessly reveals our shared psychoses and traumas, we might
well begin with the unorthodox sleuth facing up to the apparently baffling
heterogeneity of the psychic material he unearthed in his patients. Here is
the early Freud who saw himself as both a detective and "a conquistador—
an adventurer."[10] Remarkable, however, are the adept shifts he employs to
get from the theatrical to the scientific.

Of course it is self-evidently appropriate that Freud should see himself as
a detective, a solver of riddles. And this is something that his most famous
and committed patient, the Wolf Man, spotted.[11] The detective is utterly
goal-orientated and narratively determined. This mirrors the retrospective
Freudian method. Hysterics are trapped in stories and though they begin
at the end with their extant malfunctions, the vital causal element is well
in the past. Detective and analyst also have a shared problem in that their
suspects and patients are not to be approached without great skepticism.
Analysands may not consciously know the truth or they may choose to
dissemble, while in the conventional detective story we may reasonably
assume that at least one of the suspects is a liar. Above all, both analyst and
detective work backwards to fill in the gaps, to deal with what Freud calls
"hiatus." As he said of the Dora case—he has to provide "what is missing."
And just as the detective, when he has cracked the riddle, reassembles the
actors to reproduce the initial all-determining ur-act, now in its complete
and incontestable form, so Freud seeks in his famous five cases to reproduce the primal scene that, when "re-discovered," settles the matter once
and for all. Furthermore, not only is he supremely well aware of this, he is
also conscious of the aesthetic pleasure it affords.

Psychoanalysis does indeed have "a place for everything."[12] Thus, the
Wolf Man is not important solely for the famous dream and the even more
famous freewheeling interpretation the analyst "found." Everything else to
do with Serge Pankejeff serves to tell the same story. Chasing the butterfly,
the period of religious enthusiasm, the need to breathe in short deep gasps,
the oddly colored pear, the "scene" with the maid Gruscha—each element,
quite irrespective of how different in character it *may* seem, is shown to sub-
stantiate all the others. This is detective work where there are no red her-
rings, everything fits; or, at least, everything *will* fit once Freud has realized

that, in general, he was barking up the wrong tree with his initial theory of neuroses, as he excitedly announces to Fliess on September 21, 1897. It is to be noted that this famous, and for many feminists infamous, Pauline conversion (Freud being no longer prepared to believe that paternal sexual abuse of children could be as common as his female patients suggested) is, in the first instance, instigated by his "continual disappointment...to bring a single analysis to a real conclusion."[13] This lack of completeness in getting to narrative closure is the fundamental factor that makes it clear to the analyst/storyteller that he has gone wrong. And nothing marks out the Wolf Man case more strikingly than the manner in which the exceptional quantity of stuff/raw material that it generates is shown, ultimately, to be part of an integrated whole, generated by the ur-act.

The Wolf Man Story is not, however, significant solely for its narrative purity. It is placed at a critically important time in Freud's intellectual development. For he realizes that he has to move into anthropology to explain the actual evolutionary event(s) that initiated civilization. This was a move from the overtly literary to the overtly historical, the move from Sophocles's *Oedipus Rex* and Shakespeare's *Hamlet* to the events recorded in *Totem and Taboo,* events without which neither Sophocles nor Shakespeare could have written their all-revealing dramas. Well, in truth, no one could have written anything as the ur-deed of parricide is the source of all culture. After all: "Everyone in the audience was once a budding Oedipus in fantasy and each recoils in horror from the dream fulfillment."[14] It then becomes the analyst's task to see how the same theory is universally applicable in life and literature. This proposition is appealing enough as to have generated whole schools of social and literary studies. One notes, in passing, the striking case of Frederick Crews who had his own (reverse) Pauline conversion and not only abandoned Freudian theory as misguided but in a series of essays published in the *New York Review of Books,* exposed the abuses of its practitioners. Rejecting his early work (in 1970, he edited *Psychoanalysis and Literary Process*), he realized, in what is the essential Popperian attack on Freud that, "psychoanalysis amounts to a classic pseudo science .... [that] shields its postulates from falsification in indefensible ways."[15]

Serge Pankejeff's story, in which the analysand was such an eager and— as he himself proudly noted—informed participant, is remarkable because Freud is able to show not only how everything fits (all the leaks are plugged as it were) but how it does so according to his paradigmatic account of psychosexual development. There is no infantile phase (beginning with the oral) that Serge's history does not exemplify. Nothing seems to have been spared him. He trips up over every obstacle that the analyst has already posited as lying in wait. Thus the case, when decoded, can be presented as a clear refutation of Jung and Adler's "twisted re-interpretations." (G p. 153) However, the relationship between the Wolf Man's case and *Totem and Taboo* is yet more telling. It is so on two levels: one structural, the other epistemological. Both depend upon the primal scene(s).

The structural parallel is essentially the postulated existence of the scene itself—an actual event no less that is the trigger for everything that follows. In *Totem and Taboo* the primal act of parricide is the initial human interaction binding the individual psyche with the tribal collective, and it sets off *and determines* all subsequent and increasingly complex interactions. It is nothing less than the posited existence of day one and the first deed in the story of creation, at least in the creation of Man as a social animal shaped by what are now *historically* determined notions of id, ego, and superego.

The primal scene in *Totem and Taboo*—a sort of ur ur-scene—is mirrored by the primal scene that Serge witnesses at the age of about one and half, but does not realize that he *has* witnessed. That is, the sight of his parents copulating, the father penetrating from behind and the mother "bent down like an animal," (G p. 183) a matter on which Freud is pedantic as it is *supposed* to have enabled the infant Serge to observe both the erect paternal penis and the "castrated" maternal genitalia. It is this that is recalled in its encoded fashion by the Wolf Dream some three years later. Scenically, the posited observation of the parents copulating is as far back as Freud can go with Serge.

The epistemological parallel is yet more important and makes clear the unencumbered manner in which Freud moves back and forth between the personae of the scientist and the short-story writer. It has been noted by others how potent the metaphorical in Freud is, especially when he is read in the original.[16] But that should be treated as a reflection of a deeper ambivalence. The key question is: What is the "truth" basis of Freud's contentions? The answer is that it shifts. Freud permits himself an epistemological terrain that is not only very wide, erudite, and esoteric but also exceptionally malleable. The deciding element is the nature of speculation in his interpretations/solutions.

Naturally it is foolish to complain that Freud *does* speculate. The intellectual activity in which he is engaged, along with his praxis as an analyst, make speculation axiomatic. And it is not unusual to be swept along, somewhat bedazzled, by the brilliance of the speculation itself. For instance Peter Brooks, writes enthusiastically of the Wolf Man case: "We have here one of the most daring moments of Freud's thought, and one of his most heroic gestures as a writer."[17] And one sees at once that, syntactically regarded, these two qualities cannot be the same. Brooks is telling us that Freud is both thinker (scientist) *and* writer (artist), and he is very remarkable in both capacities too. Furthermore, Freud was of the opinion that scientific truth was to be found in literature not solely in respect of content. Literature was also structurally illuminating. He is impressed by *Oedipus Rex* because Sophocles carefully works back until he uncovers the truth in a manner "comparable with the work of psychoanalysis."[18] And we might see Hamlet as particularly interesting for the narrative trope. He, as Freud is well aware,[19] has wished the Oedipal deed (the death of the father and the sexual possession of the mother) but has been robbed by his uncle's haste. The consequence of this is that Hamlet has simply been written out of the story and has, as a result, the utmost difficulty in finding a context in which he can act. He is narratively castrated and becomes, for the bulk of the play, the famous inactive hero who is guilty—as he puts it himself—of "thinking too precisely on the *event.*"

Nonetheless, while we may not legitimately complain at Freudian speculation qua speculation, we might, legitimately, hope that the speculation be subsequently confirmed by the facts it uncovers. One notes that in the parallel, if fortuitous, case of the detective, there is customarily an all-doubt-removing confession or a despairing last act on the part of the criminal that puts his guilt beyond question. With Freud this is not entirely so. Of course he can arrive at a type of confession if the patient colludes, and certainly Serge Pankejeff was highly cooperative in taking onboard the basic "facts" of Freud's speculations. But that is not quite the same as the fictional parallel. Rather, Freud is inclined to a series of highly adroit and ambivalent shifts.

Presenting his interpretation with overt scientific flourishes, he is initially inclined to speculate, *making it explicit that he is speculating*; then within a matter of pages he begins to treat the speculation as no longer a hypothetical supposition but as an empirical event. Later, however, he may call even that critically important event into question, but only momentarily and under such carefully controlled conditions that the now preprogramed reader is reluctant to forgo the actual "scene" for fear of losing the brilliance of the theory itself together with the powerful aesthetic satisfaction of the tale. This is the case with both *Totem and Taboo* and the Wolf Man. It is, however, somewhat more complex and subtle in the latter where there was, after all, a subject/analysand well placed to deliver a multitude of jigsaw pieces with which the analyst so adeptly played.[20]

In contradistinction to the opening of *The Interpretation of Dreams*, Freud opens the Wolf Man story as a man of science.[21] "Readers may rest assured that I myself am only reporting what I came upon as an independent experience, uninfluenced by my expectation." But, tellingly, he continues: "On the whole its results have coincided in the most satisfactory manner with our previous knowledge." (G p. 158) Note here the modest "on the whole" immediately trumped by the absoluteness of "in the most satisfactory manner." A detective does not solve the riddle "on the whole." He solves it absolutely—that is, "in the *most* satisfactory manner." No better solution can, by definition, exist. And we see also that although we began with Freud's *personal* assurance as to the credibility of what we are about to discover, we have now moved onto the terrain of the first-person plural. It is no longer just his opinion, but "ours," or at the very least the opinion of the scientific community to which the author—if not we—belongs. Indeed it is the case that Freud shifts elegantly between different "voices," employing freely the nakedly honest first-person singular, the authoritative first-person plural, the impersonal pronoun "one" (the German "man"), as well as the seemingly objective third person "it." If, as a writer, Freud is to be properly evaluated, it will be necessary to do justice to these maneuvers, which are often simplified in the standard English translations.

After Freud has given us enough background information about the patient, above all, but not solely, of his dream of the white wolves sitting motionless in what looked like either a walnut tree or, as Serge later wanted to believe, a Christmas tree, he chooses to present the solution. This is done as speculation qua speculation. It cannot, fundamentally, be anything else given that the Wolf Man has no direct recollection of what the analyst is about to propose. And as so often when he is forced into speculation, Freud grasps the nettle boldly. His intellectual courage at points like this is not, *superficially*, to be doubted.

> I have now reached the point at which I must abandon the support I have hitherto had from the course of the analysis. I am afraid it will also be the point at which the reader's belief will abandon me.
> What sprang into activity that night out of the chaos of the dreamer's unconscious memory-traces was the picture of copulation between his parents, copulation in circumstances which were not entirely usual and were especially favorable for observation. (G p. 181)

The first paragraph of this climactic moment is nothing if not striking. The writer makes no concessions. He invites us to disbelieve him and he will not, seemingly, tag a single "if" or "but" onto the solution in order to induce us to take his side. Instead, he will tend in the pages coming— *while playing with the notion of doubt*—to supply more specificities to the scene in the way of verisimilitude, for instance that the parents copulated three times and that Serge "passed a stool." Thus, more supposed evidence will be drawn from analysis to back up the speculative dream interpretation so that, in the end, Freud is able to make out of Serge's story (which is the story that Freud has written for Serge) a paradigmatic case history.

Above all, the truth of the dream interpretation will be dependent on its explanatory power with respect to all the *other* bits and pieces that crop up during analysis. Everything will be shown to fit in order that we come to believe everything.

The technique of challenging the reader by telling him that he will not believe, or is not up to the challenge of believing, may or may not be scientific, but it is certainly literary. For instance we have seen Jane Austen come clean on the unlikely marriage between Colonel Brandon and Marianne at the end of *Sense and Sensibility*. However, her bald honesty ("but so it was") is trumped by Freud, just as it was to be subsequently trumped by Austen herself. There is also a structural difference. Austen is blatantly tying up loose ends, but Freud has a long way to go. His apparent doubts are merely there to be brushed aside by the weight of subsequent scientific analysis. For surely we will accept his challenge; we will not "abandon" him. And after all, he does not ask all that much of us: "I can assure the reader that I am no less critically inclined than he towards an acceptance of this observation of the child's, and I will only ask him to join me in adopting a provisional belief in the results of the scene." (G p. 183) Note here the phrase "this observation of the child's." It sounds as if we are being asked to consider whether the child is lying. But of course the "observation" is nothing other than Freud's postulation of what he imagines the baby Serge observed.[22] And aside from this, the statement itself is inherently humbug. Freud is not in the least "no less critically inclined" toward an acceptance of the observation. He is, after all, its discoverer—at the very least. Certainly, he cannot fairly talk as though the scene was something that had been proposed to him by someone else. Furthermore, we know that he knows enough to be absolutely certain that the dream interpretation is spot on. For him to take up, at this point, the role of the skeptical observer is merely a rhetorical device to seduce the reader to pursue the narrative further. It is, for instance, interesting that this caveat is phrased in the present tense ("I am no less inclined"). Clearly, the story will continue. But the *reader* can be under no doubt whatsoever that the interpretation will be unambiguously confirmed on every subsequent page. He knows that the writer, who is most assuredly neither he nor Serge, is well aware of how it will all work out. It is not, for instance, as if we were in for some kind of deconstruction of the detective novel in which the sleuth simply gave up and left the dinner party in the middle of the case because his "little gray cells" were not up to the job.

We see here that Freud has chosen skillfully the moment to present his interpretation. It is not some *final* trick, which reduces the reader (above all the reader of detective novels) to cries of "swindle" and "but why wasn't I told chapters ago that the school-teacher was the minister's illegitimate son?!," and so on. Nor is it the first premise of a creation story so absurd as to incline us to put down the book before Chapter 2. When Freud presents his creation story in *Totem and Taboo* he cards are thoroughly marked. But with the Wolf Man dream interpretation we are stuck somewhere in the narrative middle and, being told that we are not likely to believe, are merely asked to keep, like the author, an open mind. In effect we are to wait and see what we can now mutually discover. This is an interesting device as it puts us in the same position as the sleuth, which is to say it changes our role as readers. No longer implicitly paired off with the likes of Dr. Watson and poor Hastings, standing around stupefied or asking embarrassing questions, we discover we are helping Freud crack the case.

But what does happen *epistemologically* to the interpretation of the dream? Will its speculative status remain unchanged? That is, will the clear distinction between the inventive interpretation and the facts of Serge's life, including those fantasies he can *actually* recall, be maintained?

Not at all. First, the dream is explained as an encoded memory of a primal scene (G p. 183). Primal scenes are historical events. Consequently the dream's place is anthropologically secure. Then we are told that having been presented with the interpretation, the patient believed it. But Serge believed well-nigh everything. He did not run off like the embarrassed banker Freud mentioned to Fliess.[23] Then there follows new assertions as to the epistemological probity of dreams. This is necessary as Freud has access to the primal scene solely through dream interpretation. Serge can certainly supply him details of many other things, but the step that gets us from the dream (wolves) to the primal scene (parents copulating) is exclusively the result of the analyst's ability to decode the former. Thus, it is emphasized that dreams are not meant to be taken literally but "are intended to serve as some kind of symbolic representation of real wishes and interests" (G p. 192). Moreover, the dream "seems to me absolutely equivalent to a recollection, if the memories are replaced (as in the present case) by dreams the analysis of which *invariably* leads back to the same scene and which produce *every* portion of its content in an inexhaustible variety of new shapes." (G p. 195, my emphases). Here in an individual and unique case study is an explicit statement of elements kernel to the Freudian enterprise at its grandest: namely, retrospective narrative narrowing in focus onto a specific primal act/scene, and the completeness of analysis as judged by its ability to explain "every" aspect of the material. Moreover, in the literary context, these techniques get us to the point where Serge actually *does* (seem to) remember the sight of his parents copulating.

These strategies not only underpin the interpretation but change its truth status. For however much dreams may be symbolic, "products of the imagination," (G p. 192) they are the royal road not merely to the unconscious in general but, in this case, to an exceptionally explicit encounter with the Oedipal trauma—that great event on which, in its actual first form, civilization itself precariously balances. And however arbitrary the process of dream interpretation may seem at first, we have in fact "every" reason to believe the interpretation, since every portion of its content reproduces the same scene—namely the primal scene—and the analysis "invariably" leads back to just this scene. Thus, the "sight" of parental copulation has now taken on the patina of an event whose occurrence is no longer to be doubted. All that is necessary is to use the symbolic material of the dream to make the connection with the now unquestionably empirically grounded primal scene. Speculation thereby becomes fact.

Fortunately all of this is readily grasped by the patient himself. Furthermore, his gradual acceptance of the interpretation does not stand in an inferior ("nachstehen") ontological position to an act of empirical remembering. In fact, Freud takes a further step and claims it has the same status.[24] Thus Serge, who presumably gets to play this critical role because he is no recalcitrant Dora, not only becomes the ideal reader of a short story in which he plays the leading role, but cooperates editorially in its construction.

Besides the fundamental epistemological shifts, individual events in the Wolf Man case can change their character within a few pages. For instance, Freud speculates that Serge urinated while watching Gruscha clean the floor whereupon she threatened him, jokingly, with castration. However, when this incident is recalled it has become a "fact," a valid piece of the Wolf Man's memory. Then there is the "passing (of) a stool" when the little boy Serge wakes up and sees his primal scene. This is also a suggestion of the analyst's. Yet in being so subtly handled and so pertinent to Freud's methodology, it is exceptionally revealing. Initially Freud writes that Serge "interrupted his parents' intercourse by passing a stool, which gave him a cause for screaming." (G pp. 222–223) He then notes that the patient accepts this conclusion. But on the same page we read:

> It would make no difference to the *story* as a whole if this demonstration had not occurred, or if it had been taken from a later period and inserted into the course of the *scene*. But there can be no question of how we are to regard it. It is a sign of a state of excitement of the anal zone (in the widest sense)... (G p. 223, my emphases)

That the passing of the stool is important is not open to doubt—*whether it "occurred" or not*—for Freud wants to show that Serge progresses problematically and incompletely through the anal phase. Yet he accepts, broadmindedly, that in the mix of memory it may have happened later, although if we remain clear-sighted we will not forget that Serge had no memory of it before Freud suggested it. However, if it is now belatedly "inserted into the course of the scene" we are entitled to ask: Who is doing the inserting? Freud is using the passive here: "had been taken." Are we to infer from this that it has nothing to do with him and that Serge, no doubt getting all those memory traces muddled up, did it himself? But it is difficult to see how we can logically draw that inference, given the awkward fact that Serge had no recollection of either the primal scene or the passing of the stool. There is self-evidently only one player in the game who can effectively accomplish the act of narrative "insertion": namely the storyteller who, not withstanding his obvious modesty and skepticism, has in fact done just that.[25]

One sees here that a seductive nexus of linguistic signals has been employed so that we are able to keep parallel epistemological options open. Is it a supposition, or a fact? Is it a memory or a guess? Did it happen when Freud said it happened or some time later? And, most remarkable of all, is it actually important where we—or he—finally come down in all of this? Furthermore, one notes that if all the bases are kept open at this stage, the analyst cannot be accused of either pedantry or simplification. But even that is not the end of the matter. Freud continues straight on with another, this time wholly unambivalent, formulation.

> The *fact* that our little boy passed a stool as a sign of his sexual excitement is to be regarded as a characteristic of his congenital sexual constitution. He at once assumed a passive attitude, and showed more inclination towards a subsequent identification with women than with men. (G p. 223, my emphasis)

So now it *is* a fact.[26] Furthermore, the passing of a stool cannot be generalized by the analyst. It simply must have a specific context, be part of a particular scene, for the self-evident if mundane reason that Serge, like everyone else, will no doubt have passed a great many. This, in fact, is not the passing of a stool at all, it is the passing of *the* stool. Indeed, one might perhaps be forgiven for observing that it is the passing of the primal stool.

So having played with the notion of doubt (maybe it did not actually occur), and having shown ourselves tolerant of different timescales (a matter on which, as we all readily understand, memory is especially unreliable), having, in short, remained loyal to the open-minded investigator, albeit one who is prepared on occasions to see himself as an "adventurer" and a "conquistador," we find ourselves right back where we started: primal scene, empirical event, and actual act. But this time it is all grounded in scientific probity and we are convinced, not least because we have been actively involved in the construction of the interpretation. "Provisional belief" is now something else entirely. Doubt as a notion has thereby become a key factor in telling a story designed to remove unambiguously the fact of doubt.

However, it should also be clear that while the manner in which Freud plays with doubt may be freewheeling, it is not without certain game rules. Specific instances are only foregrounded under highly controlled circumstances—circumstances controlled, of course, by the storyteller. The principal device is to convince the reader of the veracity of the "scientific" interpretation before suddenly suggesting that maybe it did not, as a matter of fact, actually have to have happened like that. This astounding move induces a double reaction. The reader is, in the first instance, impressed by the principled and ever-present skepticism. But immediately thereafter, he realizes that he is narratively trapped to the degree that he becomes the storyteller's champion. Like many of Freud's patients—and, never let it be forgotten, their parents[27]—he colludes in the analysis. At points like this one is almost inclined to cry out: "No, no! Don't be so modest old chap. You got it right the first time. Go back. Go back to the original!"

The story of the passing of the stool is by no means the only instance of this. Freud is also prepared to suggest that maybe Serge had the Wolf Dream at the age of six or later. But then, having presented several reasons why this *may* be so, he rejects them and goes back to his first supposition of four and a half. He is even—most extravagant of horrors—prepared to toy with the idea that Serge had seen animals copulating and not his parents. But fortunately, after giving it serious attention, he dismisses that too, and we are left with the ur-act without which the whole narrative would be aesthetically gutted. Thus, in considering Freud's seemingly open-minded methodology, one should not forget the grand quotation already noted earlier in this chapter: namely, either "everything took place *just* as I have described it..." or it is "...all a piece of nonsense from start to finish." (G p. 199, my emphasis). This is hardly a prerequisite for the effective employment of scientific skepticism.

Perhaps Freud's most amazing and dissembling use of "doubt" occurs not in the Wolf Man case but in *Totem and Taboo,* to which it is so intimately linked. The enormous derision this work has elicited is of no great significance here, but we must acknowledge its critical importance with respect to the epistemology of Freudianism as a whole. It is too often dismissed as an intellectual aberration that has nothing to do with his work as an analyst, but if Freud is to be taken at his word it is difficult to see how anything at all would stand if this alleged "fairy story" were to be exploded. And, moreover, Freud is well aware of this. Twenty-five years later in a related work, *Moses and Monotheism,* he recalls "the violent reproaches" he has met " . . . for not having altered my opinions in later editions of the book." But while he acknowledges that there have been, in the meantime, changes in anthropological knowledge and opinion: "To this day I hold firmly to (my) construction":[28] namely, the primal scene and its consequences as presented in *Totem and Taboo*.

The story of the ur-act—the first step in the creation of civilization and, one is inclined to add, its discontents—shares with the Wolf Man's tale both a taste for narrative verisimilitude (a multitude of details all interpreted to confirm the general theory) and a remarkable freedom concerning a story for which one has not a single piece of hard evidence.[29] However, when the story has been told, its universal significance made clear, and the reader is in a position to appreciate its—and of this there need be no doubt—enormous explanatory potential, he is suddenly asked to consider that it did not happen at all.

The narrative punch of this strategy is difficult to overestimate. Here the reader has just taken onboard an account of something that is a good deal more interesting, if perhaps not as poetically expressed, as the first three chapters of Genesis: a tale of sexual jealousy, personal trauma, and social interaction all placed firmly within the context of actual human, as opposed to allegedly divine, actions, and climaxing in a killing and a ritualistic act of cannibalism whose psychic consequences flood down through the generations to the reader himself. And he is now being asked to consider that, *as Freud's critics have subsequently asserted*, it did not actually happen! One should note that dismissive critics do not seem to realize that Freud speculates that the *wish* to kill the father and possess the forbidden females might itself have been enough to induce the psychic reactions necessary for the creation of the universal Oedipus complex, the collective unconscious, and the superego. Are they perhaps, in what would be a wonderful irony, as seduced by his narration as the "ordinary" reader? Certainly, placed alongside the power of the original in its concrete form—that is, the actual events that took place among the primal horde—Freud's dispensation as to its empirical veracity is like an act of literary betrayal. Inevitably the ur-scene gives a great deal more pleasure than the almost offhand suggestion that it is not actually necessary to believe in it if, presumably, one does not really want to. And surely Freud is well aware of the aesthetic danger he has landed himself in with this remarkable display of skepticism. In any case he will not leave it at that. Would it not be an exceedingly odd detective who informed the suspects brought together in the drawing room that the actual murderer (or murderers) among them did not have to have slaughtered (and eaten!) the patriarch, but only to have secretly wished him dead?

The manner in which this is done is particularly telling. *Totem and Taboo* conforms to the classic detective story to a degree that exceeds even the Wolf Man case largely because the solution is kept right back until the final section of the book. In fact this sleuth steps very gingerly toward his goal and only at the climactic moment—the moment when he turns round and astounds us all with the key missing scene—do we suddenly realize that he has not merely solved the problems of exogamy and totemism, but that he has arrived back at the root of human history and civilization itself. Naturally, as we have come to expect, he garnishes his solution with a dash of doubt, but in setting before us *perhaps* mankind's first festival," (F p. 142, my emphasis[30]) namely the cannibal ceremony, which follows the initial parricide, he adds that it "was the beginning of so many things—of social organization, of moral restrictions and of religion." (F p. 142). Later he will add "art." (F p. 156). We are surely entitled to ask: What is left? In fact the formulation "so much" is misleading, while the language thereafter will become ever firmer and less open to doubt, until, that is, the final extraordinary maneuver.

Before looking more closely at that maneuver it would be good to give Freud the storyteller once again his due. The manner in which he interweaves the various strands—psychological, sociological, and anthropological—while always seeming to make clear their apparent epistemological differences, is masterly. The careful examination of systems of totemism (often accompanied by the modest caveat that he is lacking in thoroughness), the reasoned dismissal of all previous explanations (quoting Frazer approvingly, who concedes that "we are ignorant of the origin of the horror of incest" [F p. 125]), the careful claim in the middle of the story that religion cannot be deduced from a single source (F p. 100) (although, as we have already seen, that is exactly what he is going to do), the adroitly judged introduction of the Oedipus complex by way of Little Hans (this is pre-Serge, but we note that children, like neurotics, are a privileged way back to the savage and what will turn out to be the primal scene [F p. 128f]), the appearance of the primal horde (characterized first in the plural "small groups or hordes" [F p. 125], then renamed "Darwin's primal horde" [F p. 141], and finally, also singular, the "patriarchal horde" {Vaterhorde} [F p. 146]—Freudian solutions, as we have had cause to note, are singular); all of this is handled with the utmost skill. When, therefore, he comes to the explanation itself we are splendidly preprogramed. So is it any wonder that those who reject it do so in language more exasperated than is customary? The threat of seduction was very real indeed. It has been a near run thing and, hurriedly adjusting our disheveled cognitive attire we escape through an open window, only too well aware that we are lucky that our reputations for intellectual probity are still intact.

It is also worth noting an unusually blatant strategy when the ur-act is described. Freud begins his answer to the "puzzle" of everything that has formed his story up to now with: "One day the brothers who had been driven out came together, killed and devoured their father and so made an end of the patriarchal horde." (F p. 141) However, he is clearly uncomfortable with his own formulation. And certainly "eines Tages" is perilously close in tone to the opening of the standard fairy story. [31]

He attempts to rationalize this danger away in a footnote, explaining that the nature of the material with which he is dealing compels him to a certain compression and that: "It would be as foolish to aim at exactitude in such questions as it would be unfair to insist upon certainty." (F p. 143) Here it is difficult to avoid the inference that Freud's scene—a scene that happened "one day"—is a fictional portrayal that merely has an illustrative function. But the footnote remains a footnote, while the text proper gives us the singular act without any waiver. Does not the former then function as a peripheral safety net into which the writer can fall should the grand textual retelling be challenged as scientifically unsupportable? Whatever the case, one is no longer surprised at such ambivalences. This particular one, however, should be kept in mind when turning to the last three pages of the book.[32] It is here that doubt is introduced in the boldest manner, producing the most violent epistemological shift. Having got us to the end—that is, to the initial Oedipal act—he proposes that what he has just described might not have taken place; it did not need to have taken place because, just as with the neurotic (with whom the savage shares much), the psychical reality alone is sufficient to the Oedipus complex ("the nucleus of all neuroses" [F p. 157]) and thereby the factual reality becomes superfluous: "for psychical reality would be strong enough to bear the weight of these consequences." (F p. 160). "Accordingly the mere hostile *impulse* against the father, the mere existence of a wishful *fantasy* of killing and devouring him would have been enough to produce the moral reaction that created totemism and taboo." (F pp. 159–160) In the original German, the conditional and the subjunctive are ubiquitous, underlining the speculative character of the passage. After all, a suggestion is merely being put by an open-minded scientist and it is only right that it be considered. What follows is almost breathtaking.

> One ["*man*"] will object that indeed a change from the Fatherhorde (patriarchal horde) to the Brotherclan (fraternal clan) did in reality take place. This is certainly a strong argument, but not yet a decisive one. (My translation)[33]

The "one" is quite extraordinary. To whom does this impersonal pronoun refer? In this section Freud has been employing the authorial plural, but here the "one" has to be the reader whose, *utterly reasonable,* objection Freud is paraphrasing. That is, the author has suddenly placed the reader in the text to give him the opportunity of protesting to the author that he really should not start doubting the veracity of his own theory. Whereupon the author, whose modesty and open-mindedness are clearly exemplary, simultaneously compliments and chides the reader. That is, the reader's objection is a strong one but not *yet,* in itself, sufficient. And thus our pathfinder goes further down a road that ostensibly leads to yet further doubt as to the ontological credibility of the primal scene as *he* has hitherto explained it.

But we need not have worried. By a further series of shifts, the dramatic deed is restored to us and the reader is shown to have been right in his objection once full use is made of the "not yet." Having placed the savage alongside the neurotic so as to call into question the original explanation, Freud now uses the same analogy to establish the opposite. This is accomplished by pulling something new out of the hat. It transpires that while the two (primitive and neurotic) are both fixated on the deed (namely the Oedipal killing) the savage has a need of the act itself, whereas the neurotic is limited to the psychical reality. He does not need to *do* it. Thus, the analogy between the "psychical reality" and the "factual reality" with which Freud began, turns out to deliver the exact opposite of what we expected. It somersaults and establishes, not the similarity, but the decisive difference. And so the reader's objection was correct after all, although at the time he was permitted to make it by proxy, he did not (bless him!) quite fully understand why.

Freud's formulations as he pulls this trick off are suitably skilled. The last sentence of the second to last paragraph commences: "The analogy between primitive men and neurotics will therefore be far more fully established if..." (F p. 161). But what follows is not a similarity ("the analogy" further "established"), as would be consistent with the preceding paragraphs, but rather the determining difference. Namely, that while neurotics are inhibited and cannot turn the wish into action, primitives are the antithesis. Thus, given that they are uninhibited, we have good reason for assuming that "primitive men actually *did* what all the evidence shows that they intended to do." (F p. 161). Readers can decide for themselves what this "evidence" amounts to (has there been anything that could be called "evidence"?), but the formulation that an uninhibited group has simply carried out what it wanted to carry out can hardly, prima facie, sound unreasonable. And yet we have arrived at this point by virtue of a comparison that, we were told, would establish quite the opposite, namely that the two groups—savages and neurotics—were (supposedly) fundamentally the same.

In the final paragraph, Freud pushes us to a point of such quasi-divine authority that he can sprinkle one last dash of skepticism over the whole business while moving freely between authorial voices:

> The primitive is uninhibited, the idea transforms itself directly into the act; the act is for him a substitute for the idea, and therefore *I* believe—without committing *myself* with absolute certainty in the last degree—that *one* can properly assume in the case *we* are examining that: in the beginning was the deed. (My emphases and translation)[34]

It is a fine conclusion. This last gesture of doubt, initially expressed in the first-person singular, is magnificently trumped by the absolutism of the final judgment's biblical echo, ringing proudly behind the quotation from Faust: "In the beginning was the deed." Freud has indeed given us Genesis and it would be blasphemy to doubt him. Although one can, of course, only admire his determination to doubt—however feebly—himself.

Now it is necessary to look at the overriding importance of the "phylo-genetic heritage." Without it, there is no way we can get from the primal horde to Serge. It is the mechanism that makes possible a metanarrative that, just as the Marxian dialectic (class struggle and evolving forms of production), and religious millenarianism, and all the others, triumphs over death by linking the generations. But the Freudian Weltanschauung realizes the desires that give rise to a metanarrative in an exceptional, even perverse, fashion because it is both so exact in its explanation and so intense in the manner in which it binds the generations by a posited act of original sin that does not, cannot, go away. As a result there is the suggestion of a utopian form but there is not, unlike the other metanarratives we have looked at, a utopian content. Here is Klee's "Angelus Novus" who stands on the rubble of history, the proverbial messy terrain, with, as Benjamin put it, his back turned to the future. Yet he is swept into the future by the storm emanating from paradise.[35] We might place the Klee/Benjamin angel within the Freudian model. "Paradise" is a dystopia and though one can take flight from it, one never escapes the currents that flow from it. In fact, there is no flight that is not at the same time an expression of the drives emanating from the past.

Nonetheless, one can see how the psychosexual basis of Freudianism together with the attendant notion of repression might inevitably evoke its dialectic (utopian) opposite. For Freud is clearly playing with notions of (chiefly sexual) liberation while remorselessly revealing the mechanisms by which one will always be to some degree or other crippled. But this invites sabotage by virtue of sexual liberation. For instance, Herbert Marcuse in *Eros and Civilisation* remained true to the structure of the Freudian apparatus, but upturned it to produce a liberating Weltanschauung. While he enthusiastically takes onboard Freud's shift into "phylogenesis" ("psychology discovers that the determining childhood experiences are linked with the experiences of the species—that the individual lives the universal fate of mankind"[36]), he maintains that "civilization" and its repressions evolve in tandem with different social systems. Thus, rationalized "mechanisms of labor" will lead to the release of surplus erotic energy that, partly through the liberating power of fantasy or imagination (the shift to aesthetics, as we will see in the next chapter, is a popular one in German idealist philosophy), will in turn produce the triumph over repression. Civilization may have to defend "itself against the specter of a world which could be free,"[37] and we can entertain a synthesis whereby: "Imagination envisions the reconciliation of the individual with the whole, of desire with realization, of happiness with reason. While this harmony has been removed into utopia by the established reality principle, fantasy insists that it must and can become real, that behind the illusion lies knowledge."[38]

Just as in *One Dimensional Man*, we might feel that Marcuse's Marxist optimism and taste for revolution leads him to place more hope in his randy Californian students (simply, in the *first instance*, because they were randy) than turns out to be justified. But it is surely only right to acknowledge that he has taken fair advantage of both the principle of dialectics and the praxis of Freudian hermeneutics to underpin his own radical agenda on both the level of individual liberation and of social emancipation.

Interestingly, in respect of the phylogenetic inheritance enthusiastically adopted by Marcuse, Freud can sometimes seem in his early work to be a little tentative. That he needs a grand cultural DNA in *Totem and Taboo* is clear and at the end he faces up to it, although he makes it sound very speculative. He does not present the phylogenetic argument in so explicit and "factual" a manner as in the Wolf Man case,[39] where the notion allows him to throw an olive branch to Jung with whom his disagreement is otherwise becoming alarmingly sharp. Naturally the phylogenetic premise raises masses of questions—so many that one suspects Freudian analysts want to put it to one side and concentrate on the id, ego, superego, pleasure principle, death wish, reality principle, and so on. For, while Freud is certainly clear that the inherited element must be influenced by the cultural specifics of each society, he cannot present any clear mechanistic account of how cultural inheritance genetically works. It is "merely" the logic of his suppositions that leads him to baldly assert that the child "replace(s) occurrences in his own life by occurrences in the lives of his ancestors." (G p. 239). However, when he returns 25 years later to the premise (now sometimes called the "archaic heritage") he has come in for so much criticism as to have no option but to brazen it out.

Moses and Monotheism, for instance, is exceptionally bold. It is nearly all speculation and, despite the problems Freud had in getting it into shape, still able to justify his original intention of calling it, tellingly, an "Historical Novel." Moreover, the final German title (literally "The Man Moses and Monotheistic Religion") preserves the feel of biographical invention better than the English. Now he concedes his Lamarckian solecism, "the present attitude of biological science...refuses to hear of the inheritance of acquired characteristics by succeeding generations." However, he has no choice in the matter and so, while employing a nice mixture of adverbial qualifiers and, as normal, displaying a certain reticence, he defiantly asserts that he "must, however, in all modesty confess that nevertheless I cannot do without this factor in biological evolution." One way or another "men have always known that they once possessed a primal father and killed him."[40] Presumably it matters not that they do not (knowingly) know they know it. Here, at least, he is compelled to echo Jane Austen's "but so it is." In any case, biological science is sure to make further discoveries, and Freud, like the astronomer discovering a new planet, will be proved right ultimately.

But he is well aware of the thin ice on which he now stands. In the 1937 essay *Constructions in Analysis,* he notes how a "man of science" has accused him of loading all the dice so that it is a case of "Heads I win, tails you lose." This sounds like the classic Popperian objection to social "sciences" that do not allow of any strategy by which they can be proven false. And perhaps Freud did have Popper in mind for, although he is writing well before *The Open Society and Its Enemies* appeared (Popper was in Christchurch, New Zealand between 1937 and 1945), his remarks do postdate *The Logic of Scientific Discovery,* easily accessible to Freud in the original German (the English translation appeared in 1959). But what is striking is the nature of Freud's response to the criticism. One can only assume he recognized the threat in that he took the trouble to address it. However there is, in effect, nothing substantive that he can say to defend himself in that he cannot take on the falsifiability argument on its *own* terms. Instead, he is reduced to a statement of unsubstantiated personal probity: "I can assert without boasting that such an abuse...has never occurred in my practice." He then restates the principles with which we are familiar. That is, while we cannot trust the patient's initial answer: "The path that starts from the analyst's construction ought to end in the patient's recollection...[but]...it does not always lead so far." Typically, he goes on so as to remove the doubt and qualification he has just expressed, "if the analysis is carried out correctly, we produce in him [the patient] an assured conviction of the truth of the construction which achieves the same therapeutic result as a recaptured memory."[41] The key qualifier here is "correctly," which functions in rhetorical terms as a classic Freudian tautology. Freud, of course, carries out his analyses "correctly"—he has just told us so "without boasting"—and this frees him from accusations that he plays fast and loose.

There is a further matter of some interest that also follows from the dsytopian first cause of Freudian theory and which also takes expression from the tension between the supposed unique subject and the grander story of the species. For Freud does not avoid the inherent pessimism of his Weltanschauung. After treatment, Freud does not send his (former) neurotics out again into the world with great confidence. This is not because he is uncertain with respect to the theoretical principles on which the therapy rests, but because he is all too well aware that the notion of an unproblematic existence is dubious. His ideas rest not merely upon the problems of those of us who have gone awry, but rather upon problems of psychosexual development that are universal and which evoke, no matter how "civilized" we may be, fears and drives that come into conflict with a superego from whose tyranny we can never be utterly free. For the "superego torments the sinful ego" and nothing can escape its terrible power "since nothing can be hidden from the superego, not even thoughts."[42] There would appear to be no sunny uplands on which, finally liberated from neurosis, we can gambol. In this metanarrative, a happy ending is both a narrative impossibility and an intellectual absurdity.

Poor Serge Pankejeff discovered this. He never became a free man, and one wonders what the term free man would have meant both to him and his most famous analyst. There are, however, several places in *Civilization and Its Discontents* (1929) which, although not directly answering this question, do give some idea of how deep Freud's pessimism is. After all "What we call our civilization is largely responsible for our misery" and moreover "…we should be much happier if we gave it up and returned to primitive conditions."[43] But this should not be taken to mean that he, too, has a lingering attachment to a blissful beginning in the manner of romantically inclined Marxists. He is merely voicing a common feeling that we all have when we are conscious of the restrictions of civilization. Freud, of course, distrusts all forms of utopianism and was painfully perspicacious when it came to the Soviet Marxists. He points out that, while he has "no concern with any criticism of the communist system…" and that he "…cannot inquire into whether the abolition of private property is expedient or advantageous," the fundamental optimism of Marxists with respect to the nature of man is "an untenable illusion."[44] Rather it is the task of civilization, by prohibitions, and so forth, to contain the essential aggressiveness of the human being. The commandment to love one's neighbor as oneself is "really justified by the fact that nothing else runs so strongly counter to the original nature of man."[45] Abolishing private property will not make us benign, for "aggressiveness was not created by property. It reigned almost without limit in primitive times, when property was still very scanty, and it already shows itself in the nursery almost before property has given up its original, anal form."[46] Far from evoking Marx's paradigm of ur-communism, this recalls Hegel's view of primitive life noted in chapter 2. And it surely underpins the power of the Freudian argument that the above section concludes with an unsettling, perspicacious remark: "One only wonders, with concern, what the Soviets will do after they have wiped out their bourgeoisie."[47]

However, no matter how pessimistic the Freudian metanarrative may be, that has not been the root of the criticisms expressed here. And those criticisms can hardly be inferred from the fact that narrative per se has been the principal structuring device of the Freudian project. Rather, what is disturbing is the overriding authority the particular narrative, as well as the specific strategies of seduction Freud as a storyteller employs. Furthermore, one expresses doubts for the paradoxical reason that he is so good at what he does; so good that his explanations and stories deliver over a massive topography while ostensibly taking account of every detail. Here is an intellectual who seemingly reconciles completely the wood with each separate tree. Here we are blessed with an all-explanatory overview that is not contradicted by a single aberrant detail. Indeed, it would be fair to say that *apparently* aberrant details are meat and drink to him.

The chief problem with his narration has been its singularity: the notion of the unique contemporary solution (functioning in the pluralistic subject-based world of dream interpretation etc.,), but grounded in the great species event of day one—no matter that he was prepared to concede that there must have been many day ones. Everything will, must, fall into its ordered chronological place. Of course, enthusiasts excited by the complexity of the model may maintain the opposite; they may assert that the Wolf Man interpretation is not the result of some "neat Holmesian solution but rather a proliferation of narratives with no ultimate points of fixity."[48] However, in reaching such conclusions they are doing less than justice to the subtlety and consistency of the Freudian enterprise. Primal scenes turn out to be very fixed and are, by definition, nothing if not ultimate. Furthermore every effort—partly *because of* all the sham games with doubt—is made to give them as much authority as possible.

In the end, one distrusts the solution precisely because in such a vast context it has been possible to come up with *one*. Things are just not going to be that neat, either on the level of the "phylogenetic heritage" (if one chooses to accept it) or on that of individual neurosis. Freud, in seeking the kudos of a grand theory, has unwittingly betrayed the brilliance—however integrated—of his own speculative and analytical work.

Donald Spence has argued for a distinction between narrative and historical truth. Freud is then seen to deliver the former but is caught out because this cannot correspond to the latter.[49] Yet one must not forget that historical truth is axiomatically narrative too. The difference must be a difference between narrative form(s). Reality, or historical truth, is not going to be easy. In the social sciences, the very business of bringing order will inevitably mean imposing distortion, no matter how aesthetically satisfying that distortion may be. And although there is no definitive solution to this problem, the task of engaging with narrative in a manner that will take account of the *plurality* of historical reality will not go away. Although the erudite and eclectic cornucopia of the Freudian endeavor, replete with insights, will never cease to fascinate, we will have cause to remember the ultimate singularity of its archaeological chronology and its attendant shortcomings in the chapter after next. But in the meantime aesthetics—but not chiefly literary aesthetics—have to be given their due. We return to the tradition of German idealist philosophy to ask to what degree the narrative/historical enterprise can be grounded in normative values. That is, to what degree is that idealist tradition useful in establishing the truth claims of narration in respect of *lived* reality.

Chapter 5

Philosophy and Fatherland
German Transcendentalism, Aesthetics, and Nationalism

"No universal history leads from savagery to humanity, but one indeed from the slingshot to the H-bomb. It culminates in the total threat of organized humanity against organized human beings, in the epitome of discontinuity. Hegel is thereby verified by the horror and stood on his head." This is Adorno in *Negative Dialectics*[1] (ND 313–315), typically playing with concepts that he simultaneously debunks, and employs as a means of debunking. He will allow some sense of rationality—of "organization"—but only if the payoff is disorder, "discontinuity." He will allow the dialectical tradition of German philosophy, but only if its most celebrated dialectician can be hoisted, upside down, on his own petard. And he will allow history as long as it is celebrated for its disasters. As a result there is an implied teleology, for one thing does "lead" to another, but nothing satisfying can be inferred from this. If in his unremitting bleakness he seems bound to permit the category of narrative, it is only for the perverse pleasure of dialectically inverting it so that it produces technologically driven misanthropy. We might ask, what is the point of troubling ourselves with a teleology if the unavoidable telos is the abyss?

Nonetheless, the presence of narrative and teleology at least suggests the possibility of an alternative. For Adorno cannot simply recite a singular process that allows no narrative plurality. If that were so, there would be no need for any analysis on his part, dialectical or otherwise. In fact, his odd stance with respect to narrative is a product of his feeling—however

intellectually jejune it might be and however much he might deny it—
that he is at the end of the process. He has seen the Third Reich, history's
monstrous "promised land," and he cannot believe that there is a way back,
which is to say a way forward that does not amount to more of the same.
But it is his place at the end of an idealist philosophical tradition that is
instructive. And it is that tradition, the failure of its beneficent elements,
and the triumph of its malevolent ones, that is important here. Therefore,
narrative is doubly present in this chapter, as an account of a particular
intellectual and national history, and as a conceptual category that might
explain exactly that intellectual and national history.

Arguably the most productive problem with narrative explanations is
inherent in teleology, a category that, at the very least, all narratives must
evoke. It is this problem, for instance, that steers the last section of Kant's
Third Critique and drives him in the direction of both the argument for
design and a more complicated proof for the existence of God. Certainly it
appears prima facie a contradiction in itself to argue for any kind of teleological explanation that does not posit for itself a goal, even if one cannot
say anything very much about that goal. In commonsense terms, to suggest
a narrative epistemology and then put aside the question of where things
are going is somewhat odd. Nevertheless, this strategy can be employed.
When Thomas S. Kuhn, aware that his use of paradigms in *The Structure
of Scientific Revolutions* was imprecise, decided to redefine his model it was
to narrative without a goal/telos that he turned. This permitted a notion
of scientific development that, like Darwinian evolution, was narrative in
character but about whose end—if any—nothing meaningful could be
said.[2] And in general, we ought not to be surprised if even grand thinkers
steer clear of predicting ends. Telos as a category is nothing if not a hostage
to fortune.

If the last chapter was devoted to a single thinker who imposed coherence, this one looks at narrative and truth in respect of a philosophical
school so diverse that the subsequent discussion must appear arbitrary.
German nineteenth- and twentieth-century philosophy is nonetheless
essential to the considerations that drive this book. Moreover, this is not
so solely with regard to how narrative is handled by a largely idealist philosophical school—or how it is neglected and with what consequences—but
also because the actual history of German thought itself is part of the
issue. This is in some ways an odd business in that a tradition dependent
on transcendental concepts (the chief exception being Marxism) falls into
crisis as a result of the empirical facts of twentieth-century history. The
accusation against German idealism is then framed in terms of empirical
catastrophes (underpinned by the poverty of German philosophical empiricism) that can only be arbitrarily inferred from out of that philosophical

tradition. Therefore what follows is very vulnerable to the charge of polemical cherry-picking.

Contradictorily, the most important category in the cherry-picking is prima facie linked neither to narrative nor truth. It is aesthetics and it runs through this chapter as one of its organizing threads. It is Kant, above all, who turns to aesthetics to establish the normative character of philosophy. Further, aesthetics drives him to pursue the question of teleology until he arrives, as teleology when rigorously pursued logically must, at answers to the most fundamental moral and existential questions. Yet hardly any of this engages with the empirical *social* lives of individuals, or addresses the problems of practical civic existence. The best Kant can tell us is that we may "argue" and "doubt" as much as we wish as long as we "obey" (*What Is Enlightenment?* [1784]). While in the *Fundamental Principles of the Metaphysics of Morals* (1785) duty, which is the moral basis for the imperative to obey, is played off as the antipode to lying, which is thereby made impossible in every case. Should anyone feel that this flies in the face of common sense, Kant, at the age of 73, does not shirk the consequences of his strict categorical and therefore universal position. In his essay *On the Supposed Right to Tell Lies from Benevolent Motives* (1797), he argues that should we be asked by a murderer the whereabouts of his intended victim we must tell him.

Behind this there stands—how appropriately—a notion of morality that allegedly rejects any consideration whatsoever as to the consequences in mundane existence of acts deemed "good." And although it has already been noted in chapter 2 that it is not clear that Kant deals with his deontological (duty based) model in a consistent fashion, he nevertheless sticks unwaveringly to the principle that judgment with respect to the right thing to do is determined wholly by motivation ("pure Will") and is not influenced by the effects of what one does. In passing we might note that Hegel *does* allow for the historical expression of the idealized Will or Spirit to some empirical degree, but only to enfeeble the instruments of civilized social development, at least before the emergence of the "modern" state. Prior to that happy event, civic values are inferior to the merciless exercise of power in the person of the hero, as unfortunate a figure in German intellectual life as in German history. He cuts his path through the mass of little people in order to perform great deeds and attains great ends, which may amount to killing dragons in aesthetics and invading Poland in reality. Brecht's Galileo was, at the very least, on to something when he answered Andrea's observation that "Unhappy is the land that has no heroes" with "Unhappy the land that is in need of heroes." Nevertheless, if it is Wagner's dragon slayer who thrills, one might welcome Kant's stringent idealism in that it did not lead him down that path.

For Kant, judgment mediates between understanding and reason just as pleasure stands between knowledge and desire. The Third Critique (*The Critique on Judgment*) can thus be seen as working in gaps between categories central to the preceding two Critiques on pure and practical reason. It is these gaps that will be colonized by aesthetics (a category that amounts to more than mere pleasure) and thus by judgment, which, it transpires, is impossible without aesthetics. These together will engender normative values universal in character, and lead ultimately to bold claims for a teleological, and thereby ordered, view of the world. And one should note immediately how vital—and typical—for Kant this shift into universalism is. It is as essential for him as it is for Freud, but it is far harder for Kant to establish the category from out his own material. *He* is not digging down to a singular taproot, but attempting to pull the whole multifarious endeavor into stringent order. And often one feels that universalism is arbitrarily arrived at. It does not even have the underpinning of dreams as a nebulous reflection of hard reality. Nonetheless universalism is a necessary axiom for the categorical imperative, otherwise it could hardly be categorical and would not, for that matter, be all that imperative. So in the Third Critique, it is asserted as an essential category of aesthetic experience and normative knowledge of the world. Without it, the deepest claims made for aesthetics and teleology will not hold. One should also note how peculiar this sounds. For when *we* think of aesthetics we think, however superficially, of something for which timeless, unconditional rule-making is perilous. And it celebrates subjectivity. Indeed we feel ourselves flattered, our sensibilities underpinned, in finding that our taste is *not* universally shared.

But Kant asserts that aesthetics (and ultimately moral judgment) are the product of an intrinsic mental capacity, a "cognitive faculty," (§ 8)[3] that lies deeper than individual sensations of pleasure. That is, he is ultimately obliged to posit a priori a collective notion of the mind that is not, as in the British empirical tradition out of which he is *partly* working, a mere tabula rasa (as Locke would have it) dependent on a posteriori sensual experience of the world. As a result, it is claimed that judgment in aesthetics transcends the particular, subjective self-interest being not only an unwelcome ingredient in the mix but an unnecessary one: "Every one must allow that a judgment on the beautiful which is tinged with the slightest interest, is very partial and not a pure judgment of taste" (§ 2). Frankly you might not, as I do not, (and Freud most certainly would not) share either this view or the inference of a grand impartial category. However, it does allow Kant to infer three key concepts, which in descending qualitative order are: the Good (which "esteems"), the Beautiful (which "pleases"), and the Agreeable (which "gratifies") (§ 5). We note that the beautiful is superior to the agreeable because the latter is dependent on sensual pleasure, while the good rules the roost because, by virtue of reason, it "commends itself by its mere concept" (§ 4), which is to say that it underpins Kant's notion of Platonic (a priori) mental faculties. Much of what follows seems designed to get us to the "good" through the good offices of the "beautiful." And certainly the chief characteristic of the beautiful is that, as it is free from self-interest, it becomes perforce a universal, shared phenomenon: "For where any one is conscious that his delight in an object is with him independent of interest, it is inevitable that he should look on the object as one containing a ground of delight for all men" (§ 6). Furthermore: "We are suitors for agreement from every one else, because we are fortified with a ground common to all" (§ 19). In short, the beautiful will deliver the key category of universalism, and Kant will carry this category with him through to the end of his argument so that whatever he feels he has finally established he has assuredly established for everyone. And thereby when teleology surfaces explicitly in the final section of the Critique, it will be in a hardwired form, although Kant, initially, admits to some doubts in the matter. He will, however, overcome them. In the meantime, we may admire how he gets around the problem of subjectivity with respect to aesthetics and universalism. In the end, he allows himself an engaging oxymoron, "the judgment of taste, with its attendant consciousness of detachment from all interest, must involve a claim to validity for all men, and must do so apart from universality attached to objects, i.e. there must be coupled with it a claim to subjective universality" (§ 6).

This quotation is significant for another reason, which is no less paradoxical than "subjective universality." It is the reference to objects. These are said to have purpose, which is an expression of their empirical nature. But the beautiful by its apparent lack of purposiveness, or its lack of "interest," becomes a proof of the deeper and normative purposiveness of the world itself, which is to say of the empirical world of objects as well. It is as if the beautiful (and later the "sublime" in a yet more paradoxical manner) confirms purposiveness as an idea, in that it is not present in the beautiful in any purposeful, empirically useful manner. The "sublime," for instance, will be characterized as "contra-purposive" to establish much the same thing.

The sublime however is unique in that it belongs, not to external nature, but to that faculty *in the mind*, which is indispensable to the power of judgment, and thus it has a key role in the argument that permits normative a priori deductions from aesthetics. "For the beautiful in nature we must seek a ground external to ourselves, but for the sublime one merely in ourselves and the attitude of mind that introduces sublimity into the representation of nature" (§ 23), and further: "Sublimity, therefore, does not reside in any of the things of nature, but only in our own mind...we are capable of attaining to the idea of the sublimity of that Being which inspires deep respect in us, not by the mere display of its might in nature, but more by the faculty which is planted in us of estimating that might without fear, and of regarding our estate as exalted above it" (§ 28).

It was part of the agenda of *The Critique of Pure Reason* to establish that a priori judgments in respect of certain synthetic statements are tenable; that is, in respect of statements that are not of themselves necessarily true because their predicates are contained within their subjects, as is the case with analytical statements. Analytical statements are in essence tautologies; they are necessarily true in their own terms. A crude example might be "the bachelor was unmarried." Kant, for instance, having deduced space and time as necessary categories, can formulate the analytical statement that all objects occupy space. However, it is clearly a much more demanding task to establish a category of synthetic statements that are a priori true. An example here of the sort of synthetic statement Kant wishes to establish a priori—and in the teleological section at the end of *The Critique of Judgment* believes he has—is that we can deduce a moral drive within us (that is, dependent on an intrinsic mental faculty) to increase the summum bonum or the collective good. Clearly, the ability to make statements of this kind is essential if Kant is to satisfactorily establish transcendent normative judgments independent of (a posteriori) empirical experience of the world.

And in the Third Critique the move from the beautiful—found in objects—to the sublime (somehow or other an expression of the mental category of pure reason itself) convinces him that he has taken a (the) crucial step in attaining this goal. In § 29, titled "Modality of the judgment on the sublime in nature," we find that while the beautiful allows us to "love" something, the sublime permits us to "esteem" it. In short, it evokes the lofty category of the "Good" (which "esteems") that surfaced in § 5 (see above), and which is, quite consistently, also an expression of an intrinsic mental faculty. Furthermore, that there is a category of mental faculty linked to the moral is explicit: "As a matter of fact, a feeling for the sublime in nature is hardly thinkable unless in association with an attitude of mind resembling the moral."

And thus it is not surprising in § 29 to see Kant making the key shift into logical a priori synthetic judgments on the basis of aesthetics:

> In this modality of aesthetic judgments, namely, their assumed necessity, lies what is for the Critique of Judgment a moment of capital importance. For this is exactly what makes an *a priori* principle apparent in their case, and lifts them out of the sphere of empirical psychology, in which otherwise they would remain buried amid the feelings of gratification and pain (only

with the senseless epithet of finer feeling), so as to place them, and, thanks to them, to place the faculty of judgment itself, in the class of judgments of which the basis of an *a priori* principle is the distinguishing feature, and, thus distinguished, to introduce them into transcendental philosophy.

So aesthetics enables Kant to establish a transcendent philosophy that logically allows us to make judgments about the world because we have not only been initiated into its deeper mysteries, but have found those mysteries intrinsic to our mental structures. Transcendent is a key term here, and potentially a troublesome one. For what use in practical life are Kant's lofty arguments? Naturally artists have turned to him. But this has underpinned and (usually unintentionally) contaminated German idealist thinking. For there is nothing in the Third Critique that would even let us evoke Shelley's trumpeting claim that poets are the unacknowledged legislators of the world. Kant's poets are in no position to legislate. Furthermore, no reading of *The Critique of Judgment* will generate any idea of how society is to be organized on the basis of civic institutions. And his great moral axiom (the categorical imperative) makes the task of deciding how to behave in practical terms difficult. In fact it seems to maximize the conditions under which we might martyr ourselves. With Kant, we are trapped on the lofty Keatsian plane of Truth being Beauty and Beauty Truth. But we arrive at those heights only to find that we have no place on which to stand, and no agenda for collective action. Certainly Kant's teleology and the summum bonum are redolent with good feelings and they do confirm that Germany is "the land of poets and thinkers." But where are the shopkeepers?

Another consideration is relevant here, although it might appear to some as willfully missing the point or as needlessly calling into question what, for most people, is a legitimate tautology. Nonetheless, it seems fair to point out that there is no axiomatic reason why Kant's shift into a priori synthetic statements should of itself establish those *particular* elevated things it allegedly does. We might ask, on what basis do Kant's "proofs" validate as a priori moral the "virtues" of the German Enlightenment rather than the "vices" as defined by the same tradition? That is, unless arbitrary assumptions are made, we cannot find intrinsically in aesthetics the values Kant finds. For instance, he specifically mentions "gratitude, obedience and humiliation"—all supposedly enlightenment virtues. Later he asserts that the three ideas of "pure reason" are "God, freedom, and immortality" and that it is freedom which connects the other two and connects us with the "supersensible." Freedom "can extend reason beyond the bounds to which every natural, or theoretical, conception must remain hopelessly restricted" (p. 607). Now, no doubt if you can couple freedom as an a priori category on to the more humble qualities of "gratitude, obedience and humiliation" you can validate the assumptions of a good deal of enlightenment propaganda. But the question remains: Is it just a happy coincidence that Kant's deployment of aesthetics and teleology comes up with a "proof" for those values and the summum bonum, or is it because that was the moral agenda, and the hidden inscribed teleological aim, from the beginning?

No doubt for most people it is only natural for any moral philosophical inquiry to arrive at these values. And with respect to his privileged category of aesthetics, Kant treats this as more or less self-evident: "I do maintain that to take an immediate interest in the beauty of nature... is always a mark of a good soul." In addition, "We have reason for presuming the presence of at least the germ of a good moral disposition in the case of a man to whom the beauty of nature is a matter of immediate interest" (§ 42). But that does not of itself answer the objections that, let us say, a fascist would raise. He would have a quite different notion of the "good." He would no doubt be quite happy with the mental faculty, the intrinsic little voice of morality that Kant mentions in the last section of the Critique where we are told that if man deviates from "the path of duty," conscience will mutter words of reproach in his inner ear (p 593). But he would have a very different idea of what that duty was.

Perhaps Kant gets around this by his use of form, which implies order and on which beauty is (allegedly) dependent. And, of course, the whole business is axiomatically universal anyway. Aesthetics then escapes contamination by alien forms of anarchical or fascist struggle because the link between aesthetic values and democratic (enlightened) order is self-evident... for Kant. So beauty is

> the symbol of the morally good, and only in this light (a point of view natural to every one, and one which every one exacts from others as a duty) does it give us pleasure with an attendant claim to the agreement of every one else, whereupon the mind becomes conscious of a certain ennoblement and elevation above mere sensibility to pleasure from impressions of sense, and also appraises the worth of others on the score of a like maxim of their judgment. (§ 59)

However, as we have seen, the sublime escapes the bounds of form. And certainly as a concept it would be a narcotic to the inspired fascist. He would have no trouble accepting it as an innate mental faculty that allowed him, like any Heldentenor, to face the might of nature "without fear." After all, the Sublime (and the Will) attain great potency in nineteenth-century Germany. They couple heatedly with heroism and spawn a cult of death, which in turn is perfectly successful in finding aesthetic expression. We might, arbitrarily, see it in the march from Sturm und Drang to Wagner to

Ernst Jünger. Nor could a Freudian accept the Kantian agenda. Although Freud paid due homage to Kant and linked the categorical imperative to guilt,[4] the basic assumptions of the Freudian model (no less universal than Kant's and much less amorphous) are those of struggle and satisfaction. Nor could a great deal of German idealist philosophy escape what might be seen as the non-Kantian implications of his work on aesthetics. However democratic the Kantian enlightenment, however much it accords equal moral worth, it also underpins a romantic Weltanschauung that invites us to contemplate hierarchical values and suggests the superiority of certain sensibilities, embodied in individuals (or in the Volk) over others. The cult of the genius, whether poet or not, readily becomes the cult of the Übermensch, which only tells if there is a "herd" to be despised. As Adorno says of Nietzsche "It is the weak who are the guilty" and therefore pity is contemptible.[5] And all of this readily spills over into the cult of the führer. Kant is hardly to be blamed for this, any more than he is to be blamed for not being a shopkeeper. But the celebration of the sublime came at a price. It left common sense and empiricism far behind. The cost, when everything went awry, was huge—if, that is, one is, as here, disposed to entertain a proposition so speculative that it can never be substantiated.

When we approach the final section of *The Critique*, we find teleology is at first presented in a tentative form. Although the argument for design is there (and, some years before Bishop Paley, the analogy of the watch implying the watchmaker) (§ 65), Kant seems reluctant to make conclusive claims for it. Instead he warns of the circular argument of using God to validate nature and nature to validate God (§ 67). Richard Dawkins could not have made the point more satisfactorily. Initially Kant wants to hold God as a teleological necessity at arm's length, as extrinsic, a "peregrina," to the argument in that he does not wish to exceed the parameters of natural science (§ 68). In short, when thinking of teleology within the category of physics and applying that to the natural world there is no requirement to infer a Deity. At this stage the teleological argument from design is also only an inference, "strictly speaking, we do not *observe* the ends in nature as designed. We only *read* this conception *into* the facts as a guide to judgment" (§ 75).

And yet teleology soon shifts as a category: "Teleology...in the form of a science, is not a branch of doctrine at all, but only of...the critique of a particular cognitive faculty, namely judgment" (§ 79). This definition may read as slightly pejorative ("only") but, as we have seen, such is the mighty significance of "judgment" that it has to be an elevated step. Thus in gradually uncoupling teleology from the natural world (nature), Kant allows it to take flight so that, at the very least, it plays a role in establishing that which it initially seemed it could not establish: a Deity. If he is not so much moving the goalposts here as changing the playing-field, it

is to make teleology do what he wants: "We have seen...that the mechanism of nature is not sufficient to enable us to conceive the possibility of
an organized being, but that in its root origin it must be subordinated
to a cause acting by design" (§ 81). In short, we proceed beyond a teleology of the physical world because we are driven to consider the final end,
and a "physio-teleology" when contained within the parameters of nature
"can never disclose to us anything about a *final end* of creation." Again it
might appear that this shift toward a "theological teleology," now explicit,
is somehow a betrayal of stringent analysis in that the initial premises have
to be abandoned: "It is true that physical teleology urges us to go in quest
of a theology. But it cannot produce one" (§ 85). However, the introduction of new categories changes everything. In the section titled *Remark* (p.
593), we read that man "exists for an end, and this end demands a Being
that has formed both him and the world with that end in view." And we
discover that the category of the subjective, which underpins this move, is
again paradoxically defined, in that the assertion that "Man" is an expression of a divine will in a world that must itself have an end/telos is made
on "a purely moral ground, which, while of course only subjective, is free
from all foreign influence." (ibid.). This is indeed an elevated notion of the
subjective and it will duly link with the universal moral category, that is
with the mental faculty that is intrinsically an expression of the good and
which is manifested in aesthetics. In this context man, the subject, is not
a meager category. Rather, he is moral and rational and comes trailing
Wordsworthian clouds of glory.

Then we find ourselves confronted by ethical values intrinsic to us.
They have been abstracted from those—literally prejudiced—qualities
already mentioned: "gratitude, obedience and humiliation" (one *feels* that
"humility" is meant although the German is "Demütigung"). [(ibid.]).
Moreover, it becomes ever clearer that the mental faculties that allow us
to appreciate the beautiful lead us to morality as expressed in the summum bonum, and then on to a sense of the Deity. The summum bonum
does not descend into a loose generalization either. Instead it, too, conjoins
the three essential categories found in man the subject: the universal, the
ethical, and reason. The summum bonum is "formed by the union of the
greatest welfare of the rational beings in the world with the supreme condition of their good, or, in other words, by the union of universal happiness
with the strictest morality" (§ 87). It is we as "men" who, being capable of
reason, are the "rational beings in the world." In short it seems we are, if we
only knew it, thoroughly good chaps...axiomatically at least.

However, the nagging question returns as to what to do with those
subjects for whom "gratitude, obedience and humiliation" do not carry the
moral clout they should? Well, presumably in having failed to appreciate

beauty, they have remained ignorant of the higher qualities that are pregnant in their mental faculties. But what are we to say to the man who
argues, in opposition, that cruelty and egomaniacal desire are also axiomatically part of our mental structures and, moreover are not only present in
nature but fruitfully, even attractively, expressed in aesthetic activity? Such
an assertion would return us to Terry Eagleton's rhetorical question noted
in the first chapter: namely whether it is part of the liberating historical
struggle to balance the individual's capacity to torture in proportionate
relation to his capacity to love. And does not the "nagging doubt," which
Kant imagines will disturb the man who has "diverged from the path of
duty" so that "words of stern self-reproach will then fall upon an inward
ear, and he will seem to hear the voice of a judge to whom he has to render
account" (p 593), sound more like the Freudian superego kicking in, rather
than another manifestation of an immaculate Deity?

Against this it might be argued that Kant is engaged in an abstract
pursuit and is not, unlike Hegel or Marx, to be brought before the court
of history. And yet such is the nature of his "discoveries" that one could
legitimately reply that if these finer things have no effective purchase in
quotidian life, they damn well should. After all, the summum bonum
asserts collective will, collective values and, as was pointed out by Auxter,
only works if it is good *for* something.[6] Moreover it is man in the material
here and now who vindicates these grand things, "supposing we follow the
teleological order, there is a *fundamental principle* to which even the most
ordinary human intelligence is obliged to give immediate assent. It is the
principle that if there is to be a *final end* of all, which reason must assign
a priori, then it can only be man...*subject to moral laws*" (§ 87). But we
might ask how can this lofty creature be brought down to earth where he
can do some good in the community? And this is tantamount to asking if
the categorical imperative and the deontological model can deliver on the
same level.

Nonetheless, if we were looking for a theory that sublimely married the
two title terms of this book we could hardly do better than *The Critique
of Judgment*. Here is teleology (with its narrative implications) on the one
hand and truth on the other made virtual synonyms through the agency of
aesthetics. So it is a pity that one is not more happy with it. The chief difficulty lies in a teleology that, paradoxically, emerges as a theoretical rather
than as a narrative trope. If Darwin, Dawkins, and Kuhn et al. in their
different ways give us teleology without telos, Kant seems to come up with
a teleology without effective narrative. It posits fixed categories, universally and timelessly true and therefore invulnerable to the practical effects
of narrative, and thereby turns teleology on its epistemological head. Its
significance does not lie in the stories that shape it, but in the "mere" fact

that it is *there*. There is a further difficulty, which at first sight looks like a similarity. Kant insists upon universalism. But Kant's universalism is inferred from what are, for him, self-evident enlightenment values, and not, as here, from the fact of death. This is regrettable, as one would like to embrace the notion of aesthetics that Kant duly infers from out of his (arbitrary) universal values. But the universalism born of death does not, of itself, enable that. Nonetheless, aesthetics will continue to be an important and, it is hoped, productive category in the rest of this book.

Perhaps Adorno's attack on Kant (and Hegel) is the most substantive. This is because he sees fascism rooted in German philosophy. In an analysis blackened almost beyond qualification by the catastrophe of the Third Reich, Adorno finds in German idealist and dialectical thinking the irredeemable fons et origo of a horror so absolute that it becomes a negative paradigm. It is evoked by the signifier "Auschwitz," which certainly amounts to more than either the place or even the horrors that occurred there. In mentioning this now I am jumping from the beginning to the end of something that I cannot in all conscience call an argument, but rather an arbitrary interpretation on my part for which, however, a great deal of, inevitably anecdotal, evidence can be assembled.

In view of what Kant has made out of aesthetics it is hardly surprising that when the catastrophe occurs, it is expressed by Adorno as the utter failure of Art. In fact Adorno's earlier attack on the American culture industry, which reads like an exercise in unbridled snobbery, is, no less than loss of faith in poetry after Auschwitz, an expression of the Kantian importance of aesthetics. These two polarities—the reification of Art according to the principles of American consumerism, and the axiomatic inability of Art in the face of the German/European catastrophe to find a subjective correlative adequate to the objective correlative of immediate history—are equally normative in character. But now those normative values are deeply corrupted. Here the apposite textual strategy is unrelenting contradictions, every proposition is immediately shown to be ipso facto its own inimical opposite. That these contradictions are graced with the title "dialectics" reads like an exercise in propaganda, an after the fact profession of intellectual probity. Typical is: "Whoever believes in God, can therefore not believe in Him" (ND 391–394).[7]

In debunking any grounds for optimism, Adorno is also keen to show that Hegel does not produce a positive synthesis out of his triad model. Instead it is the negation that it is dynamic. And not unreasonably, he claims that Kant is compelled to accommodate evil because of his across the board category of the "transcendental, which is supposed to be founded in the subjective consciousness." Hence his "tenacious effort to demonstrate the moral consciousness as something ubiquitous, existent even in what is radically evil. Otherwise he would have had to reject, in the appropriate phases and societies in which there is no freedom, along with the character of rationally-endowed beings also that of humanity; the follower of Rousseau could scarcely have found comfort in that" (ND 217–221). And freedom as a positive concept is, of course, a complete chimera. It can have no validity separate from its antithesis on which it is not only wholly dependent but expressive, "freedom itself is so tangled up with unfreedom, that it is not merely inhibited by the latter, but has it as the condition of its own concept" (ND 258–262). Thus here too, Kant is embroiled in the dialectical catastrophe in that, driven once again by universalism, pure reason obliges him to embed freedom in societies that are not in the least free.

But in seeing that Kant has introduced an "as if" (ND 230–231), which permits every subject to speculate on what could be, Adorno unwittingly comes close to appreciating the Brechtian notion of realism, which as Raymond Williams suggested many decades ago is best understood as a form of subjunctive action.[8] As Adorno was to mount a contemptuous, misplaced attack on Brecht, it is a pity he did not pursue the Kantian argument a little further. In fact it is remarkable how aware Adorno shows himself to be, elsewhere, of the optimistic and narratively conditioned "what if" element secreted in every aesthetic discourse: "Even in the most sublimated work of art there is a hidden 'it should be otherwise.'"[9] However, it does him little good.

Surely Adorno is caught in a structuralist bind of his own making. What is the point of this unremitting pessimism calling itself dialectical if it is intellectually monothematic? It simply becomes invalid in dialectical terms. Inevitably then, his determination to cling to his own stringent dialectical credentials compels him to summon up the opposite of his own jeremiad. And when Adorno does let in the redemptive category, he lets it in as an intense illuminating beam.

Adorno and particularly Horkheimer—if Habermas's account of who wrote what in *The Dialectics of the Enlightenment* is accepted[10]—were always aware of the "aporia" intrinsic to their analysis. Ironically their criticism, on a deeper level, celebrates enlightenment values, because they have not managed to mount their attack from outside the box of their own "enlightened" cultural milieu. As a result they are obliged to take on board just those premises they are determined to eradicate. Neither can they— even before Auschwitz—foreground the sort of doubts expressed above with regard to the arbitrary status of Kant's enlightenment values, nor do they find in Marxism the structures that would facilitate a deeper analysis of the "culture" they are debunking. For although those Marxist structures are there, it is the priority of cultural and philosophical factors that cripples their thinking. They can never, even in the attacks on commodity fetishism and reification, escape an idealist humanist Weltanschauung. As Habermas points out, Adorno is convinced that art maintains its independent ontology.[11] It is no surprise then that it is always culture that has to express the failure of real history. Naturally when "Auschwitz" breaches Adorno's Weltanschauung, at least to the degree that he is projected onto a wholly new level of despair, that failure is expressed in the old terminology made absolute. "Auschwitz irrefutably demonstrated the failure of culture" and "All culture after Auschwitz, including its urgent critique, is garbage" (ND 358–361).

But if that "garbage" applies to the "urgent critique," does it not also apply to Adorno's? So even here the absolute takes advantage, under its own dynamic, of the dialectical twist. For not only is there a form of hope, there is even some kind of acceptable response to Auschwitz after all: "Perennial suffering has as much right to express itself as the martyr has to scream; this is why it may have been wrong to say that poetry could not be written after Auschwitz." (ND 354–358) And a great deal can be made out of this scream. Its very bleakness gives rise to its untarnished antipode: utopian thinking. Adorno acknowledges that all art contains a utopian moment implicit in the assumption that "it should be otherwise." Furthermore, the Kantian transcendental subject can never be extinguished and "no assessment of his aesthetics can overlook this semi-miraculous persistence of the subject in a conceptual schema that posits its complete reification."[12] Here the formal parallel between Freudian and dialectical thought becomes disturbing. In both cases the intellectual game is glib in that both devise a blank check with respect to empiricism. The former tells us that we cannot, ipso facto, trust what we perceive because culture is the product of fantasy and sublimation, while the latter insists that everything is other than it seems because it is constitutive of its antithesis.

Furthermore, the dialectical argument as theory formally evokes a Marxist solecism that can surface, with tragic consequences, in empirical political action. If in the 1930s Marxists regarded fascism as the perverse but logical product of capitalism, they should have colluded with it. It was the "bad" predestined to do "good." In 1923, Clara Zetkin was confident that fascism was "condemned to...disintegration,"[13] while the leader of the German Communist Party Ernst Thälmann in 1933 warned of any "opportunistic overestimation of Hitler fascism."[14] Here dialectical theory was realized in praxis at a cost that beggars belief. Furthermore, critical theory almost cost several members of the Frankfurt School their lives. Adorno, naively packaging fascism in the standard dialectical manner, only succumbed to common sense at the very last moment and fled, thereby avoiding an all too empirical experience of Auschwitz.[15]

Yet, it is to the allegedly contaminated category of culture that Adorno turns to accomplish what we might see as his most remarkable back-somersault. Like many German thinkers, he imagines music, as opposed to literature, will do the business.[16] It, for instance, is best equipped to resolve the dichotomy between the spiritual and the subjective:

> Every expression of hope, which emanates from great works of art...is con-figured with that of human beings...[and] nowhere more unambiguously than in the moment of Beethoven. What signifies that not everything is in vain, is the self-reflection of nature in subjects, through the sympathy with that which is human; solely in the experience of its own natural base [Naturhaftigkeit] does the genius escape from nature. It is to Kant's last-ing honor that he, like no other philosopher, registered the constellation of the human and the transcendental in the doctrine of the intelligible (ND 386–391).

Now what is this if not the Kantian sublime? What is the figure of Beethoven as celebrated here if not the elevated German hero performing great deeds in the sphere of transcendental art because he is the authen-tic child of nature, unencumbered by communal or familial responsibil-ity? In this he is, as Adorno also makes clear, unlike poor Bach with his huge family and weekly labors for the paymasters at the Thomasschule. Adorno is reproducing the very categories of idealist thought that he has hitherto tarred with the negative paradigm of Auschwitz. Certainly there is no place for empiricism or common sense. In fact the rhetoric prais-ing Beethoven could just as readily be applied to Young Siegfried out on the hunt for heroic deeds, except that here it is not dragons or wondrous women but art, once again slipping the epistemological reins that ham-string everything else, that redeems us all. It is as if the Übermensch as a creative force, binding nature with human essence, steps into the room in the form of Beethoven, who has obligingly brought his own storm clouds with him. Perhaps we should not be surprised. The one thing you can say about the German romantic tradition is that it never lacked for atmosphere.

That Adorno makes much of music is hardly surprising. The elevated (abstract) nature of German philosophy made music the ideal aesthetic category. So at this point we can allow music to take us back to the imme-diate post-Kantian world. Of all the German philosophers post-Kant and pre-Adorno who succumbed to music's mystical authority none asserted its allegedly far-reaching powers and its ontological uniqueness more ambi-tiously than Schopenhauer.

One notes, at first, that the elemental energy of the Schopenhauerian Will, which underlies everything, is in fact not wholly denied us as experience. For although he thought it impossible to experience things in themselves, he did concede that we have some intimation of the deeper unity of the world through the subjective experience of our own bodies. In fact, Schopenhauer accords significance to physical gratification, to the genitalia, even to the bacchanal. But in the end such pleasures are transitory and dissatisfying, and merely contribute to the suffering we have to endure in a world were nature is anarchic and Hobbesian. So although the body is privileged as the Will "objectified," we can never reach a truly painless experience of the world. We are condemned to be mere playthings of the Will. Indeed it would seem that nothing can gainsay the lived fact that we are here to suffer.

Furthermore Schopenhauer, whose transcendental disposition is difficult to outbid, also makes use of the Platonic "Idea." As a result we can conceive of absolute qualities. Love, justice, and so forth are thus present. And we are not surprised to learn they are to be found through aesthetics. Aesthetics enables us to rise above the struggle and facilitates a further, wholly Kantian step, in that, as it is universal, the subject in this instance will become so too. (Section 33 of *The World as Will and Representation*) Moreover art, being contemplative, purges one of desire and thereby leads us away from impoverished bodily intimations of mortality. We can then infer that anything that arouses is clearly decadent and Schopenhauer duly substitutes for the dissatisfactions of sensual pleasure the ideal of renunciation and the virtues of asceticism, best embodied by St. Francis and Christ. (Sections 68 and 70)

It is music that offers the most promising way into these, albeit extremely nebulous, categories. For unlike the other Arts, which are representative, music is not merely a reflection of the Ideas, but "a copy of the Will itself."[17] It is thus immediately comprehensible. It connects in an unmediated fashion to the spirit. So in this instance, Schopenhauer can ameliorate our suffering and direct us to the transcendental. And the transcendental is experienced directly through a transcendental category (music) and not in any way mediated through lived—let alone shared—experience. In fact we are so estranged from one another that shared experience is wretched.

This undiluted transcendentalism was to have an enormous effect on German thinking. Nietzsche made out of the compliant Schopenhauerian Will a dynamic and ruthless force that denied God and freed the ego from any inhibitions that might curtail it. And, quite naturally, he remained true to the notion of aesthetics in general and music in particular, which read as sublime substitutes for the Godhead that he otherwise dismisses. Expressive of higher striving, they place the individual as hero above the vulgar mass and underpin his contemptuous but admirable indifference to the sufferings of its members. For "it is only as an aesthetic phenomenon that existence and the world are eternally justified."[18] The Übermensch, in turn, imposes order on his passions, just as the artist controls the work of art he creates. Thus obsessive, if controlled, egoism triumphs, while the communal is only allowed onto the stage in the most debased form possible: the herd.

The divine associations of the artist/creator were, at one time, most strikingly clear to Nietzsche in the person of Wagner, who was himself a devoted disciple of Schopenhauer. Like him, Wagner mixed Christian and Eastern philosophy, expressed the same tension between sensual satisfaction and ascetic renunciation, and was fascinated by Death. What Schopenhauer saw as the otherworldly denial of the "Will to live," Wagner saw as redemption, which he employed, by highly sensual means, as the inevitable and hypnotic climactic signifier (both ideological and narrative) of his music dramas. Nietzsche is a worthy, that is to say a perspicacious and enraptured, disciple of the famous Wagnerian Rausch (intoxication). And so we celebrate again the unqualified uncoupling of art from the world and we prostrate ourselves once more before its mystical dissolution into the categories of Will, Idea and, now, transcendental oneness.

Nietzsche is particularly inspired by Isolde's Liebestod where a text that makes no concessions to common sense whatsoever is flooded by ecstatic waves of sound, all of which are designed to convince us that she and her conventionally "dead" lover experience an ethereal triumph over death as a mundane category—which is, nonetheless, the only possible (and crushingly unavoidable) category *for* death. Nietzsche rhapsodizes on Wagner in a manner that does not seem to exclude, at the very least, a feel for the "Godhead":

> So we remember the experiences of the truly aesthetic listener, the tragic artist himself, as he, like a voluptuous divinity of individualism, creates his forms—in which sense his work can scarcely be understood as an "imitation of nature"—and as his immense Dionysian drive then devours this entire world of appearances in order to allow him, through its destruction, to have a premonition of the original and highest artistic joy in the primordial One.[19]

As we now seem to have arrived at some form of a climax, if only stylistically, it may be appropriate to make a short diversion and consider, to state the matter somewhat melodramatically, an opportunity lost—an opportunity that, had it been taken, might have militated against some of the extreme excesses of German idealist philosophy. Furthermore, it is a diversion that should throw into particularly sharp relief the dangers that followed when nationalism colonized the nexus formed by philosophy and aesthetics. To do this we need to return, by implication, to the body.

German communication theory and discourse ethics after the Second World War is clearly given form and methodology by the upfront respect for all those who enter, on terms that must be axiomatically equal, the interactive speech community. The theory and praxis of this, as a form of communicative philosophy, is both materialist *and* egalitarian, and by virtue of its privileged category of intersubjectivity, it wipes the slate clean of all the assumptions that follow when universal moral categories are hijacked, whether by superior sensibilities or heroic actors. However, elements that were later to influence discourse theory were present much earlier in the history of German idealist thinking.

Habermas argues that the young Hegel, lecturing at Jena up to the time Napoleon's army defeated the Prussians outside the city in 1806, came close to pursuing the agenda of twentieth-century discourse theory.[20] Put baldly, Hegel's lectures at this time wriggled free of Kantian transcendentalism and programmed a form of intersubjectivity. Although beginning with Cartesian and Kantian notions of the subject (Hegel talks of the "Subjective Spirit" [Geist]), he subsequently moves into human *relationships*. There he starts with love relationships, which allow a complete immersion of the subject into the other and makes out of the assertion of the self a wholly interactive statement, notably because the subject becomes aware of himself as a result of the intensity of the relationship with, and the devotion to, the Other. Indeed this talk of a love relationship (Liebesverhältnis) recalls the argument and, most importantly, the values Habermas employed in his essay *Glauben und Wissen* dealt with in chapter 2. In general, we note again that a shift to the body is the obvious reaction to the elevated, if unsatisfactory, attractions of idealism. But, unlike Schopenhauer, the young Hegel does not end there; rather he broadens out the category of interaction to talk of family and society, which he then couples with the "Objective Spirit." Although Habermas does not make the inference explicitly, the Objective Spirit at this point in Hegel's thinking should perhaps be distinguished from the later Spirit of History working out its own metanarrative through the ruthless agency of Great Men, one of whom was not only just about to cause Hegel to gather up his draft of *The Phenomenology of the Mind* and flee Jena but would soon march his troops into Berlin and impose humiliating surrender terms on the Prussian state. Rather the societal/communal values that are celebrated in the Jena lectures imply that the Objective Spirit is linked to social structures and civic institutions. Terms like "gegenseitiger Anerkenung" (mutual recognition) in human relationships preecho later fundamental, practical, and ethical assumptions. In fact: "Hegel disputes that the knowing speaking and acting subject is faced with the task of bridging an imagined chasm that separates him from the Other. A subject that is from the very beginning *with others* is conscious of no such lack," and further, the subject is articulated, and articulates himself, "in a pregiven latticework of discourse formed by concepts and actions."[21] In this manner Hegel is shown to have foregrounded two crucial elements on which discourse theory is, later, to be wholly dependent: the category of intersubjectivity, which shatters the classic dualism of subject and object in German philosophical thinking, *and* the constitutive, binding character of communal language, which itself enables intersubjectivity.

But this all goes awry. Germany philosophy cannot escape the transcendental Kantian tradition any more than Hegel, who, out of his own intellectual struggle, develops the "Absolute Spirit." This ultimately generates a totalitarian model. Platonic idealism triumphs where Aristotelian empiricism had been in play. Now the Absolute Spirit works out its omniscient destiny through "the cunning of reason" ("die listige Vernunft"), and thus makes out of the Real a transcendental category. Despite appearances, the world is the utterly satisfactory expression of an ethereal ontology, driven by a Spirit that is eminently comprehensible *and* thereby end-focused.

This "return" to transcendental thinking comes about as a result of a dilemma from which Hegel was not able to free himself—although no doubt Habermas thinks he might have managed it had he pursued his initial agenda more stringently.[22] The problem arises with revolutionary activity. Hegel is thinking of the French Revolution. Here the second manifestation of the Geist—the Objective Spirit—fails in that there are no strong and legitimate social institutions in place, which allow and control change under such violent and chaotic conditions. As a result, Hegel sees that the revolutionary is compelled to appeal to an abstract moral category; he must resort to the manufacture ("Herstellung") of a higher absolute Reason under whose artificial protection bloody radicalism can take place. Now Hegel may have, here or later, found this act of rationalization unappealing, but it does not lie at odds with the logical thrust of his (later) notion of history, which employs both the World Historical Individual and the State to work out its grand plan.

In this manner Hegel is confronted on a profound level by pressing contemporary events. Furthermore, what one senses is a more prosaic contradiction common to a lot of German nationalist thinking of the period, in particular that of Fichte and Ernst Moritz Arndt: namely a highly ambivalent attitude toward Napoleon. This may seem a rather constricted consideration, but its consequences will emerge in the pages that follow as significant. On the one hand Napoleon is the "arch-enemy" (Arndt) while, on the other, he perversely embodies a nexus of attractive qualities. He emerges as both an unknowing and, in respect of the extinction of numerous tiny German principalities, a knowing agent of the German revival. He is a thrilling phenomenon ("Napoleon, this synthesis of the inhuman and the superhuman" as Nietzsche later put it[23]) and has a correspondingly massive effect on German thinkers, poets, and playwrights. He underpins the, above all Prussian, disposition toward a führer principle. And when in 1813 and 1814, Blücher and Gneisenau triumph against him on the battlefield, the lasting significance for Prussia across the board—from the contemporary philosophy of Hegel to later expansionism under Bismarck and all the extravagant, heroic, death-obsessed nationalism beyond—is correspondingly decisive.

There is a further characteristic of this general culture, which is likewise decisive. Art, literature, and philosophy; politics and civic administration; conquest and the cult of the military; an exotic longing for a mythical Germany of the mind together with a passionate and at times arrogant celebration of the native hearth—all these exist in an unusually deep, intertwined, and contradictory form in the renaissance of German (often explicitly folk) culture initiated in the Napoleonic period. The productive capacity of this promiscuous nexus of factors, along with its dangers, is only enhanced by the subsequent headlong rush toward industrialization. There is a general and highly excited sense of change taking place at speed throughout all the material and ideological apparatuses of society, of history being made on the run. It is no accident that many of the key figures of the emerging Great Power play out their lives as eclectic actors, intermingling the roles of poets and musicians, and philosophers and warriors in a manner that today seems almost bizarre.

Nonetheless, whatever regret Habermas may feel as Hegel returns to transcendentalism to avoid the challenge of the French Revolution, the move does raise an important issue (one that should cause Habermas some trouble) with respect to human agency. It is surely impossible as a general rule to expect dictatorial regimes be replaced by democratic ones by virtue of democratic means. "Velvet revolutions" in dictatorships are atypical. It is clear that Robespierre (to take Hegel's example) was compelled by a logical dilemma to resort to higher powers in order to "manufacture" a rationalization for violating the very principles the Revolution was about to embed in French society. He needed the God of history, the cult of the Supreme Being, to morally sanitize radical intervention. He proclaims:

> a whole nation, grappling with all the oppressions of the human race, suspends the course of its heroic labors to elevate its thoughts and vows toward the great Being who has given it the mission it has undertaken and the strength to accomplish it...Is it not He whose immortal hand, engraving

on the heart of man the code of justice and equality, has written there the death sentence of tyrants? Is it not He who, from the beginning of time, decreed for all the ages and for all peoples liberty, good faith, and Justice?...Our blood flows for the cause of humanity. Behold our prayer. Behold our sacrifices. Behold the worship we offer thee.[24]

Of course Robespierre can offer no basis that is not wholly arbitrary for this overblown rationalization. Nevertheless it is easy to see how appealing this sort of thing must be. Divine authority that justifies earthly bloodletting, itself designed to produce the conditions that will make such bloodletting obsolete, is very convenient.

Habermas does not face this problem—at least not in these terms—because he claims there is a necessary interdependency between philosophy and democracy, which allegedly turns them into a kind of double helix, each driving the other forward. "In respect of their origins philosophy and democracy are not only indebted to the same historical process, they are also structurally dependent on each other."[25] Furthermore—or so one assumes—this pairing leads one to reject any argument for widespread violence justified by anticipated but deferred improvements as a result of that violence. This makes anything like The Terror impermissible. Here Kant's loaded, a priori, moral categories assume an extreme, albeit nontranscendental, expression in that philosophy must fundamentally embody universal values that place, as a first principle, everyone *equally* within the community. Its distrust of guilds, of oligarchies, of, above all, the *Führerprinzip*, is a measure of its freedom from the philosophical past. It could even be said, as a practical methodology, to have gone beyond Anglo-Saxon empiricism in that it employs sociology to colonize philosophy.

But the problem that Hegel encountered when he attempted to come to terms with the French Revolution (and Robespierre circumvented by appealing to the Supreme Being) remains. That is, communication ethics seals itself off from the "necessary" use of nondemocratic means and thereby expresses a contradiction that discourse theorists themselves have had to confront: namely, we employ one set of principles with respect to domestic matters and quite another with respect to foreign ones. For discourse theorists, domestic issues take place within the contemporary German democracy where all sorts of convenient moral givens are in place. But a wholly different set of problems surfaces when they are faced with external action that will obviously not be effective if heads do not roll. No wonder they were so uncomfortable when confronted by problems, too close to home to be ignored, that followed the collapse of Yugoslavia.

Early nineteenth-century hostility toward, and fascination with, Napoleon expresses a deeper dilemma intrinsic to the development of German nationalism. In the first instance the cult of the Volk, given a massive fillip by Johann Gottfried von Herder and Fichte, functioned as a convenient reaction against French arrogance and as a rationalization of native roots. But it was, as a direct result, compelled to hold onto the foreign without which the particularity of the native was indiscernible and meaningless. Condescending Frenchmen could be easily dismissed as falsely cosmopolitan and likely to pollute the earthy if less sophisticated domestic culture. But a respect for the uniqueness of each Volk would also lead to an understanding not only of the particularity of the German Volksgemeinschaft, but also of the particularity of every other. To go beyond France and the French would be, ultimately, to become fascinated with other peoples, some of whom would inevitably emerge as more attractive points of comparison than others. This leads to the contradictory strategy whereby German nationalism in its obsession with what is "German and genuine" (to quote Wagner's Hans Sachs) induces not merely an admiration for certain alien cultures, but also an attempt to marry Germanness with those cultures. Ideally, the best of the ancient will then be shown preserved in the higher more developed German form. And this is to touch, for the moment at least, on another contradiction. The celebration of the homeland and its frontiers—not least because one might set them ideologically in neighboring countries, as in the now banned first verse of the national anthem—shares its cultural justification with the contrary notion that geographical boundaries are, anyway, superseded by higher cultural considerations. Moreover, given that this ambivalence is already present in Herder and given that it leads to a notion of historical and racial development-cum-evolution, it is not surprising that the urgent inquiry into what is German and genuine gives rise also to the question of racial and cultural origins.

The search for a foreign genesis for the German people and for the fountainhead of German culture leads to some obviously attractive speculations as well as to some pretty bizarre ones. Understandably ancient Greece had a bewitching appeal. For instance, Nietzsche's "blond beasts" were a crude but admirable northern race who had yet to succumb to debilitating Christianity,[26] and thus they recalled the "splendid and lionhearted Greeks, with their child-like minds" who had used their gods to keep enfeebling guilt at bay.[27] This sort of thing lasts well into the twentieth century and influences philosophers such as Hans Georg Gadamer who is much taken with a mystical notion of the Volk and Plato's Guardians. Heidegger saw in the classical Greek language a linguistic partner to high German. Both were uncontaminated and uniquely able to tackle the great ontological question of Being. The Nazis in parades and propaganda evoked an Hellenic heritage, while those in the Stefan George circle, notably Berthold and Claus von Stauffenberg, who conspired to assassinate Hitler, claimed to be acting under the double benediction of a sacred classical past and a mystical Germany best embodied in the figures of the Hohenstaufen Holy Roman Emperors Friedrich Barbarossa and Friedrich II. The oath that Claus von Stauffenberg composed for his fellow conspirators before the attempt on Hitler's life on July 20, 1944 rests in part on the profound link between Hellenic culture and an idealized Germany. [28]

But it is the quintessential contradiction of the Volksgemeinschaft, which leads to truly fanciful theorizing. One cannot propagandize the domestic without recourse to the, quite possibly forbidden and therefore seductive, exotic. Wagner, the uncompromising anti-Semitic artist and theoretician, is fascinated by the Wandering Jew and turns him, in the form of the Flying Dutchman, into the hero of his first truly "Wagnerian" (that is to say redemption-based) music drama. This is typical of much German culture and results in further contradictions in that Christian, non-Christian, and pagan Weltanschauungen become entangled.

That was clear with the Nazis. They made propaganda films mocking claims that Egypt was the cradle of civilization. I have seen one in which a benign German professor chuckles over the idea that the pyramids prove the historical priority of the Nile civilization, after which we are shown scenes of happy hairy blondes, dressed in animal skins, dancing and singing in a village-based ur-Gemeinschaft. Meanwhile Himmler, who was among those most seduced by the holy (but not necessarily Christian) heroic German past, promoted the cult of the Teutonic Knights and recreated them in the tall blondes of his SS. Much influenced by the occult and cosmology, he attempted to control the diet of his supermen (apparently there is a lot to be said for leeks); he wanted to be surrounded by 12 of his knights at table (like King Arthur); he organized ceremonies in the cathedral at Quedlinburg to commemorate the early Saxon/German king Heinrich I (Henry the Fowler), whose reincarnation he imagined he might be; and —until the outcry of their wives forced Hitler to order him to back off—encouraged his SS men to breed with Aryan women uninhibited by marital strictures.

Moreover, the international breadth of Himmler's cultural search for the fons et origo of the master race led him to fund anthropological expeditions to Tibet, the standard central Asian homeland of the Aryan people. Ernst Schaffer and his colleagues, who went along with this in 1938, were for the most part reputable and duly made plaster casts of the natives, took the necessary body measurements, and met the Dalai Lama. And although it is true that several of them despised the Nazis and were essentially taking advantage of an opportunity too good to miss, one or two later got so involved in racist theories that they actively colluded, for purposes of "research," in the murder of the mentally ill and concentration camp inmates, selected by them according to stipulated physical characteristics. But perhaps the most bizarre example of the contradiction inherent in theories of the Volk surfaced when the Nazis went so far as to entertain the idea that the lost island of Atlantis had been the ur-home of the German people.

Johann Gottlieb Fichte, the most influential nationalist voice immediately after Herder, was well aware of exactly this problem: namely the "misleading" nature of geography. The notion of the Volk, although clearly needing a coupling notion of the Heimat, cannot, however, be limited by the physical frontiers of that Heimat. All sorts of contradictory considerations flow into this dichotomy.[29] There was certainly a Germany universally acknowledged by people who regarded themselves as Germans, but there was no consensus as to what, territorially, that Germany was. To say that this would be a problem is to state the obvious, but it is, nonetheless, a banality that best expresses how intractable the matter was. Germany at the beginning of the nineteenth century was still a patchwork of small states with one growing northern power in Prussia, and a vast heterogeneous imperial power in the south that stretched from Vienna through lands, and peoples that were most certainly not German. Furthermore, the history of the Fatherland offered the poet and patriot a cornucopia of possible models, all more glorious than the contemporary reality that made of the Heimat little more than the plaything of French hegemony. Chief among these was the Holy Roman Empire—an even more heterogeneous and unstable phenomenon than its godchild, the Austrian Empire—which at one time extended as far as Sicily, where the emperor Friedrich II was buried. Under these circumstances, any discourse as to Volk, Heimat, and culture was going to be a mess. It would always be compelled to propagandize in an irrational manner. The seeming modesty of the model inferred from Herder's idea of the Volk, expressed through language, myths, mundane customs, and so forth, would always be undercut by notions of nation and culture that would spring those boundaries so radically that the very idea of fixed boundaries itself became a matter so difficult that there was a great attraction in simply getting rid of it.

If Fichte insists that "internal boundaries" make the Germans German, it is to have intellectual space in which to diminish the role played by territorial ones. In his 1806 *Address to the German Nation*, he begins with first nationalist principles. The "original, and truly natural boundaries of states are beyond doubt their internal boundaries. Those who speak the same language are joined to each other by a multitude of invisible bonds...they understand each other and...are by nature one and an inseparable whole." The racial consequences of this are stringently pursued so that geographic considerations become incidental, although one is grateful when protected by rivers and mountains.[30]

Fichte anticipates a type of thinking about the nation that will trouble later German intellectuals. Nothing is more threatening than the loss of that which is common. Fichte is clear about this.

> Only when each people...develops and forms itself in accordance with its own peculiar quality, and only when...each individual develops himself in accordance with that common quality...then only, does the manifestation of divinity appear in its true mirror as it ought to be...which is the highest law in the spiritual world![31]

But it transpires that the mix of the (seemingly) unproblematic homogeneous with the disruptive "alien" is constitutive of what it means to be German. Not only do regional differences in mundane life mean that the strong ethnic position with respect to the Volk is compelled to celebrate internal, sharply delineated variety in popular culture, but the bitter anarchic history of religious warfare, the inevitably uneven pace of modernization, and the independent foreign policy of different states and their differing entanglements, expose the strong ethnic position as a chimera.

Wagner's Hans Sachs declares a propaganda-based reconciliation of these tensions. Poet and shoemaker, intellectual and worldly, he synthesizes the key qualities, aside from heroism in battle, that are German and genuine. But the would-be homogeneous polemic flies apart in his final peroration in which we are instruction never to reject the Masters of German intellectual and artistic life. Thus, the very heterogeneity of *Die Meistersinger,* with its detailed musical and textual celebration of a variety of guilds and social classes, is, when all is said and done, only able to maintain the integrated whole by virtue of a foreign threat that Sachs invites us to consider in apocalyptic language. Moreover, the danger of this threat and the confusion it would bring, is polemically expressed, as it ought to be, in language that again raises the idealized character of a people above the incidental boundaries of their geographic presence. Fichte had also seen this threat, had witnessed—or so he thought—the damage it had done and blamed the "seductive craft and cunning" of foreigners for Germany's problems.[32] Sachs is supremely conscious of the same danger: "Beware! Evil tricks threaten us: if the German people and kingdom should one day decay, under a false, foreign rule soon no prince would understand his people; and foreign mists with foreign vanities" would contaminate the land. And though the geographical parameters are ambitiously set by Wagner, art and idealism remain transcendent, "even if the Holy Roman Empire should dissolve in mist, for us there would yet remain holy German Art!"

But the mixture of alien threat and domestic plurality becomes most horridly unstuck when it is claimed there is a domestic element that is, nevertheless, "non-native," an element that can be immortalized in propaganda films as virus carrying rats; but rats disguised and secreted among the Volk. For the Nazi characterization of "German" Jews was exceptionally fruitful as a political and nationalist move not because German Jews were obviously alien. They were in fact highly integrated. Just how many Aryans who were to support Hitler had put the health of their children into the hands of Jewish doctors? Rather, the deep-seated problematic discourse as to what it meant to be German provided a subtle and well-established context for anti-Semitism; this was something that Freud, astutely aware of how a community exploits the fear of the exogamous, understood better than most—certainly better than most Marxists. Nor should it be imagined that this was solely an opportunistic electoral strategy at a time of mass unemployment. The most disturbing aspect of Nazis racism is its absolute sincerity—a sincerity that is at least as clear in the absurd attempts to unmask Jews by codifying their physical characteristics (shapes and sizes of noses etc.,) as in the gas chambers of Auschwitz. For the alien is doubly terrifying if those confusing Wagnerian "mists" mean you cannot get a clear view of it.

Several other considerations, wry and bitterly unpleasant, surface when speedy military and industrial growth upset the balance between native and foreign so that the latter is increasingly at the mercy of the former. What, for instance, would be the appropriate *ethical* stance for the German nationalist (conceivably of a post-Kantian disposition) when Prussia started to export warfare at the end of the Napoleonic period? This might be seen as a considerable act of overcompensation to Fichte's complaint that Germany had been treated as a battlefield by foreign powers. Logically, once the Prussian army had been modernized, a massive fillip to patriotic feeling followed victory against the condescending enemy.

As a result post-Napoleonic Prussia (and later imperial Wilhelmine Germany) would find itself ideologically in hock to a "modern" army, heavy with tradition, and carrying weighty ideological baggage. It was an army able to colonize the internal life of the state to a degree that was not equaled in France and Britain, who were thus less hamstrung when it came to developing democratic institutions. After all, the German military did not enjoy the same access to colonial and exotic pleasures as the British or French. Rather, the military overhaul from 1807 to 1813 was to create "the school of a new nation,"[33] while the army, answerable directly to the king or emperor, became an alternative apparatus to that of elected government.

It heavily influenced foreign policy (the annexation of Alsace-Lorraine in 1870–1871 owed a lot to pressure from the General Staff) and consumed increasingly vast sums from the treasury. Already at the time of Friedrich the Great, the French diplomat the Comte de Mirabeau, had remarked that Prussia was not a state with an army, but an army with a state. Later Bismarck complained he was not able to exercise full civilian authority over the Chief of the General Staff von Moltke and derided young staff officers as demigods. The arrogance of the Prussian officer, schooled in reactionary student fraternities (they are still to be found) and decorated with a dueling scar, became legendary. D. H. Lawrence unpacked its perversity, and in a rather lampoonish fashion it transferred as stereotype to Hollywood and turned out to be a nice little earner for Erich von Stroheim. More tellingly, the peculiar arrogance of the man in uniform within the domestic community was brilliantly satirized by Carl Zuckmayer in *Der Hauptmann von Köpenick.*

There is, it should be admitted, a marked element of the anecdotal in the above and one may now be accused of trivializing German militarism if the plumed figure of Wilhelm II is pulled onto the stage. But he does embody wonderfully both the comic and the tragic aspects of the narrative. An unstable man, he was obsessed with his place as head of the armed forces and happily treated Berliners to a plethora of parades.[34] He duly made his own contribution to the aestheticizing of public life.[35] This reached full bloom with the Nazis, as Walter Benjamin readily grasped in the Afterword of *Art in the Age of Mechanical Reproduction,* "aestheticizing of politics climaxes in a single point. And that point is war."[36] But before the Nazis made their contribution to turning violence into aesthetics and vice versa, Wilhelm was given his own opportunity in the spotlight, to star in a production that would lack for nothing in costumes, extras, or special effects. Declaring war in 1914, he announced that parties and debates were extinguished and proudly declared himself to be at one with his people. This could only mean that the army, the highest representative of the state and uncontaminated by factions, would now settle matters in the best, which is to say in the most elevated, manner possible. And moreover he would attempt to lead it...disastrously.

Before reality hit hard in the trenches, warfare had taken on the character of domestic theater in which it was assumed battles were staged on green fields with color-coded professional soldiers. Victory might still be decided between sunup and sundown, perhaps as the result of a dashing cavalry charge or, as at Königgrätz (Sadowa) on July 3, 1866, by the last minute arrival of fresh troops. Meanwhile the Berlin Kriegsakademie was working on the finer points of the Schlieffen Plan, calculating the divisions it would need to knock out France with a huge right hook through the lowlands. Behind the polished buckles and boots a massive apparatus was in place, straining to be used. Men were compelled by their very professionalism to fantasize about the coming war. Many were concerned that they might miss out. War, which ratcheted living up to the highest experiential summit until it became an expression of death, was hardly a feared destiny. Before the First World War gutted a great deal—but certainly not all—of such thinking, battle was for the professional officer his raison d'être. And it never lacked for artistic and intellectual verification. A hundred years earlier, the romantic poet Novalis had remarked that the spirit of the warrior was expressed in his desire for death[37] and the Prussian historian Heinrich von Treitschke declared at the end of the nineteenth century that "the ideal of perpetual peace is not only impossible, but immoral as well."[38] And when war did come, the ideological passion for death had its own field day and produced its own extraordinary ecstatic apologists in the likes of Ernst Jünger. Mass death was intellectually justified because "it was shaping of a world yet hidden in the future."[39]

A love of Death is the odd, if apposite, consequence of the paradoxical—chiefly aesthetic—ingredients that are easily brewed in the nationalist pot. A culture that chose to privilege the native hearth and the, allegedly unthreatening, plurality of völkisch life, ends up creating a cult of sacrifice. And the poetics born of such a culture readily lubricates xenophobia, racism, and conquest. Above all, it discovers in death not only a glorious triumph, but a mystic narcotic. The paradoxical result can be a culture that starts to morbidly feed off extinction. A longing for downfall is, says Richard Wolin, "a classic trope of reactionary German Kulturkritik."[40] This has roots in the passive ascetic Schopenhauer and in the worldly striving Nietzsche, but Oswald Spengler was to give it greater supranational purchase. Committed to decline as destiny and hooked on a risible system of cycles, Spengler emerges as pessimistic as Schopenhauer: "All rational schemes are at the bottom nothing but revolts against the uncertain, tragic, and mysterious rhythm of life."[41] But that does not mean there is nothing to do. Instead one fights against fate, one grasps the downfall with drunken enthusiasm. Life may be "endless murdering"[42] but when man struggles against destiny, he creates great things.[43] He becomes an artist. A grand death is the minor actor's chance of stardom. In the 1933 film *Morgenrot*, a German submarine captain says: "Perhaps death is the only event in life. We Germans may be bad at living—but at dying we are fabulous."[44]

The mystical character of the German people is a felt experience for a whole range of intellectuals, artists, politicians, and soldiers. It is not, intrinsically, let alone exclusively, a Nazi phenomenon. Spengler and Jünger both felt it deeply but were contemptuous of the Brown Shirts.

And there was a general distrust of democracy because it diluted blood and spirit. Thomas Mann, later a public symbol of German democracy, had in *Reflections of an Unpolitical Man* (1917) rejected it, preferring instead the authoritarian state, creative irrationalism, and the inward Germanic spirit. In short, he reproduced the classic-nineteenth-century pairing, dismissing synthetic French civilization in favor of rooted German culture. Here again is the Volksgemeinschaft and the same Führerprinzip to which Heidegger was so committed, and which was a key factor in his flirt with the Nazis.

The Führerprinzip was a necessity for many pre-World War II thinkers, no matter how they may have (later) despised Hitler. Heidegger, Spengler, Gadamer, Jünger all accepted the need for a great leader whose authority did not come from the herd. So did the members of the Stefan George circle. Devoted to a notion of Germany that extended geographically as far as Palermo but which remained an idealized manifestation of a divine Geist, the Stauffenberg brothers believed no less passionately in the Volksgemeinschaft and the Führerprinzip when they set out to murder Hitler than they had when they fought for him and Fatherland. Furthermore, in his last words Claus von Stauffenberg declared his loyalty to Stefan George's holy Germany and not, by proxy, to the democratic nation that after the war opportunistically adopted him as a national hero.[45]

The aesthetic underpinning for all of this is, in the last instance, a matter of pure speculation. But the idealized character of German nationalism should, I think, be seen as a reflection of transcendental German philosophy that had aestheticized thinking long before totalitarianism aestheticized life. Practical utilitarianism was hardly a philosophical category, while influential philosophers such as Heidegger and Adorno (and the committed "Marxist" Ernst Bloch) wrote like poets or prophets for whom truth is always linguistically encrypted.

In general, German intellectuals imagined that ideas and culture, and not railways and autobahns, would bind the people. The Nazis, of course, were not so simplistic. But such was the faith in the German spirit, that "unshakeable life force" best expressed in Wagner's Holy German Art, that an artist-intellectual like Wilhelm Furtwängler, who despised the Nazis and had had the courage (unlike his colleague Herbert von Karajan) to stand up to them, still believed in a German triumph—expressive of his unassailable faith in an uplifting and unblemished German culture—until the downfall was at the door. It would have been intolerable for him to entertain the idea that the high culture he worshiped could have produced the poison. His contemporary Thomas Mann, who had to flee and was subsequently quite capable of examining both Wagner and his earlier self critically, had once felt the same instinctual and elitist faith. Naturally it was in music—and not in his own field, literature—that he found this power to "bind and unite," and declared the Prelude to Lohengrin (I assume to the first act) to be the very "Heimat" of his soul.[46]

And what of Marxist philosophy—of dialectical *materialism*—in all of this? After all, the German SPD was the largest left-wing party in the world, while the Spartacists, later the German Communist Party (KPD), had a highly organized urban proletariat at their disposal that, when mobilized in 1918/1919, was to seize power for a few months in Berlin and threaten the Bavarian establishment. KPD voting figures were high and usually grew until the Nazis came to power.[47] Party organization and infrastructure were considerable, left-wing publications printed in left-wing publishing houses were plentiful, meetings were held exhaustively.[48] It is calculated that by 1929, there were 180 agitprop groups reaching a public of around 3,600,000.[49] KPD members were not afraid of either the Brown Shirts or a fight, and, at least going by the semidocumentary account of a Berlin rally in Brecht, Ottwalt, Dudow's film *Kuhle Wampe* (1932), well read.

But all this was not well served by left-wing philosophy. Perhaps, from a strictly dialectical materialist position, it should not have been. On that basis, we might want to congratulate German Marxist intellectuals for effectively establishing unambivalently their constituted place in the superstructure. But were we to do so, we would have to acknowledge the extraordinarily apolitical—or at the very least hopelessly idealist—nature of those theoretical labors with respect to the revolutionary struggle. We would be hard pushed to see an easy causal link between material and social conditions on the one hand and the philosophy it supposedly generated on the other. If Marx had turned Hegel on his head, clearly a lot of Marxist intellectuals, who may have paid lip service to the axiom, had yet to take it to heart.

In fact leading left-wing thinkers never lost their fascination with transcendental philosophy and were never going to dismiss Hegel. As we have seen, when Lukács found an expression for the dialectic in an evolving consciousness defined as class dependent and needing no agency outside of itself, he offended Lenin. Karl Korsch, who was thrown out of the Party in 1926, had committed a similar sin in *Materialism and Philosophy*. Clearly empiricism and common sense were not something that frightened the Russians. They had often dreamed of them in *their* philosophy. But German Marxist intellectuals could always take refuge in aesthetics. Arguments over the avant-garde versus naturalism in the pages of, among other journals, *Linkskurve*; the theatrical experiments of Piscator; and Brecht and Eisler and Weill developing radio drama, oratorio, and proletarian theater, and so forth, generated an abundance of creative work. It should not be imagined that this could escape hard political reality either. The Soviet dictatorship was obsessively concerned with the evolution of theoretical positions that might, it imagined, threaten its own authority. Aesthetics became a matter of life or death—something that many German artists and intellectuals who sought refuge in the Soviet Union were to discover. When Lukács attacked the "reportage" style of the novels of Bredel and Ottwalt in the pages of *Linkskurve*, he was also mounting an assault on Bertolt Brecht and Epic Theater, and everyone interested in left-wing philosophy knew it and, moreover, also knew he had the lethal authority of the Soviets at his back.[50]

However, while debates on aesthetics among novelists and playwrights immediately became debates about concrete praxis, Marxist philosophy often found in aesthetics and/or dialectics a flight from material reality. Left-wing philosophers, like Benjamin, coped with history's disappointments by a deliberate and inventive inversion of Marxist categories, or gradually collapsed like Adorno and Horkheimer into despair, or later like Marcuse saw an exit in the hedonism and rebellion of the young, or like Korsch turned into passionate anti-Communists, or like Ernst Bloch succumbed to Panglossian optimism as to a revolution always on the cards but forever postponed together with a belief in the transmission of souls and the redeeming power of (what else?) Beethoven.

Indeed Bloch's ascent into philosophical fairyland is the appropriate antipode to Adorno's collapse into nihilistic despair. It is not that Marxist thought was betrayed by both men simply because neither took on board adequately the challenge contained in the dual terminology of dialectical materialism. Rather, it is that both engineered exits (two directly opposed exits) courtesy of a free use of language that, however skillfully employed, either simplified reality or made no effective encounter with it at all. That the discourses chosen were, in one case, ecstatically uninhibited and, in the other, a mesh of overelaborate paradoxes, is merely a question of style. Both Bloch's transcendental romanticism whereby no mundane misery can corrupt the blissful, but deferred, coming paradigm, and Adorno's mocking of transcendental Kantian values within a wholly transcendental pseudo-dialectical epistemology, amount to forms of capitulation that are equally two-dimensional and equally useless.

It should now be clear that holding on to a workable and nondestructive form of narrative has been this chapter's chief difficulty. And that is as it should be. The starting point was an explicit engagement with teleology that made, however cursorily, gestures as to telos, but in effect sacrificed narrative to "truth." Kant's teleology is not an interpretation of history, nor are his fundamental categories in their intrinsic character vulnerable to narrative flux. Perhaps Hegel's greatest contribution is that he changed this and made the temporal a necessary tool without which analysis was jejune. Certainly for Hegel truth still exists (as the Absolute Spirit) and seemingly floats above the flux of history. But it has meaning and is open to interpretation only when seen within that flux. It might sound like a fixed category, but is in effect an opportunistic and unstable one.

At no point in this chapter have the two title terms of this book been effectively coupled in that one might be happy with the consequences. The philosophical undertaking makes narrative an ethereal category largely because it resolves (by virtue of aesthetics) a series of problems intrinsic to transcendental thinking. As Gert Ueding, talking of Bloch's utopianism, remarks: "The aesthetic sign is seen as a manifestation [literally "Träger"—or carrier] of extra-aesthetic significance, which cannot up to now be experienced except in this aesthetic form."[51] Nonetheless, the theoretically fertile and creative category of aesthetics enables, when suffused by nationalist notions of culture, a *return* to a real but overly patriotic narrative that mixes the hard facts of the battlefield with the wild romanticism of the sublime in a dangerous stew. The end result is a history in which both terms—narrative and truth—end up debasing each other, generating intoxicating but irreconcilable drives that march to the abyss.

Nevertheless, it is scarcely credible to lay the greater part of the blame for the subsequent disaster on aesthetics or idealist philosophy. Within the complex and, in part, accidental flux of history the victory of the Nazis in 1933 had more to do with weaknesses within the Weimar Republic which, in turn, had their roots in the Versailles Treaty, a proportional voting system that gave too much influence to small parties, and an inability to handle problems such as hyperinflation and mass unemployment. But there were elements readily at hand in the general cultural climate that made the Nazis takeover and the subsequent dismantling of libertarian institutions attractive. There was a readiness to willfully rewrite history (Germany had been stabbed in the back by a Jewish/Capitalist conspiracy in 1918), an elitist contempt for democratic institutions, a longing for a strong leader evocative of past greatness, and a racially susceptible sense of nation. Clearly, many philosophers, and artists, and intellectuals did not—as many later acknowledged—put up the best defense against National Socialism. There was much in it that many of them found seductive. Worse, that may well have been, given the intellectual tradition in which they were placed, only right and proper.

But Goethe, whatever his penchant for the immortal feminine might lead us to believe, was not immune to those qualities whose absence from the German intellectual tradition have been much insisted upon here: empiricism and common sense. Given that he was also a practical scientist and statesman, this should not be a surprise. For instance, while German intellectuals thought culture rather than railways would bind the Volk, Goethe was not so simplistic. Johann Peter Eckermann records him saying that he was not worried about the future. Germany would be united and "our broad roads and coming railways will do their work." It is an encouraging observation and pushes us a productive step beyond, or away from, the mystic nationalist message. Nonetheless, it is the tragedy of German history that common sense of this sort did not successfully colonize notions of native culture. The idealist norm is more to be found in the likes of Bogumil Goltz, who declared grandly in 1860 that German culture had transcended national fixed boundaries and "we must not trade for the thing or phantom that the French or the English call nation."[52] Goethe however had stressed practical, and binding, considerations: a common currency, weights and measures, and "a hundred similar things, which I cannot now name."[53]

A particularly interesting figure that can be tossed into this arbitrary mix is Heinrich von Kleist's *The Prince of Homburg* (1821). He is anything but unambiguous. We meet him as a sleepwalker and he remains ambivalently placed between fantasy and reality, never able to reconcile the two except—inevitably—by embracing his own death. But this death is likewise ambiguous. He is to be executed by the Elector of Brandenburg for having disobeyed orders during the battle of Fehrbellin. However, his intervention (a cavalry charge) was heroic and guilt can only be established by the most stringent notion of (Kantian) duty, which is here turned into a perfect expression of the military values that were to become an obsessive codex of Prussian life. And surely Kleist's drama—which preceded his own suicide by six months—recalls the notorious events at Küstrin in 1730 where the young crown prince of Prussia, Friedrich, having defied his father and fled with his friend Katte, was captured. Both young men were to be court-marshaled. However Friedrich Wilhelm I, who practiced iron disciple and had built up the Prussian professional army to an astounding 83,000 men without employing them in battle, compromised in so far as he pardoned his son. Debasing himself before paternal and military authority Friedrich was made, nevertheless, to pay a horrible price. He had to watch while Katte was beheaded. One imagines this sort of thing is not easily forgotten. Later Friedrich, who turned out to be—proverbially—the most enlightened monarch in Europe (he wrote a book attacking Machiavelli, was admired by Kant), a patron of the arts (a distinguished musician), a serious thinker (friend of Voltaire), employed the army his father had created in wars against the Austrians and the Russians; wars which enabled Prussia to absorb Silesia and take part in the shameless partitioning of Poland.

If we were to apply the Kantian philosophy of duty (deontology) to Kleist's prince it is not clear that he would wholly escape guilt, any more than the actual crown prince. The Prince of Homburg's intoxicating imaginative life makes him vulnerable to dreams of military glory. Yet there is no evidence of a lust for power. It is hard to deny him the status of a man behaving according to his own notion of duty (albeit an overheated one), but in a context where notions of justice and the appeals of the heart are always in play. Friedrich might even meet one of the key criteria of the categorical imperative in that he could wish that everyone placed in his situation would have done the same. In the end, the fascination he exerts makes his execution impossible. Instead he is allowed to replay his initial dream and sleepwalking scene, but this time it ends happily. Here again is a narrative, as in *Persuasion,* replayed in order to arrive at the beneficent outcome.

Perhaps we should return to Claus Schenk Graf von Stauffenberg as the final anecdotal embodiment of the themes that intertwine in this chapter. Handsome, a splendid sportsman, heroically wounded in battle, imbued with a deep sense of Kantian duty, highly cultured, possessed of a disciplined intellect, he was pure central casting. Furthermore he, too, is enmeshed in the conflicting threads of culture, nationalism, and militarism. The Stefan George Circle to which he was devoted had its roots in Schiller, Heine, Hölderlin, Hebel; it was "mysterious" or "secret"—favorite adjectives. And it was most assuredly not empirically grounded. Max Kommerell, one of the George "disciples," wrote in his 1928 *The Poet as Führer* that Hölderlin was the "prophet of a secret Germany."[54] He imagined a people that would "awaken" in the spirit of the dead poets and German masters.

For Claus the modern expression of this past spirit could only be found in the army. It was "the State and the heart of the people" and its officer corps the lofty "embodiment of the nation."[55] Peter Hoffmann believes that the destruction of Weimar democracy little disturbed the Circle. Their party was the secret Germany of *their* führer (George) and only a few were called to join.[56] It is for this Germany that Stauffenberg died. How ironic it is then that he has been adopted as one of the founding heroes of the present bourgeois democratic German republic.

If this chapter has told the story of a meaningful failure, the next will push the matter onto more fruitful and ambitious territory. But oddly, this will not mean, in the first instance, abandoning aesthetics. One turns to Bertolt Brecht because, although his theatrical practice foregrounds plain commonsense thinking, it does so in order to expose the dangers of vulgar empiricism, to show that our dominant perceptions of social organization are false and that by, paradoxically, commonsense analysis, a deeper understanding of the world is possible. Furthermore, because this is accomplished in a narrative framework, it facilitates an unusually percipient and deep form of realism which, in turn, facilitates a deeper marriage between narrative and truth than has hitherto been possible. It is not, however, imagined that Brecht's undertaking is unambiguously successful or that he can escape the antinomies generated by his own endeavors. The consequences of these failures will further elucidate the challenge of holding on to narrative as the privileged trope of truth.

Chapter 6

Realism
Brecht, Sport, the Bible, Lenin, Conspiracy Theories

In Aristotle's *Poetics*, we find a definition for the epic, "by an Epic structure I mean one with a multiplicity of plots."[1] Bertolt Brecht was familiar with Aristotle and was quite happy to describe his theater as non-Aristotelian. Empathy, catharsis, the homogeneity of the poetic elements, and so forth, are all Aristotelian qualities that Brecht has rejected. However, the Aristotelian defining quality of epic poetry as having a multiplicity of plots isolates the key quality of the Brechtian theatrical endeavor, and one should keep that in mind when confronted by Brecht's characterization of his own theatrical praxis as "episches Theater," not least because the term "epic" in English sends out different signals, all misleading.

Furthermore, Aristotle, in that his values are a-Brechtian, lays out the problem Brecht was to face as a practicing playmaker. The drama "should have for its subject a single action, whole and complete, with a beginning, a middle, and an end. It will thus resemble a living organism in all its unity, and produce the pleasure proper to it." And the reasons for this are purely technical. "In Tragedy we cannot imitate several lines of actions carried on at one and the same time; we must confine ourselves to the action on the stage and the part taken by the players. But in Epic poetry, owing to the narrative form, many events simultaneously transacted can be presented."[2] To see Brecht as trying, ultimately, to overcome this limitation, to do exactly what Aristotle said could not be done in the theater in order to realize an Aristotelian notion of the epic by non-Aristotelian means, is to grasp his theatrical aesthetics on a profound level.

It is also to grasp why, ultimately, his type of theatrical praxis is meaningful outside of the theater. That is, not only are the specific stage techniques non-Aristotelian, they result in a wholly different relationship between the world inside the theater, both with respect to the auditorium and the stage, and the world outside of it. Brecht's epic theater attempts a "radical transformation of the mentality of our time,"[3] so that what we see on the stage with respect to making new people and "transforming human relationships,"[4] has its true purchase outside of the theater. It is only in this manner that Brechtian realism can be appreciated. His theater is neither a place of escape, nor of spiritual enrichment in that the subject/spectator feels a yet deeper sense of belonging to the community. Instead it is, in the first instance, a place of experimentation and comedy in which the spectators, who must not be allowed to check-in their brains with their hats in the cloakroom, are confronted by a reality that is brazenly drawing attention to the world outside of it. And this is accomplished by continually making clear how the "world" within the theater is artificial. Brecht's realism is, as one would readily expect, highly loaded, but his use of Marxist theory is far from an exercise in left-wing platitudes. He wishes to examine the world in such a way that we see we are deluded as to its very nature. It is an endeavor that not only exposes as contradictory "empirical facts," which we have hitherto seen as unproblematic and authoritative, but it also explodes the ideologies that have, in a seemingly unproblematic parallel manner, underpinned our naivete. Brecht is a realist writer in a very special sense. And his encounter with realism generates the fundamentals on which his theatrical praxis rests. And that praxis is best seen as the Aristotelian notion of the epic as a multiplicity of competing narratives.

Although Brecht crops up in this book for a wholly instrumental reason—to elucidate a type of "Realism" that couples narrative and truth on a deep level—it might in all fairness be appropriate here to make three polemical points concerning the manner in which he is, and has often been, mistakenly, even badly, treated.

The first concerns the techniques of epic theater, a convenient list of which can be found in Brecht's notes to *Mahagonny*. The techniques of epic theater have had a wide currency *as techniques*. The alienation effect, the half-curtain, the masks, the Gest, the "beat," actors speaking about themselves in the third person, the mixed media stuff (songs, choruses, projections, etc.,) have all been adopted by directors irrespective of whether they had any awareness of, or interest in, Brecht's notion of (Marxist) realism. In fact, many seem to have equated Marxism with sloganeering and propaganda, elements that are certainly there but which do not mean Brecht is bent on agitprop. In general, epic theater has been appropriated because of its stylistic elements, as though it were a toy box. This is, in itself, fair enough. Brecht himself was a great thief. But the results have got nothing to do with Brechtian realism.

The second point concerns a deployment of Brecht that is far from unfair. He has been of much use to philosophers of language and the "sign." Those who have exposed the unstable relationship between signifiers and signifieds, the tendency of texts to break down into heterogeneous plurality in defiance of the author's attempt to assert control, and so forth, have found a great deal to admire and recycle in Brecht, who is not only willing to question the authority of the text but also employs a theatrical practice that involves perpetual dismantling and reassembling. A Brecht play most certainly should not "resemble [an Aristotelian] living organism." Linguists and semioticians find here a ready ally and have, at least since Roland Barthes, quarried a good deal from both his theory and praxis.[5] Nonetheless, as far as Brecht is concerned these matters are wholly instrumental. The explosion of unity and coherence in that dominant ideology is unpicked, is both an expression of a general ontological position (the world is disharmonious and contradictory in its deepest nature), with which linguists and semioticians would quite likely agree, and the more epistemological position that this can only be understood by dialectical materialism (seen as a revolutionary praxis), with which linguists and semioticians might well not. And because this point is so fundamental in that without it there would be no way into the manner in which Brecht couples narrative and truth under the rubric of realism, his instrumentalism in this case is also the instrumentalism of this chapter.

The third point is hardly unconnected to the other two. It is, however, of more significance because it is not only more vulgar but also more influential. There has been a widespread disposition in the West, perhaps most clearly expressed some time ago by Martin Esslin and Peter Demetz, to see Brecht as a great playwright in spite of his theoretical and ideological agenda. That is, as an artist Brecht "the eagle...sharply view[s] the future of the arts—but the eagle's feet drag the rusty chains of Marxist iron and lead."[6] Yet he triumphs over his political commitment, which being a-aesthetic would have debilitated his work if his natural creativity had not got the better of it. As a result he can be placed within the canon of great Western playwrights. This is both disingenuous and glib, having more to do with the prejudices and outdated aesthetic disposition of the critics concerned. But to appreciate this, it is necessary to have a view of Marxism that recalls the Marxist humanism discussed in chapter 2, which means we must momentarily backtrack.

This will also lead us to a deep tension in Brecht's work. It is a tension that is entirely at one with the fundamental problem of Marxist humanism. As has already been mentioned, Marxist humanism is caught in a necessary bind whereby it is foregrounding two radically different historical epistemologies. The notions of prehistory and real history can readily be seen by critics, of whatever persuasion, as fraudulent in that they require a fundamental shift in respect of how both the individual and the collective are defined. The Marxist classless paradigm as a posited historical fact needs a world in which "man" the individual is placed harmoniously within the collective in such a way that there is no tension between the full realization of his own nature and that of everyone else's. But this is to come about as a result of exploitative class relations reaching their fullest antagonistic expression before exploding in violent emancipation. This contradiction can certainly be contained and rationalized under the rubric "dialectics," but it is always going to sound a little too neat and an overly convenient fit between two irreconcilable notions of history.

It also has disturbing consequences, one of which is that new people are to be "created." In fact, creating new people is a standard task revolutionaries all too willingly set themselves. For Marx and Engels, it is necessary to the communism of the future, but it need not be postponed. Hitler, ecstatic before the adoring ranks of the Hitler Youth, announced that the creation of his new people was well underway and that he was, in effect, looking at work in progress. These young men were to be "as fleet as greyhounds, as tough as leather and as hard as Krupp steel." And it has already been noted in chapter 1 how Soviet intellectuals self-confidently declared that they too were in the process of creating the new "man." It is, of course, merely a technical matter as to the manner in which the new people are new. Whether they spend their energies bringing in the corn, and/or doing criticism, or whether they drill for war, is secondary to the question as to what degree and in what time frame one can change the parameters of human consciousness.

Brecht, as he takes on board more Marxist theory (through his "great teacher" Lenin), ends up in exactly this territory. He had begun with plays that center the ego as sensual, self-indulgent, and asocial. Brecht's Baal is too clever—and poetic—to be one of Nietzsche's blond beasts but he is not morally estranged from them. He celebrates the joy of both pain and gratification, and spits in the face of all and everyone, and is happy to swallow the spit that lands on him in turn—he likes the taste. Sex (heterosexual and homosexual) is naturally the principal means of gratification and the instrument of defiance. But despite sex, he is man alone. However, those that follow Baal are not. In fact, although the stage-play as form may be self-evidently inclined to foreground the hero/subject (of whatever moral stamp), it will have precious little dramatic tension if that subject is not placed within conflicting relationships. It might be seen as the literal, stage-based, expression of Althusser's condemnation of—for him pre-Marxian—humanism: namely that it is unavoidably the "drama of the subject."[7] But Brecht will show in his most explicitly Marxist plays that it is a subject who must attempt some kind of reconciliation with the collective.

Brecht's first shift into the territory of conflicting relationships is that of the battle between two men. It might be noted that boxing was his favorite sport and he admired and knew the German middleweight champion Paul Samson-Koerner. This conflict is clearest in the characters of Shlink and Garga *In the Jungle of the Cities*. Here the battle is one of identity, of getting into some else's skin—a favorite image of Brecht's at this period. The result is a confluence of theatrical and intellectual considerations that undercut the ostensible egocentric agenda, in that they introduce elements that make that agenda untenable. Of great importance is the city. Although Baal can only be contained—if at all—within the universe, the heroes who come after him are essentially urban. Whatever truth there is, is in the cities. The mass—whether despised or embraced—is not to be gainsaid.

A second consideration is that the notion of identity is problematized by Brecht without any recourse, initially, to Marxism or to psychoanalysis. True, both of these will come when he studies under Korsch at MASCH (The Marxist Workers School) in the mid-1920s and reads Reich in 1930.[8] But initially it is as if his own unbounded egomania, engorged in Baal, is so absolute that there is no way forward but the introduction of elements that being alien must undercut it. So it is his very egotism that compels him to a notion of identity that is changeable, even unrestricted. After all, why should a man be limited to but a single skin? As a result Brecht is predisposed to the axiom that one can indeed create new people. And as he works his ideas out, he produces stage figures/things such as Galy Gay in *Man Equals Man*, the Elephant Calf in the Interlude of the same play, the Clown in *The Baden Teaching Play* Interlude et al.—all of whom will be taken apart and reassembled before us. As Brecht was to declare: "The continuity of the ego is a myth. A man is an atom that perpetually breaks up and forms anew."[9]

Both these considerations—the city and the artificiality of subject identity—give rise to a third: the collective. This is largely the result of debunking *in* the city the conflict/sexual pairing. This pairing is exposed as incapable of handling the problems its own propaganda engenders. For instance, the hero of *Drums in the Night*, Kragler, turns his back on the Berlin Spartacist uprising that is going on offstage but which we can hear, and declares himself for sex. At the end he takes his girlfriend home to "the great, white, wide bed. Come!"[10] In doing so he debunks the stage qua stage, mocks the flats that make up the set, and punctures the moon. Consequently the very egotism and sensuality of his solution is undercut by foregrounding the bogus quality of the theatrical "experiment"—an experiment, moreover, in which he is as trapped as any other thing or "person" *on* the stage. His solution unavoidably trumpets its own fraudulence and is further trapped in a more general dilemma, namely: "For art to *refer,* even protestingly, is for it to become instantly collusive with what it opposes; negation negates itself because it cannot help positing the very object it desires to destroy. Any positive enunciation is compromised by the very fact of being such."[11] Eagleton is here marking out an Adorno-like dilemma, but Brecht, at his best, (unknowingly) embraces it largely because of the productive character of the multiple and contradictory viewpoints it promises. Meanwhile, we can see that Kragler's flight is not a substantive act of defiance against the world. Did Baal not copulate in the slime and under the stars, not in a warm clean bed? Nor has Kragler's flight any purchase on events outside, not because they are not real—everyone in the theater knew the Spartacist uprising was real in a sense that the stage characters could not match—but because he cannot present any basis for rejecting the world, and the uprising, other than his own inadequacy. If Baal is the great egotist, Kragler is the petty one and he is not going anywhere where Brecht can fruitfully follow.

What come after are unambiguous attempts at getting the collective on stage: namely those *Untermenschen* despised in the first plays and those derided workers and revolutionaries heard but not seen in *Drums in the Night.* This attempt reaches its apogee with the *Lehrstücke* (the Teaching Plays). It is usually shaped by a configuration of four characters, one of whom—like Galy Gay in *Man Equals Man,* Fatzer in the *Fatzer* project, Lindbergh in the nexus made up of *The Flight of the Lindberghs/The Ocean Flight/The Baden Teaching Play of Acquiescence,* and The Young Comrade in *The Measures Taken*—is kernel and defined in terms of his relationships, progressive or reactionary, exploitative or fraternal, with the others. So while previously the interpersonal conflict of the pair maintained its egotistical character in that the Other had been necessary only in so far as he was either fucked or killed (or, ideally, both), it is now clear that the Subject is nothing without the *Others.* Fatzer (the hero of Brecht's massive, unfinished project, which occupied him from 1927 till 1930) may declare repeatedly that he needs to "breathe with four lungs,"[12] but in fact, holed up with his three comrades and the wife of one of them in the industrial city of Mülheim, he discovers he needs more. All Brechtian heroes thereafter must make the same discovery.

This move means that Brecht confronts Marxist humanism in an ambivalent manner. It also means that he engages with morality in a sophisticated way. It does not mean, however, that he resolves any of these problems definitively, but he does illustrate—and to some extent establish—that these are the questions and tasks that face us if we are to grapple honestly with history.

Once Brecht has carried over the egotism of his early work onto the terrain of Marxist theory, the collective structure made up of the three plus the ambivalently placed leader allows him to throw into the structure both notions of history (class exploitative and communist), albeit in simplified forms. Just as the sexual drives of the egotistical hero compel him to forgo his place above the herd and enter into relationships, so the need for food and booze leads those in relationships to a deeper understanding of how class-based production distorts values on all levels, turning men and women into commodities. During this period Brecht's fascination with the city, the collective, and material productivity, led to an equal fascination with America, above all with the Chicago livestock market. But before he tackled the appropriation of labor and the character of commodity fetishism, the sensuality of his early work had predisposed him to foreground the crude materialist facts of life. Meat and drink, cooks, bakers, and butchers (and at the beginning whores and whiskey bars) are vital and weighty considerations for Brecht. And so he moves from the capitalist, albeit escapist, world of *Mahagonny* to the explicit Marxist polemic of *The Measures Taken* where a merchant declares that he does not know what rice is, only the price. Of course it is the same answer when asked: "And what actually is a man?" But the communist agitators know all about reification, just as they (but, fatally for him, not their Young Comrade) see through the false sentimentality of capitalist ideology. Instead they evoke the Marxist humanist ideal, now disguised in the capitalist body politic (the agitators wear masks, have new "skin"), but to which that body politic will give revolutionary birth.

Fatzer, however, is initially trapped in the earlier historical phase. The brazen assertion of self-identity through sex is still present (he seduces the wife of one of his comrades), but at least the materialist drives are ambivalently placed in relation to his three fellow soldiers—all four have deserted during the First World War. He acknowledges in the first instance how they need him solely for food and drink, and he has duly made friends with some butchers and a soldier with access to a supply train. However, the goal of the *Fatzer* project is his realization that *he* needs them and that without them he is "nothing," although he is confused as to what self-fulfillment might mean, complaining that after the others have taken from him what they need, that which is left "is Fatzer."[13]

In one of the more striking scenes Brecht sketched, Fatzer goes walk-about in Mülheim and begins to comprehend his own alienation from the mass. Workers meet in pubs in an atmosphere that recalls Marx's idealized portrayal in the *1844 Manuscripts*. Fatzer cannot enter.[14] Still, he gradually becomes more deeply conscious of things he would previously have either not recognized or have dismissed contemptuously. He even has a sense of how the proletariat is locked into an ambivalent relationship with tools and machines; this is something that Marx also placed within the category of alienation in the *1844 Manuscripts* but of which Brecht, like most Marxists at this time, was not likely to have known. Gradually, then, Fatzer goes further than his predecessors. Merely being aware of the presence of the proletarian community from which he is excluded by his own vulgar materialism, and being strangely fascinated by the machines along the canal (Brecht wrote several contemporaneous poems about dockyard cranes),[15] he is caught in a process that would have led him (does lead him in some sketches) to a consciousness of both the revolutionary struggle and the communist ideal. For while the soldiers are holed up in the room, Lenin is in his sealed carriage traveling through Germany to join the progressive Russian proletariat in order to make revolution.[16]

It was claimed above that all this means Brecht engages with morality in an unusually sophisticated way. The argument for this is weighted a priori in favor of Marxist humanism and it takes us back to the distinction between the two notions of morality mentioned in chapter 2. Brecht's plays are exceptionally expressive of the tension between these double moralities. Above all, they expose the false ideology of capitalist social relations by exposing the contradictions in the capitalist mode of production, while evoking the morally deeper paradigm to come.

Brecht seeks concrete means to make the dialectical contradictions of capitalism clear. Tools, as in *Saint Joan of the Stockyards,* can become weapons; that is, they may be means of both enslavement and liberation. Texts are equally dialectical. Brecht often turns to the Bible not least because it is customarily employed as an expression of unproblematic compassion and used as a narcotic to intellectually pith the masses. As a schoolboy, he wrote a small play called *The Bible*. It dealt with the tensions between the one and the many in that the salvation of the single soul was only accomplished because a city was raped. In *St. Joan*, the Bible is unambivalently a commodity and who owns it is a matter of market forces. The heroine's former "bible-basher" colleagues in the Black Straw Hats are therefore merely being rational when they aid Mauler in buying up all the "bible shops" in the district. And in *The Mother,* there is a brilliant moment when the Bible as book—as object—is the site of a battle as to who owns the dominant ideology. It then becomes an actual tool/weapon with which someone is indeed bashed.

Motherhood also becomes the site on which the dual moralities conjoin and struggle. That is, the iconic ideal of motherhood as the embodiment of sacrifice and unconditional love is exposed from the polarities of both historical stages. The communist mother realizes (like Pelagea Vlasova in *The Mother* and Señora Carrar in *Señora Carrar's Rifles*) that she will best serve the cause of true (maternal) compassion by escaping the false capitalist portrayal of motherhood even if it means accepting her children's right to sacrifice themselves for the revolution. Meanwhile, the mother trapped in false consciousness (the classic example being Anna Fierling in *Mother Courage and Her Children*) not only has to watch her children perish but also is stringently exposed as the capitalist agent who brings about the disaster. On the other hand, true motherhood is explicit in *The Caucasian Chalk Circle*. What counts is solely the ability to effectively care and love; this is something that as a principle is made clear in the Prologue where the valley goes to those who can best make it fruitful. Consequently the play proper argues that the "real" mother is the one who saved the child when it was in need and not the biological mother who was at first selfish, and later interested in it more as a possession and a fashion accessory, rather in the manner of some media stars. As a result The Judgment of Solomon is upended.

Upending is the basic strategy whereby the two antagonistic worldviews are staged. This upending is critical for Brecht in that it embodies not only deep dialectical truth (he regretted he had not called his theater "dialectical" rather than "epic"[17]), but also because it implies revolution. He tells us repeatedly that those who are at the bottom should come to the top. His most striking metaphors for this usually have to do with water: the notion of swimming with or against the stream, the idea that the river might flow backwards (which according to one of the books in his library, the Volga, thanks to Soviet engineering, actually did[18]), and, above all, the image of rain/water that "falls" from below to above, a possibility raised at the conclusion of *Roundheads and Pointedheads* and realized in the "Ballad of the Waterwheel."[19] There is a parallel in the imagined orbit of the sun around the earth, which is shown in *The Life of Galileo* to be the opposite of the truth. Were the church to allow this "upending" it would be difficult for the ruling elite to enforce the dominant ideology and the peasantry might, as a result, forget their place in the rigid and dying ("Ptolemaic") social system. It is, however, chiefly through stories that Brecht attempts to reveal how dialectical truths shatter the "self-evident" assumptions of dominant ideology.

Contradictorily, one of the best ways of appreciating how remarkable, if theatrically intractable, the narrative endeavor is, is to consider one of Brecht's best, that is to say most fruitful, concrete symbols: the wallet in

Herr Puntila and His Servant Matti. Here the dialectical struggle is contained within the person of the landowner Puntila and the two social systems in conflict are precommunist. Puntila finds himself on the cusp of the change from feudalism to capitalism. The world of contracts, legal obligations, money based methods of regulating human relationships that generate reification, are present in embryonic form. And they tear Puntila psychically apart. He wants to retain the system of mutual dependency and obligation, which is part of the feudal order (without acknowledging that this, too, is a form of exploitation), but is compelled to function according to early capitalist principles. Above all, he has to learn to treat men as commodities. Brecht's trick is to split him into a drunken feudal lord and a cold sober capitalist. Throughout the narrative, Puntila oscillates between these two polarities, giving promises—showing generosity—when drunk that he regrets, or on which he reneges, when sober. His servant Matti understands this perfectly. And Puntila trusts him. Therefore he gives Matti his wallet before he starts drinking. It is his insurance policy so that his descent into an impaired form of humanist life in which men and women are, at least, still men and women, does not cost him more than he is prepared to pay when he is once again in full possession of his "reason." This tension is pursued throughout the narrative producing incidents that gain comic and political point from what is an irreconcilable but ever present dialectic.

But *Puntila* is a relatively late play and soon after it Brecht, unfortunately, started to compromise on his epic/dialectic program. He comes to insist on the coherence of the integrated form as evidence of the playwright's professional skill.[20] Moreover, he is worried that he has made a mistake in excluding sympathetic, associative feelings on the audience's part. Where once they should have laughed when the characters cried and cried when they laughed, they may now get emotionally involved, something that is rationalized by a glib verbal distinction permitting "feeling" but rejecting "empathy."[21] As a result narrative plurality is sacrificed. Where once the happy ending was mocked and MacHeath was arrested twice in *The Threepenny Opera;* where scenes were replayed with different outcomes in *Fear and Misery in the Third Reich;* where characters were confronted with, or invented, their dialectical opposites; where a Teaching Play such as *He Who Says Yes* could be debated and rewritten with a different telos as *He Who Says No,* we have instead the tragic heroine Mother Courage and the tragic hero Galileo, who are wholly integrated, emotionally involving figures.

Naturally it is exactly these plays that were (and still are) fervently adopted by lovers of conventional (Aristotelian) theater, whether anti-Marxists who wanted to save Brecht from himself, or sincere Marxists who needed their "tragic" fixes. For instance Raymond Williams (1971) argues that *Mother Courage and Her Children* is an example of Brechtian "complex seeing." This sounds encouraging, but it turns out to be the result of an a-Brechtian psychological rectitude. We become emotionally torn because the lead character is obviously "flesh and blood." This is hardly an incentive to play with subject-based alternative narratives. *Mother Courage* is indeed "perfect," for there is no way in for the spectator and no opportunity for him to exercise Brecht's playful notion of "Spaß" or fun. Ironically, this is rather removed from Williams's own key explanatory notion: subjunctive action (1981). It poses the question: "If we were to do it another way, what would...?" and clearly evokes the realist goal of epic theater. But the techniques of epic theater are hard to find in the late plays. Not surprisingly, they are praised as "seamless works of art."

Nevertheless there is another genre to which Brecht was drawn. It is, moreover, a good guide to what we lose in the later plays. As a young man, he declared: "We pin our hopes on the sporting public."[22] There are two overriding reasons why we should. The first concerns the spectator and the second the narrative nature of a sporting contest itself. We should pursue both in turn.

The spectator at a sporting match is far more percipient and better behaved than the man in the auditorium during a play or an opera. Who, having experienced both, could doubt the truth of this? In fact, had Brecht paid more attention to football rather than boxing he would have better appreciated just how right he was to place his faith in the sports spectator. A football fan is an expert, the theatergoer, a dilettante. The football fan knows the players on his team, knows their strengths and weaknesses. He brings with him a huge history, a library of shared experiences—shared that is with his mates on the terraces. But consider the opera fan, who has to follow the text projected above the stage, so he can laugh knowingly at one of Mr. da Ponte's witticism, and that before the baritone has actually sung the relevant words. And look at the programs sold in theaters: full of cribs to help the wretched punter cobble together a pretentious remark or two at the wine bar during the interval. The football fan, however, buys his program for facts and statistics, and the fanzine for humor and argument.

It should not be imagined that the fan's deep knowledge is restricted to the players on "his own" team either. The Brechtian debate, the dialectical battle over competing opinions, would be but a meager affair if it were. But in fact the football aficionado is clued up about the opposing players too, knowing exactly which type of derision is most likely to put them off their stride. I remember a first division (as it was then called) game in England when the goalkeeper of the visiting team (Peter Shilton of Nottingham Forest) had been involved in a minor traffic accident the day before. When the police arrived, they found him in the car with a lady who was not his wife. On the Saturday, the Tottenham supporters had the perfect ditty: "Peter Shilton, Peter Shilton, does your missus know you're here?" He duly made the sort of blunder that gives goalkeepers nightmares and loses games.

The reservoir of knowledge the football fan possesses means not only that he enters the discourse better equipped than the theatergoer, but he is also far more productive, both qualitatively and quantitatively, of argument. These days he is likely to be blogging and at greater length and seriousness than ballet lovers gushing clichés ("divine darling!") about a new star. Football stars are not divine; they are "magic," performance artists of flesh and blood who create something fresh every time. Indeed, the fan uses "artistic" language to describe the star player because he instinctively knows how sport as a genre outbids the conventional playhouse in aesthetic terms.[23]

However, no matter how serious and informed the sports fan may be in theoretical matters, it is at the event itself, in the act of Brechtian praxis, that he best exercises that knowledge. Fans do not colonize the genre; they create it. And at the final game of the season, they customarily do something they know is "forbidden" in that it violates the official parameters of the genre but which nevertheless expresses unambiguously their participatory role: they invade the pitch. In fact, it has been known for fans to do this during a key (usually a relegation) game in order to abort a narrative that is going badly.

Statistically a team will win more games at home than away and will do so by wider margins. Therefore, even given that his example is not football, Roland Barthes comes up short when he observes that "a boxing match is a story which is constructed before the eyes of the spectator."[24] Boxing spectators are also participants; they are invasive. Boxers, too, prefer fighting in front of their home fans. Nick Hornby suggests that in football, the players are representative of the fans and are manipulated by them. When Arsenal won, Hornby quite rightly says the victory belonged to him "every bit as much as it belonged to" the players and the manager. After all, he "worked every bit as hard for it as they did" and "...the only difference between me and them is that I have put in more years...and so had a better understanding of the afternoon, a sweeter appreciation of why the sun still shines when I remember it."[25]

At this point it would be nice to have recourse to Kantian aesthetics. Then one could invest the witty and creative community on the terraces with moral virtues. And when Nick Hornby claims that "bad teams attract an ugly following"[26] we can see how the connection might be made. However, this is difficult to sustain as Hornby, who surely spent many years listening to the chant "boring, boring Arsenal" before his team imported the French and got panache, must know. Certainly it is hard to see why the boring must be aesthetically superior to the ugly. In any case, loyal fans by definition stay the course, while aesthetically satisfying teams also enjoy the support of racist swine. Winning invariably takes precedence over style when the choice is reduced to an either/or involving only these two factors. True, aesthetically satisfying teams attract support because they are that, but so do successful—that is, winning—teams even if they do not play attractive football. Therefore unless a firm, positive correlation can be established between aesthetic appeal and winning (and as all West Ham United fans know, it cannot) the Kantian and ethical argument that marries aesthetics with morality will not hold in sport either…at least with respect to how fans behave. Although, as will be suggested below, it may hold in respect of how they think.

Addressing now the formal characteristics of sport, we see at once that it is a better embodiment of the epic form than theater, largely because it realizes in a lively and immediate fashion competing multiple narratives. Brechtian doubt and not textual authority is its very raison d'être.

That this is self-evident should not dilute its importance. The spectator is caught in a mesh of narratives and actively struggles to confound those he finds hostile. In this instance his chief cognitive role is, surprisingly, to fight intellectually with his fellows, that is with those who want the same outcome as he does. Together they are pushing the grand narrative to the same telos/end (the final whistle), but they do so as much by pluralistic disagreement as by consensus. Thus, the fan is engaged in a double debate: a larger one shaped by the opposed narrative aims of the two sets of supporters, and a more elaborate one in which those with the same objective argue exhaustively among themselves. The fan who yells for a substitution, which is then made and results in a goal, experiences a rare egotistical and aesthetic gratification. It is not necessary for him to crow. He knows that the narrative was written for a moment in the manner he wanted. In fact, he is sure *he* wrote it.

Sport does all this in a profound way because while narrative plurality is infinite, the telos is singular and focused. Supporters who leave before the final whistle when they know that the unwanted outcome is unavoidable, do so out of a respect for telos so strong they cannot cope with it when it is not benevolent. Narrative and telos are for them in deep conflict. But the real fan is supposed to stay loyal until death; the relevant terrace song for "defeated" fans being "United, we'll support you ever more." In general, winning fans do not leave early. The final whistle is for them a utopian moment to be indulged utterly. True, there need not be a winner. But even a draw is seldom evaluated as equally satisfying. Instead there is usually consensus as to which team profits more. Nevertheless winning is the unambiguous objective of sport. And it has about it the agreeable aroma of (momentary) utopian bliss. It is the positive expression of teleology, of which death is the negative.

This deep pleasure cannot be dismissed as a false God simply because it is fleeting. Not only does one remember those perfect moments; the paradigmatic experience has long-term potency in that it does not work unless at the same time it makes transparent just how wretched mundane life is. It becomes, like all utopian concepts, a yardstick, and therefore has the same formal relationship to the everyday as Marxist utopianism has to class history. However, while both forms are identical in that both are narrative, the sporting paradigm has the additional and not inconsiderable advantage that it actually occurs empirically...and then disappears, reduced to "mere" memory. No wonder the football fan is living life at a higher emotional and intellectual level than the theatergoer. In fact, there is about the utopian moment the whiff of a narcotic death. To have attained the ineffable moment is to tempt both fan and sportsman with suicide. Certainly both fantasize that there would be no better time to die. The sportsman if he is sensible in the matter will retire. But the fan will simply renew his season's ticket knowing that he must be in for disappointment. After all, the Boston Red Sox can lay "The Curse of the Bambino" only once, although if they are true to the imaginative world of sport they are obliged to do so from a seemingly hopeless position— a position in the final series when all seemed lost. But while, in general, the matter of "blissful death" should be postponed until the next and final chapter, it should be acknowledged here that sportsmen and fans both are aware that they are dealing with categories of this sort.

Sportsmen and fans see their collective activity as transcending death not merely because perfect victory makes it, paradoxically, a momentarily wished-for category, summed up by the phrase: "Now I can die happy." They also see sport as transcending death in that death is downgraded and becomes conditional on other things. In the face of the unstable inventive struggle going on, death, unlike in warfare, becomes a secondary category and is dismissed from the field as overvalued, irrelevant even. Karl-Otto Apel, examining whether sport as a rule-based praxis can provide the normative model for discourse ethics (it seems it cannot), notes the remark of an American basketball trainer: "Defeat is worse than death, because you have to live with defeat." Apel is disturbed by the vulgarity of the "victory/defeat" reduction and calls this sort of attitude "un-human" (unmenschlich). Although this may be true, it marks out clearly the gap between his attitude and that of every fan, player, and manager.[27] They understand exactly what the great Liverpool manager Bill Shankly meant when he said in 1981: "Some people think that football is a matter of life and death. I can assure them it is much more serious than that." And, he might have added, it is also much more satisfying. To realize—or to imagine that one has realized—the impeccably beautiful moment is to tempt fate, to evoke death, it is the (sexual) self-dissolution at the climax of pleasure. Are not goals the orgasms, the climactic moments, of what is now known as "the beautiful game," a remark attributed to its most beautifully creative player—Pelé?

Furthermore, the utopian element embodies not only the narrative character of the undertaking but also its beneficent core. Things not normally possible in life are created by sport. Aesthetics is thereby empirically verified. Knockout competitions are particularly important as they maximize upsets. In sport, it is not merely every dog that has his day, it is every underdog. Brecht's wish that those at the bottom be at the top, is repeatedly realized, although never made permanent. But big names can also experience the same utopian moment especially if there is a good narrative twist. A golfer who has been going through a bad patch will like Ben Crenshaw after winning the Masters break down and cry. The *Guardian* correspondent David Davies got the form—at least—right when he wrote: "Fairy tales can come true. It can happen to you." This sort of thing now "happens" enough to have become a cliché. If the class-ridden Neanderthals who run English cricket ban Ian Botham, it is decreed that he should on his return take a wicket with his first ball. The batsman duly obliges. A jockey who has overcome cancer will win the Grand National. How much better it is if his name is Champion. I suspect that narrative wish fulfillment has become so psychologically powerful that in Botham type situations, opponents are under (unconscious) pressure to play ball and lose. Certainly sportsmen and sportswriters are now fully au fait with the narrative trope. The cricketer Alan Border described his last innings for Queensland as "perfectly scripted," while the *Guardian*'s headline on the 2004 Ryder Cup ("Montgomerie leads the charge as Woods loses the plot") has everything: heroics, competition (battlefield violence as metaphor), and narrative. "Losing the plot" is now a standard expression in sportswriting. Still, if the journalists were better Brechtians, and thereby better sportswriters, they would talk, at the very least, of *plots*.

However, if the narrative category struggles after truth, realism, even of the sort we find in Brecht and sport, will not fuse them. For if truth were merely a tautological synonym for narrative, it could not evaluate narrative action in normative terms. To fulfill such a function it must have a discrete identity. The only alternative to this would be the determinist argument that whatever happens is not only destined to happen but is the best that could happen. At which point, truth loses all normative function and ceases to be of any independent interpretative value. As all types of Panglossian thinking of this sort, including Hegelian (and "scientific" Marxism), which make synonyms out of history and reason, are rejected, any suggestion of a pure *tautological* bonding between narrative and truth becomes impossible.

This conclusion could be avoided if it were shown that not only is truth dependent on narrative, but that narratives, irrespective of historical plurality, are of necessity productive of only one coherent normative position. This is something many religious faiths, certain as to both correct behavior and the goal that awaits the believer, make unproblematic. However, this is a jejune form of wish fulfillment for which no rational historical validation is possible. Nonetheless, the question of a possible normative status for narrative that can in part be adduced from within the category itself, without being a tautology, will not go away. But for the moment it is necessary to return to the practical consequences of buckling narrative and truth together in order to ask what we can do to bring about those goals for which we can claim a normative status.

This is, in plain terms, the question of permissible violence, of the morality (if any) that underpins our right (if any) to take the historical narrative into our own hands and cause harm to some in a cause for which adequate moral justification can, we argue, be adduced. Brecht addressed this question in a powerful manner. So powerful in fact that subsequently his moral and political courage (of which he never had much at the best of times) deserted him and he colluded in suppressing the plays, chiefly *The Measures Taken,* in which he had conducted the experiment. Therefore, it should be acknowledged that to build the remaining discussion on the foundation of *The Measures Taken* is to confront Brecht's critics on the terrain where they feel their own anti-Brechtian polemics most unproblematically rest. And if their arguments can be shown to be flawed in this limited context, it may well transpire that the character of those "flaws" will in turn be instructive with respect to narrative and truth in general.

The Measures Taken has an ambivalent relationship to epic theater chiefly because it embodies, in common with all the Teaching Plays, the tyranny of the text. This is expressed in two ways. First, the plays being short can be repeated during a single "performance" period with, as was intended, the participants playing different roles. But there is no chance of a different outcome. Therefore, a degree of "complex seeing" is possible, but only if the participants realize that it is noninvasive.

Second, the text is secure because we are repeatedly told so. For instance, the implied text from which *The Measures Taken* draws authority is the writings of Lenin. When The Young Comrade strays from the path of effective revolutionary agitation (he and his fellows have been sent to China to agitate among the coolies) the others "consoled him the words of Comrade Lenin."[28] But even given that Lenin's writings are not explicitly used (his *Left Wing Communism—an Infantile Disorder* is, however, heavily implicit), the text that reflects them is explicitly authoritative. At each stage of the story, the actions of the agitators are validated. They have killed The Young Comrade to preserve their mission and are now reporting—playing back—the story to the party members. The repeated statement "We are in agreement" is a verdict whose authority is beyond question.

Moreover there is another text that, also implicitly, stands behind the text being performed. This is the Bible. It has a complex function in *The Measures Taken* in that it is not merely an ironic commentary, but an ethical point of reference, which raises the question as to what true compassion and effective help amount to. As such it, too, even when it is upended, is an authoritative text. It will be necessary to return to the Bible, but for the moment it is important to acknowledge what Brecht's critics would surely see as grist for their mill: that in *The Measures Taken* text qua text and judgment qua judgment are melded into each other so that each is incontrovertibly validated by the other. The only way out of this bind, and it is a bogus exit, is to do what was done with *He Who Says Yes*—rewrite the play as *He Who Says No*. But while this strategy permits of textual pluralism—though not *simultaneous* textual pluralism—it unavoidably confirms exactly that which it is designed to undermine: the tyranny of textual authority.

Clearly when it comes to the question of truth, the authoritative (Leninist) text seems to deliver Brecht into the hands of his enemies. For surely all he has done in *The Measures Taken* is write a propaganda piece that has the unambiguous purpose of justifying murder. If this work is to be the ethical core of revolutionary action in the flux of history, then it is nothing more than a justification for the coming Stalinist horrors. And several of Brecht's critics took exactly that line. Ruth Fischer, who was thrown out of the German Communist Party in the mid-1920s, is a particularly striking example. Once a fervent Marxist on the Rosa Luxemburg model, her book attacking Stalinism also attacked Brecht (*The Measures Taken* "is a preview of the Moscow trials"[29]). It might be noted that one of Fischer's brothers, Hanns Eisler, wrote the music for *The Measures Taken,* while another, "Gerhardt Ende," was, like The Young Comrade, sent to China as an agent of the Comintern (The Communist International).

David Pike and, of course, Theodor Adorno are at least as severe as Fischer, the former arguing for an intrinsic wickedness in Brecht's politics that made him, and Lukács, into "tyrannophiles."[30] One notes also how many contemporary Marxists were disturbed. O. Biha in *Linkskurve*

(January 1, 1931 pp. 12–14) was ambiguous. The song in praise of the party was splendid but the party itself was "an alien, almost mysterious power" and would never have shot the boy. That "did not correspond to revolutionary praxis." The critic in the December 16, 1930 number of *Die Rote Fahne* was in no doubt and declared: "We regard the entire conception as false and unmarxist," and after the premiere in Moscow in 1930, Alfred Kurella missed the Leninist argument altogether and declared The Young Comrade for correct and his three fellow agitators for criminals.[31] Postwar, the play remained a problem for both the Brecht family, who continued to forbid "performances," and the East German establishment. The GDR's (German Democratic Republic) leading Brecht expert, Werner Mittenzwei, could hardly attack its alleged "Stalinism" in 1955, but was deeply uncomfortable with its overriding emphasis on the collective. In his eyes Brecht progressed beyond this.[32]

Others commentators such as Martin Esslin attempt to rescue Brecht in that they argue, like Kurella above, that the play either establishes the opposite of what was overtly intended or opens up interpretative possibilities that counteract its apparent unambivalent message. In what reads as an entertaining exercise in intellectual gamesmanship, Esslin puts the classic anti-Marxist ("Brecht the genius in spite of himself") argument in fine style and goes so far as to claim the play is Brecht's "first modern masterpiece" in that he had "with the *intuition* of a poet ... grasped the real problem of Communist discipline with all its far-reaching implications."[33] In short, with *The Measures Taken* Brecht is damned, whether with praise or condemnation, by enemies and friends alike. It is something that honors him greatly.

The overriding solecism behind all this blame and praise is twofold. There is a loss of nerve with respect to the principal dramatic act of the "play" (the ambivalent murder/suicide of The Young Comrade) and there is a commensurate failure to appreciate—but quite possibly not to feel— the full range of Brecht's analysis. Both of these considerations will be discussed in tandem in the remaining remarks on *The Measures Taken*.

The first is among the saddest of reactions, for it is symptomatic of the inability of the intellectual to face up to violence although it is all around him and an inevitable premise—though not always to the same degree—of the regulation of social life. Above all, it is a necessary element of the relations his own nation enters into with other nations. That is, it is accepted here that Merleau-Ponty is self-evidently right when he asserts that: "Violence is the common origin of all regimes. Life, discussion, and political choice occur only against a background of violence."[34] This is surely something that Adorno, among others, has said many times over. It is not however accepted that Merleau-Ponty's blanket judgment means that violence has the same expression and is equally inimical—or beneficent—in all societies. But in respect of any kind of emancipatory action against tyranny, the axiom that: "He who condemns all violence puts himself outside the domain to which justice and injustice belong"[35] is taken as read.

However, this does make plain how careful aesthetics must be in respect of death. Aristotelian catharsis in tragedy seems obligatory, but to stage a nominally tragic death in such a way that it escapes the parameters of conventional empathy is to take a risk. And to discuss it in a seemingly clinical manner so that an agreeable, well-intentioned young man is martyred because of his tactical "misuse" of compassion is clearly asking a lot. And then to manipulate the audience/participators so that they collude in the martyrdom, is outrageous. *The Measures Taken*, irrespective of—and also because of—its poetic language and shape as a parable, slaps you in the face with realism while depriving you of any of the customary aesthetic and culinary theatrical exits. The hostile reaction, whether by appalled Marxists ("Of course we would never do such a thing!") or anticommunists ("There, we told you so!"), is a product of Brecht's considerable subtlety, although that subtlety is disguised by the apparent disingenuousness of both style and form.

Given that *The Measures Taken* rejects, on the one hand, classical theatrical tragedy and, on the other, the jolly celebration of like political minds drinking up the wished-for propaganda, what is the nature of its effectiveness? Ironically its effectiveness is an expression of the very thing the piece does not seem to be. For, while it sends out aesthetic signals as to its transparent simplicity, it is in fact subtle and complex. Certainly, as has already been made clear, it cannot realize the principal formal agenda of epic theater, which is best exemplified in sport. But while simultaneous narratives or *overt* textual plurality are not in play, an elaborate set of implied simultaneous discourses are. Hidden texts (Lenin and the Bible in particular) color the undertaking. And they are not simply neat dialectical opposites. Furthermore the competing discourses imply different theatrical forms and values. In *The Measures Taken*, one nexus made up of bourgeois naturalism, cathartic experience, and Christian humanism confronts a second made up of historical realism, detached analytical rigor, and Marxist humanism. But this should not be seen as a battle in which the second group simply vanquishes the first, although on a superficial level that may appear the case. Certainly naturalism (the unproblematic presentation of a coherent empirical "real world") will give way to realism, in that narrative dialectics reveal deeper contradictory "truths," but that does not mean that Christian values and Christian ideology are merely exposed as misguided. Rather they are co-opted, on their own terms, and employed as a vindication of Marxist humanism. Many will see this as an illegitimate shift, an intellectual swindle, but no one interested in dialectics should. *The Measures Taken* does then allow of a type of synthesis; and this is something that makes its encounter with realism all the more unpalatable for its critics. The best way of looking at this is to return to the Bible. There are few texts that influenced Brecht more. It was not a book from which he could—or wanted—to free himself.[36]

The Measures Taken has the form of a Christian parable of the sort that guarantees authoritative (divine) judgment. It foregrounds pity, and in consequence the apparent sacredness of each individual subject is on the agenda. That is, whereas the chief performance unit is the collective (the chorus, the masked agitators etc.,), the language and the morally loaded iconography is focused on the forsaken soul. The biblical parable of the lost sheep, whose *singular* recovery (salvation) causes more joy in heaven than in the "ninety and nine just persons" (Luke 15: 1–7) is always present. And in this context one notes the odd, but effective, rationalization at work in the Christian Weltanschauung in that it is able to marry the multitudinous particular with a singular omniscient authority that is all-seeing and knows every hair of a man's head (Luke 12: 7). Thus, while incontestable authority is ever present the particular is never out of the equation, for how else is the insignificant man in the multitude, the unhappy figure from out the crowd who plucks Christ's robe as he passes and is promised justice and bliss in the beatitudes, to believe in salvation?

Naturally it is worldly salvation that the communists are to bring to the masses. Yet the communist knows that any promise as to immediate *universal* salvation is fraudulent. History willfully claims its particular victims long before the inevitable category of death makes unambiguously clear *its* universal hegemony. Of course heavenly redemption is in the untroubled position of being protected by its own ontology. Indeed it makes of worldly amelioration a lesser virtue. As a result, Marxist humanism is ironically placed vis-à-vis Christian humanism in that the latter is supposedly impeccable by virtue of sacrificing the collective (the 90 and 9) for the one (the theme of Brecht's first play: *The Bible*), and accepting with some nonchalance the probability that millions will be thrown into eternal torment. After all, there is little point in positing a hell if you decline to take advantage of its generous spatial possibilities, just as it may be cultural snobbery on the part of some Christians to mock Christian fundamentalists because they cannot get enough of Satan. But that still leaves Marxist humanism open to the accusation that it is, in itself, wicked — and intrinsically so— since it is morally obliged to find the widest expression of worldly salvation while accepting *without quibble* that this will mean worldly sacrifice on the part of some. Yet even if omelets mean broken eggs, it is reasonable to claim that the Marxist model is theoretically more democratic. For the

Christian promise as to divine love and universal salvation functions in a highly partial fashion in respect of both this life and the next. The Marxist humanist position, on the other hand, seems more promising. But it is vulnerable to the test of delivering empirically and, moreover, within a given time frame. And when confronted by the latter consideration, the revolutionary will always quibble tenaciously.

The Measures Taken works busily within these conflicting models, throwing the praxis and ideology of each into a double conflict, in that it questions the ability of each discourse (whether Christian or Marxist) to deliver not only with respect to its own epistemology but also in respect of the other's. That the "experiment" is partial, that Brecht has, as it were, made his mind up as to which discourse can best validate its own (and quite possibly the other's) ideology, should not blind us either to the sophistication of the exercise, or to the weight of expectation that is then laid upon the ideological shoulders of the victorious Leninist discourse... not least because that weight is not free of Christian connotations.

Given the closeness of the two discourses, it is not surprising that both groups (communist agitators and Christian evangelists) are implicitly bracketed in that the ideology of the latter is evoked in the story told by the former. Both accept the premise of rebirth. The Christian knows that "Except that a man be born again he cannot see the kingdom of God" (John 3. 3), while the agitators take on the yellow skins of their Chinese brothers. Both groups know they will be despised, and that the path is perilous, and that they will be derided and cast out of the hostile cities (Matthew 10: 23). Thus, these two texts, *The Measures Taken* and the Bible, are dancing a strange pas de deux, essentially in opposition, but almost exactly in step.

The chief expression of Christian iconography is found in The Young Comrade himself, who is the only figure in *The Measures Taken* that can claim the status of a character and thus able to elicit audience sympathy. This is a dangerous strategy in that Brecht has asked us to approve the sacrifice of the one "person" who is ostensibly a human(e) being. That is, the very form is contradictory; its emotional disposition is at odds with its polemics. We cannot, as a result, come to the desired conclusion unless we deny our immediate emotional inclination and with it the customary theatrical gratification. This is the (unacceptable) message that *The Measures Taken* is teaching us. Therefore, we are to understand that The Young Comrade is not merely attempting to change the story in that, animated by Christian and bourgeois compassion, he is diverting his comrades from the most effective revolutionary path; he is also attempting to undermine the aesthetic form. In effect, his structural function is to suggest how the Teaching Play might be pulled out of shape so that it becomes a naturalist drama with him as the cathartic, tragic hero. But we are invited to forgo bourgeois morality by rejecting as decadent, however emotionally powerful, bourgeois art...and vice versa. It is not then surprising if the bogus move, seductively held out to us by The Young Comrade, of entry into an alternative reality made up of bourgeois humanism, aesthetic naturalism, and Christian iconography, is disturbing. And when at the end the endearing "hero" approves the act whereby he is to be liquidated, and thereby implicitly tells us that Christian humanist is self-defeating, injury is added to insult. There is no problem disagreeing with someone who offers illegitimate arguments to arrive at a conclusion one finds, in any case, repugnant. But it is intolerable if, driven at the end by a desire to see *earthly* redemption attained to the greatest degree, you are compelled to arrive at a conclusion in one context that you have always understood to be profoundly wrong in another. In fact, no matter whether one accepts the verdict of *The Measures Taken* or not, any serious encounter with the piece is likely to leave doubt in the mind of each participant, whether it is doubt as to the apparently overwhelming rigor of the Leninist argument or doubt as to the probity of slaughtering a benign lamb of God. But that doubt does not mean that there is not a correct conclusion. The trouble is that if we accept it we are left upset by its (traditional, sentimental) consequences, and if we reject it, we may be disturbed by the suspicion that we have been intellectual cowards.

One key difference between the two discourses is apparently simple. It is tactics. Whereas the Christian is proverbially on the straight and narrow, Lenin makes it clear that the agitator is, in accordance with dialectical principle, using a more complicated route map. He frequently employs mountain imagery. For instance in the *Me-Ti Book of Twists and Turns,* Brecht was following the agenda of Lenin's *The Conquest of High Mountains,* and it has already been observed that *The Measures Taken* is a direct expression of Lenin's "teaching" to German communists in *Left Wing Communism—an Infantile Disorder.*[37] When in the latter he points out that to get to the peaks it is necessary "to move in zigzags...[to] retrace one's steps"[38] and that "absolute centralization and rigorous discipline [are] an essential condition of victory,"[39] he is laying out the arguments that The Young Comrade doubtless heard from his fellows. Lenin does not quibble in respect of the necessity of collusion either. Brecht is doing no less when he talks of "embracing the butcher" to "change the world." These mark out the dilemmas in which The Young Comrade is psychically and morally trapped and from which he would like to free himself but cannot. Lenin puts the matter lucidly when he warns that:

> a state of mind is *by itself* insufficient for leadership of the masses in a great revolutionary struggle, and that the cause of the revolution might well be

harmed by certain errors that people who are most devoted to the cause of the revolution are about to commit [40]

This reads as nothing less than the program of *The Measures Taken* and it is Brecht's accomplishment to realize all the consequences that follow from it. For The Young Comrade is the victim of naturalism (in aesthetic terms), of vulgar empiricism (in philosophical terms), and of infantile communism (in political terms), and, when, unable to endure further the suffering of the coolies because "misery cannot wait," he rips off his mask (his face is "humane, open, and innocent") and (demanding material redemption here and now) declares that "I can see the world with my two eyes," all these well-meaning follies are brought together in the one moment. At that point he has violated realism in every respect.

What follows is stringent and could not be more unpleasant to those who have been, or have nearly been, seduced. The matter is put plainly by the Control Chorus. It tells the three surviving comrades that: "It was not you who sentenced him, but Reality." If the consumer cannot accept this, he is perfectly entitled to flunk. But it will be a flunk. To attempt to remove from the equation the exercise of violence as part of an emancipatory struggle is also to remove oneself from reality. And to make the equation with the Gulag is to inflate a sentimental disposition into an invalid historical generalization. There is scarcely an international action (including those explicitly designed to save lives) that does not inevitably have the consequence of harming those whose names are not, for whatever reason, on the agenda of compassion. If we are keen today to talk of "win win situations," it is because of the feel good factor. Were we to examine the matter more carefully, we would have to face the fraudulence of the terminology. Such situations are sustainable only in as much as the arbitrary parameters of their definitions are accepted. But there is not a trade agreement, or even an aid, or domestic public welfare program—to leave all intentionally belligerent actions out of the matter—that does not have unpleasant consequences for some of the weak and is not made on the *necessary* basis of deciding who, among those who could be compassionately included, to in fact shut out. But in this case Brecht has tackled the basis for such decisions. And should such decisions be abused, that abuse is measurable within the morality—a morality that does not hide behind either sentimentality or, ironically, propaganda—on which the decision has been based.

Therefore, *The Measures Taken* does not rationalize the coming Gulag, but provide the means by which it should have been condemned. The appeal to history (which is a synonym for realism) does not (merely) busy itself with the question as to whether the given task has been accomplished and then use that as a rationalization for (potentially mass) murder. It is also to keep in the equation the moral core, which is the long-term paradigmatic goal of the narrative struggle that also has its *immediate* term of reference in the pressing need to get to the peaks in reasonable time...whether by backtracking or not. One could say that The Young Comrade does not understand his own ideology. He is determined to offer immediate compassion because it seems to him an absolute ahistorical virtue. And this would apply equally whether we define that compassion in Christian or communist terms as long as narrative is excluded. But, in fact, his real argument is highly narrative. It concerns the time frame. And though it is true that The Young Comrade is mistaken because "an impetuous revolution...will not last a day," he *does* have a point, not least because he requires of the revolutionaries that they explain in historical and moral terms *their* delaying actions. And it is that challenge—to explain before the court of history—that is painful. We, however, should remember that to die for a cause—or to kill for one—does not become immoral when it is taken out of the soft-focused world of fiction ("It is a far, far better thing that I do" etc.,) and placed within the analytical parameters of a real struggle, albeit one that compels us to make decisions we find unpleasant and that we normally leave to apparatuses over which we, thankfully, exert little control.

And so, ironically, we might make out of The Young Comrade's death as much as we make out of Sydney Carton's. Indeed the boy's sacrifice has a poetic power that takes full advantage of the mix of Christian and Marxist ideologies. There is, of course, no redemption. No second chance. He has ceased to be a lost sheep and now accepts his fate as a sacrificial lamb. A dreamer certainly, but not one who, such as the biblical Joseph, comes back wiser to his family and tribe. He is not allowed another "go"—a rewrite— at the narrative. While Joseph the dreamer is let out of the pit into which he is thrown, The Young Comrade is shot and a lime pit erases the deed. But he dies a fine death with his head on the arms of his executioners. They have asked him if he wants to do it alone and he has answered "Help me." It is the one (bitter) occasion when he realizes what *real* help actually means.

In this manner Brecht tackled the question of truth within narrative form. Certainly the extrinsic elements have been added in a flagrant manner, and the narrative plurality in play is, when all is said and done, bogus. But what is also clear is the unvarnished way in which the great normative questions with respect to realism attain full force. Perhaps the best measure of this is that Brecht, too, ultimately flunked. He was explicit as to the exceptional importance of the form and was planning to use it for the *Garbe* project in the 1950s. Hans Garbe would have been The Young

Comrade come out of the lime pit to judge what his fellows had—in fact—accomplished.[41] In the immediate historical context of its composition it would have evoked Marxism as the Jameson/Dowling "providential fable" mentioned in chapter 2. But it was too dangerous in the GDR to write. It is a sad fact that of the major Teaching Plays the *Fatzer* project comes to nothing because it is beyond Brecht at the time; *The Measures Taken* is completed, is clearly a masterpiece, and is then suppressed because it is too stringently rational and poetically powerful; and the *Garbe* project is aborted due to intellectual cowardice and political opportunism. Brecht is not equal to his own encounter with realism. Nevertheless, that encounter is exceptionally rich.

There is a structural parallel between the above discussion with respect to narrative when coupled with the normative element of truth, and the view taken by Karl-Otto Apel and others with respect to discourse ethics. It has been pointed out that several philosophers sympathetic to discourse ethics are skeptical as to its normative standing in that they see the normative elements as transcendental in character and extrinsic. Apel, as we have seen, has turned to football to show, analogously, how this is the case. The result is "a two-step ethic"[42] where the performative principles of the activity cannot produce the fundamental ethical norms that validate them. The same could be said—common sense suggests that it should be said—about the relationship between narrative and truth in this book. Namely that the normative element (truth) is just as transcendental and extrinsic to narrative, as the ethical claims of communication theory are to its practice. However, I am still far from ready to bite this bullet. And although this question should be postponed in large measure until the next chapter, something more might be said here, not least because sport has been such a key factor. This will also lead us back to narrative in order that we might appreciate how dubious, at the very least, it can be when liberated from any normative consideration.

In fact, the key attraction of sport in this chapter—the manner in which it expresses the epic as an unstable nexus of competing narratives—is not relevant for Apel, who is interested in the epistemological and pragmatic status of the rules and the players' duty to accept them under the rubric of fair play. As a result, we can see that Kantian deontological values are again on the agenda. It is notable, however, that Apel does concede that a player may break the rules with good reason—to prevent an injury for instance. Furthermore, when the issue of rules is abstracted out of the specific context of a controlled sports event and applied to the wider world where one might confront corruption and violence, it becomes clear that one cannot always act morally and pragmatically at the same time.[43] This is not so far removed from the principles on which the three communist agitators killed their comrade. This implicitly underlines the constricted range of the analogy between the wider world and sport. Certainly Apel is well aware that he is using sport reductively, stating that it is not "identical with the real lived world" but is rather a "fictional game-world" within that world.[44]Nonetheless, Apel's examination of the status of the rules themselves is instructive because—for our purposes—he misplaces the balance. What he wants is fairness. It does not matter that there are cheats, as long as it is understood that they *are* cheats. But I suggest cheating should be seen as an inherent characteristic of the rule-based activity. More than that even, it should be seen as a welcome, albeit contradictory, expression *of* the "rules."

Because fans and players are engaged in creating/writing providential fables, they exercise imaginative powers that transcend what would be appropriate for mechanical activity. Simply going to the stadium "When Saturday comes" is to turn one's back on the world of repetitive labor. However, they exercise these creative powers in a praxis they know to be unfair. Every football fan is in no doubt that sometimes the better team (with respect to aesthetics) loses, even though the winning side has not violated the rules. In this, sport betrays its fundamental aesthetic and moral raison d'être. Put another way, we can see that a superficial notion of "fair play" as praxis (of the sort Apel is examining) has defended its constricted ethical realm (the rules of the game have been respected), but that a deeper notion of fairness (the providential fable) has been violated. This is also to underpin the moral connotations of aesthetics in that a fair result (in the deepest sense) would reward the team whose play was more beautiful. Here, then, is a clear difference between sport and democracy. The Habermasian argument that makes of democracy and philosophy a double helix also means that, as long as the rules are dutifully followed, the democratic outcome is unimpeachable. No one may question the election scoreline. However, every sports fan knows that the sports scoreline can be unfair (immoral in fact), irrespective of the rules.

This is a bitter experience. But it can be ameliorated by the implicit morality of the epic form, in that the form itself keeps the beneficent fable in imaginative play even when it is no longer present on the pitch. This is the rationale that urges the fan, and more particularly the player, to cheat. And, if he is true to the epic form and its aesthetic burden—in an impeccable world the beautiful game would not produce *ugly* winners—the player *should* cheat. In fact, the categorical imperative and universalism work well here in that the impartial fan must concede he would have wished that every other player had behaved likewise in the same circumstances. Perhaps narrative also gives grounds for believing that we have a duty to produce aesthetically satisfying (that is, "fair" in the deeper sense) outcomes. One sees here the extent to which the universal quality is (once again) aesthetics, but this time it possesses enhanced (moral) authority in that it is wedded to both immediately creative storytelling and telos... or goal scoring. In other words, there are grounds that permit us to infer, at the very least, a causal and category relationship between narrative and truth. This will be pursued in the next chapter, also in the context of moral violations of what might be perfectly upright procedural rules and legal prohibitions. But for the moment it is still necessary to remain with sports and to do justice to the fan's encounter with cheating.

The fan's attitude to cheating is by no means unsubtle. Although biased by definition, he is able to maintain fine distinctions. Not all cheating is the same, and it is telling that the narrative/aesthetics pairing plays the determining role in evaluating the (moral) validity of rule-breaking. Brutal tackles, spitting, and so forth, are generally despised across the board. But there is respect for Brechtian cunning. The Schweykian cheat is admired as someone who has swindled the system and got away with it. However, the real, morally admirable cheat is the one who accomplishes something actorly, which is to say he shows off his aesthetic skills. The "dive" in the penalty area is the classic example. The player who has learned to successfully manipulate referees and linesman is (secretly) admired. And when the opposing fans (in Britain) bay their disapproval, they cannot help but voice aesthetic-based respect. They call out "Hollywood." A German fan may cry "Schieber," which suggests a trickster, that is a cheat blessed with Brechtian craft(iness).

Perhaps two examples might be looked at here to give some idea of how complex this matter is. Consider two famous and disputed goals: Geoff Hurst's second goal for England against Germany in the 1966 World Cup final (Germany lost), and Maradona's first goal for Argentina in the 1986 World Cup quarterfinal against England in Mexico (England lost). German football fans (indeed almost all Germans) have never been able to come to terms with the former. There is scarcely a retrospective that does not pick over this wound until it bleeds afresh. English fans, on the other hand, have never had anything like the same trouble with Maradona's goal. Yet not merely the timescales, but the empirical differences between the two would suggest that the reverse should be the case. Hurst's goal was entirely legitimate in that there is no suggestion he did anything unfair. The goal was duly awarded by the referee, and there is no hard evidence that the ball did not cross the line. But Maradona's goal was a deliberate act of cheating (he handled the ball into the net) and neither referee nor linesman was sharp-eyed enough to spot it. Furthermore, the German defeat should not be so bitter in retrospect as Germany has won the World Cup twice since 1966 and the national team invariably does well. The same cannot be said for England. It is clear, then, that the German obsession in the matter has nothing to do with sport as such.

The Maradona example is initially the more instructive because it is almost wholly restricted to the terms of the discussion hitherto. That is, it is concerned with the relation between narrative, sport, and truth. Maradona is forgiven because of aesthetics. There was no doubt that he was the most creative player at the 1986 World Cup and in fact he scored another goal (entirely "fairly") in the same match, which will bewitch football lovers as long as there are any. There is also no doubt among England fans that Argentina were the better team and though there is some bitterness at the swindle, the aesthetic and narrative justice of it all is generally accepted. That is Apel's notion of fairness is ignored out of a respect for a deeper notion of, nominally, the same virtue. Even Maradona's own rationalization is, being clever, acceptable. He made a pun on his Christian name (Diego) and said that the goal had been scored by "the hand of God."

When seen from the German point of view, the 1966 example takes us out of the realm of the normative value of aesthetics (they were not a particularly attractive team) and even out of football as narrative, in that England clearly deserved (aesthetically) to win the final. But it does not escape the narrative trope in general. But its meaning can only be guessed at in the bigger history of postwar (West) Germany. The Germans were deeply, if unconsciously, pleased that they lost the final in 1966 and this is why they have obsessively held onto it. After defeat in 1945, the postwar renaissance was symbolically completed in Switzerland where Germany won the 1954 World Cup against a much superior (more creative) Hungarian team. The Germans have always called this "the miracle of Berne." But it was a victory that generated some ambivalence. Football fans interested in notions of morality and aesthetics were hardly pleased, and German triumphalism still had an unpleasant aftertaste. So if the 1954 victory was a miracle, the 1966 defeat was a Godsend. Here it was possible to replay the narrative to, paradoxically, arrive at the conventionally unwanted result. But to arrive at it in a manner that was unblemished. And to attain the status not of losers, but of victims, and on the "holy grass" of Wembley (as the Germans insist on calling it), was a blessing from which it was impossible to be sated. Moreover, this was a victimhood that was free from any suggestion of manipulation on the part of the victims, or any hidden vindication that they in fact deserved what they had suffered. In short there was no parallel with the bombing of Dresden, which is otherwise the chief event used by Germans to change the narrative discourse. In 1966, they were impeccable. If, that is, one insists on the almost laughably banal "fact" that the ball did not cross the line.

In this manner the Germans turned to an inflexible narrative option (any plurality of opinion as to where the ball landed is utterly impermissible) in order to make out of it something providential . . . but perversely providential. For to violently force a singular, wished-for, teleology onto the pluralistic terrain of history is to generate difficulties that lead to blindness and massive acts of cheap intellectual collusion. Ultimately one is compelled to believe the dominant narrative irrespective of either the alternatives or the facts, all of which have to be airbrushed out of the record. And *this* is what leads—and it does lead—to the Gulag. A violent single-minded intervention into the field of narrative plurality amounts to the disfigurement of truth. Which is to repeat the premise that although narrative plurality may not be unproblematically productive of normative values, it is nonetheless the necessary epistemological framework for such values. In this case the distortions (concerning ostensibly one goal in a football match) are a reflection of a refusal to pay proper respect to narrative pluralism. At the very least one can argue that because any narrative interpretation and any posited alternative outcome can be tested against what in fact did happen, judgment and historical validation are not only present but susceptible to moral evaluation. The trope of multiple narratives will always demand of a dominant interpretation that it justify its propaganda in terms of what did not (allegedly) happen and what, therefore, in the future should not be permitted to happen. That is, we can see that in the case of the 1966 World Cup final, a particular group has intervened en masse to willfully distort reality so that any question as to the ball is merely a device to move the discussion onto the desired terrain of victimhood—something that in the long term can only damage the psychic health of that group. However, Germans have been compelled to realize some of this as the result of another goal. In the 2010 World Cup, a perfectly fair English goal (the ball crossed the line) was disallowed. Nonetheless, they are still loath to give up their 1966 status as victims.

All of this gives us some feeling for how dangerous narratives can be. But the dangers do not come about solely by distorting reality until it is illegitimately expressive of a singular truth, whether that truth is seen as a fact ("we beat the bastards!") or as an expression of something unfairly lost ("we were robbed!"). It can also come about by virtue of the opposite, when heterogeneity is unshackled and invulnerable to the claims of judgment. Therefore, in having moved between the terms narrative and truth with respect to sport and Brecht, this chapter should end by acknowledging, in more general but largely theoretical terms, the two obvious dangers: first, what happens when narrative is freed from normative judgment so that it attains its most unconstrained pluralistic form; and second, what happens when normative judgment takes such a firm hold that plurality is squeezed out of the model.

In respect of the first danger, the necessity of normative values is most clearly apparent when they are absent. The result is conspiracy theories. They are now one of the dominant cognitive forms of popular culture. They are by their very nature multitudinous, they are liberated from serious testing, and they make invariably fraudulent claims to imaginative thinking. They are related to "spin-doctoring," which is able to make-to-measure any silk purse out of any sow's ear. In not knowing whom to believe, we either believe no one (which is tantamount to believing everyone), or we subjectively pick whatever scenario best appeals to us and duly hoover up the necessary "evidence." For extreme skepticism, inclined to disbelieve everything, dialectically flips when pursued enthusiastically and becomes credulity—but a credulity for which there is always an abundance of bizarre proof. As a result, it willfully asserts not that something extraordinary is true, but that everything is true no matter how extraordinary. And it can be proved. This general disposition even shows signs of invading academic life. After all, if everything is the plaything of interpretation then there is no reason why evolution should not be made to share the same epistemological status as creationism—both being merely "theories."

But what is the origin of this? Well, it is hardly new. Faced with the refusal of people to believe in atrocities, Arthur Koestler in 1944 screamed (it is his own word), "split thinking... [has become] a uniform disease; never did human psychology reach such a height of phoneyness. Our awareness seems to shrink in direct ratio as communications expand. The world is open to us as never before but we walk about as prisoners, each in his own private portable cage."[45] Koestler has isolated the chief causal factor in the problem, which is, paradoxically, that which should make us better informed: communications. But what he does not appreciate, given that his concern is the USSR and the atrocities of the Second World War, is that the danger lies in the plurality of communications. We are swamped with information, with alternative interpretations, so that it no longer matters whether we are dealing with serious investigative journalism, or gossip, or fantasy. Our thinking is not so much "split," as shattered.

Who can complain then that a large section of the American population believes their astronauts did not land on the moon, that Elvis is alive and well and working in a gas station in Tennessee, and so forth? In the world of conspiracy theories, the category distinction between hypothesis (as something that can be tested) and pure invention has been utterly erased. It does not matter whether the nonsense is alleged fact

(*The Protocols of the Elders of Zion*) or alleged fiction—"sort of"—(*The Da Vinci Code*). Anything can be believed, not because evidence is deemed impermissible but because it has attained a fluid status with respect to both its traditional functions: that is, whether it underpins or debunks. It *all* stands to reason.

In teeming popular culture, it is understandable if consumers see no difference between believing a conspiracy theory that is credible in that it is underpinned by evidence (let us say that the Warren Commission was naive in concluding that Lee Harvey Oswald acted alone), and a conspiracy theory that is all free invention (let us say that the September 11, 2001 attack on the Twin Towers was an Israeli plot.) When trying to stay afloat in the flood, is there really much point in distinguishing between these two positions? Meanwhile no conspiracy theorist, as Jonathan Kay points out in his 2011 book *Among the Truthers*, is going to change his mind.

Which brings us to the second, and obverse, expression of narrative in a dangerous mode: the dominant interpretation that allows of no plurality whatsoever. Clearly religion is the principal, but hardly the only, example of a metanarrative that knows all the answers and brooks no dispute. Christian preachers—to whom this discussion is limited, although much the same could be said of psychics—are inclined to play a double game, taking advantage where possible of both realms: the spiritual and the worldly. That is, full use is made of the category of faith to escape the dangers of empirical testing on the one hand, while benign events are celebrated as evidence of divine will on the other. Thereby religious propaganda rejects any challenge to test a hypothesis in the here and now, while still being able to celebrate the material world as a miraculous manifestation of the transcendental love of God.

Even so, religion has had to give up a lot of epistemological ground over the centuries. Since the Reformation, there has been an accommodation between dogma and secular values. As democratic societies have evolved the Christian Church has, ultimately, accepted humanist principles with regard to the law, human rights, and freedom of expression, and in many cases has done so to an exceptional and civilizing degree.

Yet today we see this is changing. There is a remarkable growth in forms of fundamentalism expressive of a deeply felt need for certainty. The consequence is the overriding authority of fixed forms. History is a danger unless seen as a classic struggle between the Lord and Satan. This leads to an enthusiastic adoption of doctrinal positions shaped by various forms of Bible literalism, no matter how absurd the conclusions to which they, in turn, lead. To this can be added, in the case of the United States, an excessively confident nationalism, which assumes that the world's most powerful and Christian nation has a special responsibility to fulfill the program of the Lord and is intended by him to do so. For instance, Pat Robertson, a politically influential TV evangelist, prays on camera for vacancies on the Supreme Court, which is to say he is praying for the death of serving liberal justices. He has also used his program to advise the White House to have the president of Venezuela, Hugo Chávez, assassinated.

This yearning after certainty is an entirely comprehensible reaction to the plethora of information and conflicting interpretations with which the citizen is confronted. Therefore, it is entirely logical—necessary even—that Protestant fundamentalism set its face against history. Moreover, a great moment is well-nigh upon us. There is to be a "Rapture." This, too, can have a political and international dimension. Religious millenarianism is not frightened of a grand political narrative as long as it is unambiguous and redemptive. All of this has led to an opportunistic alliance between Protestants and the state of Israel, as well as between protestant religious ideologues (many influential in the American Republican Party) and conservative Catholics as part of the ECT (Evangelicals and Catholics Together) movement.[46]

What is promised here is twofold, and contradictorily so. That eternal bliss is on the agenda is hardly surprising. That has always been the "reward" with which the oppressed have been bought off. But placed alongside it is something new. It is the promise of happiness now because God wants us to be happy; he wants us to be successful. He even, as I discovered when listening to one telly evangelist, wants us to find a parking place. The axiom that it does not profit a man if he gains the whole world but loses his immortal soul is hardly relevant when one's chief worry is parking the car. Even The Young Comrade when most distressed about immediate suffering did not imagine he could fix *that*. God has become a convenience tool. A telly evangelist will give him credit for beneficent acts, above all miracles (cures for terminal illness are, for obvious reasons, especially welcome), while moving the goalposts when it comes to misfortune. Then we are told that the Lord moves in mysterious ways, and we are suddenly back, but briefly, in the vale of suffering.

Faced with narrative distortion, whether due to unbridled plurality or singular authority, it is not surprising if many Americans appear to have thrown in the towel. Disenchanted with corrupt political practices where seats in the House of Representatives are gerrymandered and politicians are in the pay of lobbyists, they retreat. No doubt they live good lives, helping their neighbors, working in their communities and going to a church that asks them to think for themselves—even, perhaps, to consider that doctrine can be wrong. But for many, notably the educated young, voting becomes distasteful. The worst, meanwhile, are full of passionate intensity. They have faith, and they live in a simple world, and they know whom to ask to tell them what to do. When narrative and truth get this much out of kilter the potential for trash and the danger of reactionary social developments—even in a democracy—are considerable.

Chapter 7

Death

Giving the commencement address at Harvard University on June 8, 1978 Alexander Solzhenitsyn was keen to impress upon his audience the West's spiritual degeneracy. He duly employed a paradox that one might entertain as dialectical. He claimed that the Soviet dictatorship had engendered a high spiritual level among the Russian folk precisely because they had been forced to suffer so much. That is: "Through intense suffering our country has now achieved a spiritual development of such intensity that the Western system in its present state of spiritual exhaustion does not look attractive." He did not pursue this line of thought stringently and recommend yet more suffering for the Russian people together with something similar for us, in the expectation that they would rise to a yet higher spiritual level and that we would escape our own benighted state. But he did use this strangely perverse first principle to attack what the godless call secularism and he, surely suspecting that many among his audience were vulnerable to the charge, chose to call "humanism." It is fair to see this as an assault on principles that go back to Kant and the Enlightenment. Certainly it is striking that, unintentionally or otherwise, Solzhenitsyn evoked the same teleological and thereby narrative categories that we have already met in that context. Also notable is that although he was much concerned throughout the address with "man's responsibility to God," he left the Deity unnamed, but heavily implicit, when he produced his clinching teleological proposition: "If humanism were right in declaring that man is born to be happy, he would not be born to die."

And that, we might think, is that. For certainly one can initially (if one does not think too seriously) defend Solzhenitsyn's categorical principle on the grounds that its unambiguous causal terminology with respect to suffering, and death, and spirituality (and God) seems to establish its conclusion within the parameters of its own commonsense axiom. It is, in other words, a neat statement that has little cause to appeal to anything outside of itself, although, as has already been suggested, some feeling for divine intention is necessary. So, despite the Deist premise, we might entertain the proposition that Solzhenitsyn has made a contribution to Kantian and enlightenment thinking with respect to analytical and synthetic statements in that his aphorism while not a tautology—in the sense that Kant has in mind with analytical statements—appears to be self-evidently true nonetheless. That is, it reaches that elevated status that Kant struggled to reach through the agency of aesthetics: it is a synthetic statement that is a priori true. For surely we have no difficulty in going along with its basic, all-determining premise. Seen in purely subjective terms, death is indeed a bummer.

Furthermore, in this context any empirical difficulty the aphorism might get into is irrelevant. Its logical and causal probity defends it against empiricism. Even so it should, out of fairness, be acknowledged that there is an ocean of empirical evidence that the aphorism's claim as to God's intention (he must get the credit for "inventing" death) has not been at all appreciated by the Russian people in the manner Solzhenitsyn hoped. Far from being spiritually uplifted by the dialectical mysteries of suffering and, consequently, viewing the "spiritual exhaustion" of the West with contempt, it emerged that when some degree of choice was open to the citizens of the former Soviet bloc, they were not in the least troubled by the degeneracy of the very people Solzhenitsyn was addressing at Harvard in 1978. Rather, they were all too brazenly interested in, and attracted by, their materially abundant, and quite possibly godless, lives.

But, of course, the self-evident aphorism can be readily upended. It does not follow that the Almighty's touch of genius in inventing death incontrovertibly means that we are not meant to be happy and therefore humanism (or the Enlightenment) is bunk. That would be tantamount to arguing that the pains of childbirth (in the Solzhenitsyn context presumably another divine masterstroke from which women might draw spiritual comfort) mean that we should not have happy, procreative sex.

We can also just as easily infer from the presence of death an alternative aphorism, no less valid and convincing in its own parallel if inverted terms. That is: eat, drink, and be merry for tomorrow we die. Solzhenitsyn's evocation of death no more or less readily establishes out of its own (synthetic) character a proposition that unquestionably proves (a priori) the virtues of suffering, than it does its opposite: namely, the carpe diem virtues of hedonism. It can only produce the morally uplifting—or least divinely sanctioned—category of suffering if it resorts to other synthetic arguments that, in not being a priori true, cannot deliver the certainty of (divine) judgment that Solzhenitsyn, mistakenly, sees as self-evident. We might in the end think that Milton in "Il Penseroso" does a more convincing, if not so ambitious, a job in dealing with similar material.

Nonetheless, in turning to death to underpin an across the board normative deduction, Solzhenitsyn does us a favor. We might follow him, and make of death a key explanatory category. This is a key category because it offers us our best bet to effect some kind of reconciliation between the empirical and transcendental elements that have repeatedly surfaced during this book. These elements have hitherto been seen as clearly irreconcilable in as much as any claim to normative principles as a guide to empirical practice has unavoidably entailed an appeal (whether acknowledged or not) to transcendental values, which themselves cannot be wholly grounded within the parameters of the original empirical categories. But now we turn (again) to death not solely because it is the incontrovertible vindication of a narrative Weltanschauung—as was claimed at the opening of the first chapter—but because it also has unequaled value in intellectually underpinning that Weltanschauung in such a manner that narrative and truth may, at least claim, not only an unparalleled explanatory richness in empirical terms but, more importantly, an intrinsic philosophical status that has an unmatched epistemological range. After all, Schopenhauer tells us in Chapter XLI of the Supplements to *The Word as Will and Representation* that death is an inspiring genius and the muse of philosophy. So perhaps it can smuggle into the argument a type of validation previously thought impossible. It is on this basis—or hope—that the remaining observations of this book are made.

If all forms of religious consolation guaranteeing a spiritual afterlife (*pace* Solzhenitsyn et al.) together with the various forms of the transmigration of souls promising an extension of corporeal life (*pace* Bloch et al.) are put aside, we can see that the most attractive ontological function that death fills is that it inevitably gives rise to its obvious conceptual antipode: life. This is, prima facie, exceedingly glib, but not without significance. For although death can certainly be said to give life meaning, it does not give life meaning in the rather meager way that life itself does. Paradoxically it does more for life as a *concept* than life can.

It is death that teaches us greater respect because it links the individual's destiny most clearly to the grander destiny of the tribe. Death, to remain on the level of significant banalities, is both the most personal and the most universal of phenomena. It is therefore expressive of both the finite and the infinite, although both must be manifested and mediated through life, not least because death qua death is not a commodity that has a tangible extant presence in its own terms—something that may explain our interest in giving it anthropomorphic form on the stage, in parades, and at carnivals, and so forth. On the other hand life (which we seldom theatrically personify) has to be experienced as a category that is wholly compromised in that it can never be merely and entirely of itself. It is compelled in its very nature to foreground its opposite, which is to say its extinction. Certainly on one level death, too, is expressive of its opposite in that it needs life as a concept and the act of dying, by which life is annulled, if it is to have any meaning *for us*. But we can readily conceive of a world without life—a dead world. We know that quite possibly an infinity of such planets exist and rather fear that we are willfully bringing another one about here. But life is impossible without death. And at the end, it is exactly this axiom that is empirically experienced without exception.

And if we are prepared to face up to the fact of death, we find that we do so doubly, both as individuals and as social creatures. Furthermore, we may well discover that our responses to death differ in a profound way on the basis of just this distinction, quite irrespective of other, finer, but more variable distinctions. For our encounters with death as a personal reality and as a general category apply across the board and are the richest element that death brings to our (narrative and epistemological) experience of life.

Death, as finite and ineluctable, is always most readily experienced by the individual subject when engrossed in his personal life, or when psychologically and emotionally disturbed by experiencing the temporal fact of the lives of those closest to him. He has to learn about death, and he busies himself with it to a degree that he may not wish to admit. Clearly he will fantasize about it, he will to some degree be tormented by it, and to some degree he will desire it. Nonetheless, the various theoretical interpretations on which psychologists base their speculations as to the role of death in the individual psyche need not be an issue here. It is enough merely to accept the presence of death as an inescapable and finite destiny for the individual.

However, at that moment when the individual confronts history as a category, even as a category limited to the members of his own family generationally ordered, he is compelled to see the life-death pairing as a universal and—at least with respect to the future—a potentially infinite phenomenon. At this point his narrative thinking, no matter how crude, effects a qualitative shift, which diminishes the finite ego. Nor need this awareness of the universal be the result of abstract thinking as to teleology and the nature of history. It can be experienced in a personal manner as the subject—to take one example—considers his own lineage. These days with DNA research he can trace the biological facts about himself and his tribe back over millennia. "Family" history is no longer contained within the covers of the photo-album.

The matter, however, can be confronted in a yet more personal and focused manner. Childbirth is often experienced as a paradigm shift— a forced move in which egocentrism is replaced by an entirely different Weltanschauung. That is, parental love (or possessiveness) changes the narrative parameters. Death loses its restrictive identity, in that the new parent is likely to think in less self-obsessed terms. Now life is seen as having meaning beyond individual gratification and the life span of the subject. This is no less radical when the explanation is framed in terms of genetic struggle. That is, it does not matter with respect to the emotional and intellectual shift experienced by the parent if it is assumed this is due to the machinations of Dawkins's selfish genes as they manipulate their corporeal carriers to biologically reproduce. Rather what is determining is generational thinking, which springs the immediate parameters of death as experienced selfishly by the subject. For instance, a parent who has to bury a child endures a unique torment, and feels that a great narrative injustice has been done.

We can see in respect of both cases (the finite history of the individual, and the universal and potentially infinite history of the species) that death is the necessary ingredient by which we are interwoven on all levels by multiple narratives. Clearly, it does this on a much more generalized level than the sophisticated explanations devised by Freud to link the destiny of the individual with that of the clan. But in consequence it calls into question the indulgence of the singular ego. We may, for instance, argue that for all existential purposes the world ends when we die. However, we know that *in fact* it does not and thereby we are aware that extreme egotism is no less bogus a way of overcoming the fact of death—in this case by monopolizing it as one's own exclusive possession—than resurrection or reincarnation. Instead death demands we make a story—no matter how modest—out of our lives. And it must be a story that has to take cognizance of what has preceded us and what will come after, even if that cognizance is framed in terms of bloody-minded indifference. Therefore, whether explicitly or by implication, our death-shaped story is compelled to account both for that which is selfish or subject-focused and for that which—appears at least—to transcend the ego. It does not matter in principle whether the narrative is heroic or modest—whether we have in mind the grand defiance of Byron's Manfred whose lasts words are: "Old man! 't is not so difficult to die," or the heartbreaking plea made on behalf of the doomed Willy Loman in Arthur Miller's *Death of a Salesman*: "His name was never in the papers...But he's a human being, and a terrible thing is happening to him. So attention must be paid."

It is not merely a stylistic question as to whether we stay loyal to the Aristotelian principle that tragedy "is an imitation of persons who are above the common level."[1] If we have long since violated that classical axiom, we have done so partly out of universal moral considerations that are rooted in the universalism of death, which is itself the paradoxical but logical bedrock for the declaration of human rights. And in this we are, morally at least, superior to the Greeks. The power of the quote from Arthur Miller lies in the implicit indifference of the world to the destinies of the Willy Lomans. In this case, we need to be *reminded* that attention must be paid. If the Aristotelian assumption is valid, we would not need to be if it were a president whose picture was regularly in the newspapers. Nevertheless, the self-evident justice of the Willy Loman plea, irrespective of the literary power of the text, obviates any need for either an aesthetic or a philosophical argument. We see at once the justice of the appeal. We *understand* that tragedy is a universal category that is thus experienced by everyone, and in understanding this we are conscious of our own coming encounter with death. And even were the tragic figure a hermit and the drama a one-man show, it would still evoke those that are absent, to say nothing of the more pressing community of those watching. Death will always be private and public simultaneously and can have meaning only as long as both aspects are respected in that attention is paid to both.

As a result of binding the particular and the universal, death has an unavoidable normative core secreted somewhere in its narrative baggage. Furthermore, the antithetical notion that might rob death of its ethical significance—namely the claim that it is the triumph of nihilism, or that it can plausibly justify a nihilist Weltanschauung—is intellectually jejune. Even Adorno, as we have seen, is compelled to infer something hopeful out of history's dark narrative. What we have called the subjunctive mode ("What if...") is incontrovertible. Marcuse is paying the same respect when he writes: "This 'if' is essential to historical progress—it is the element of freedom (and chance!) which opens the possibilities of conquering the necessity of the given facts. Without it, history relapses into the darkness of unconquered nature."[2]

Likewise the fascist argument as to the nobility of violent struggle unencumbered by respect for the disadvantaged, which was used in chapter 5 to question the "self-evident" enlightenment values Kant abstracted from aesthetics, will not hold if it is restricted to the idea of life as a bloody steady state. The anarrative quality of fascism in theoretical terms invalidates its Weltanschauung. True, fascism can sketch a vague narrative in that it asserts there will be, in the world of butchery, winners and losers and that, in accordance with a "principled" social Darwinism, the winner is morally vindicated simply because he has won. This, after all, is in effect the position Hitler logically assumed at the end, claiming that the Germans had failed (him) because they had lost, while the Slavs had exceeded expectations. But this is a miserable thing when placed alongside the richness of narratives as they are universally experienced. That is, its wretchedness has, in this instance, nothing to do with any moral qualms due to its cruelty, or its racism, and so forth, but is simply an expression of its self-evident vacuity. And given that the fascist argument, like the fascist narrative, is not really going anywhere which is not just more of the same, it is not all that far removed from the vulgar egotist's claim that the world ends with his own death. Moreover, should the fascist accept the interwoven narrative complexity of individual and tribal life, his blood and struggle mentality would be compelled to come up with grander interpretations. These, in turn, would then be vulnerable to historical analysis and thus exposed, as is every other interpretation, to empirical disproof and analytical criticism. Fascists do not like grand or complex interpretations as they smuggle into what is essentially a fixed attitude of mind too much analyzable material. Instead, for them the world is self-evident, and once nation and Volk have been wedded to racism all the fundamental theoretical questions have been satisfactorily answered. Ironically it is a category much glorified by fascism that should really be its undoing. Fascists are not paying enough attention to death and its implications.

These considerations are also relevant for discourse theory. One of discourse theory's difficulties is its sublime, seemingly complacent, attitude to participation. True, it sets out strict, ethically based principles with respect to the communicative activity—that is, performative rules to do with access, and participation, and so forth, based on a respect for all those involved. But what should it do with the subject/citizen who rejects the activity as intrinsically worthless? On one level this is merely an incidental matter limited to the (non) "participant." After all, if someone will not play ball that is his lookout. But it also raises the possibility that the undertaking is flawed in empirical terms. It has misrecognized reality. Perhaps the world is more accurately seen as a place of arbitrary power where winning is more important than being "right," especially when that "rightness" is determined by who is popularly thought to have the better arguments. This problem is not adequately got round by foregrounding the democratic values that are present in the society from which discourse theory has arisen. These, it might be argued, are essentially window dressing masking deeper structural oppression, as Merleau-Ponty and Foucault et al. would claim. Democratic values appear dominant simply because that society has been so successful materially as to develop obedient social habits, and, anyway, those consensual behavioral patterns are, ironically, underpinned by a guilt-based taboo born of the crimes of the Third Reich. That is, Germans today are just very receptive to the moral claims of "talk." After all, look at their TV programs.

One possible response to this was touched on in chapter 5 when it was noted that Jürgen Habermas viewed democratic and philosophical developments as an intertwined duality. But this seems too good to be true. For if there was no lack of either democracy or philosophy in the Weimar Republic, how can "they" be absolved of responsibility for that republic's collapse. And if "they" were guiltless, victims of forces beyond their power to control or influence, then what use is the philosophical underpinning of democracy and vice versa? In this matter history is too often on the side of Adorno. For instance, the difficulty of making philosophy and democracy interdependent recalls Voltaire's exasperation at the horrors done to Jean Calas. His "murder" (sanctioned by "the sword of justice") perpetrated in Toulouse 1762 in an atmosphere of religious bigotry, drives Voltaire to the outburst: "And this, in the present age! this at a time when philosophy has made so great a progress!... It should seem that enthusiasm enraged at the recent success of reason, fought under her standard with redoubled fury."[3] We, however, know of vastly greater violations of reason's "recent" successes. Therefore, if the Habermasian assumption is to have a sphere of reference it would be better if it were entirely abstract. To submit the democracy-philosophy pairing to empirical historical judgment would be to obliterate it.

Nonetheless there may be something in it. True, the likes of Heidegger would, one assumes, reject the idea out of hand. For much of his life democratic values were secondary to Hellenic wisdom. Willy Loman has no place in his philosophy. Foucault meanwhile would—and does—dismiss discourse theory as naive in that it takes little account of the topologies of repression, which are for him the necessary foundations of social organization. And all of this is to put aside the influence of thinkers such as Machiavelli and Nietzsche for whom democracy is either practicably impossible or degenerate. Yet discourse theory embodies universalism, and if the foregoing argument as to death and narrative is entertained, it has some claim to an intrinsic normative status. All of which means we are still dealing with the possibility that the universalism of death when folded into narrative will deliver something more than mere arbitrary ideology.

However the principle of equality, inferred from universalism, should not be taken as an argument for pacifism. The Leninist considerations of the previous chapter are not in any way negated and will resurface below. Even so, the teleological function of death necessitates a respect for the story the individual makes of his own life and this, in turn, necessitates an equal respect, on *his* part, for the stories of others. Death is a shared, democratically unimpeachable, category over which it is not necessary to fight. There is quite enough of it to go around.

And with respect to discourse theory one should not overlook the strengths of intersubjectivity simply because the Habermasian pairing of democracy and philosophy appears so arbitrary. Intersubjectivity marries the subject and the collective in such a deep manner—it would seem to establish a new ontology for human animal(s)—that it, too, makes inferable the normative status of death. That is, by changing the nature of the ego it transcends the notion that life must be a selfish struggle that has no meaning beyond the individual's extinction. Consider this in the light of the recalcitrant citizen/subject mentioned earlier. In refusing to participate in the democratically structured activity of communication ethics, he is obliged to deny the universal validity of his opinions. It is not simply—or even chiefly—that he rejects the rights of others or argues that some people are just plain inferior and, as such, should be written out of discourse. Rather, in refusing to participate he is forced to deny something much more significant. Namely, that any right-thinking person would agree with him. He does not need to win the argument, but if he believes he is right he cannot refuse the challenge to establish the universal validity and applicability of his opinions. Should he fail to accept this challenge he denies, in effect, the category of death, for he claims for himself a position explicitly outside of and opposed to the collective. Which is to say he denies the one unambiguous thing he shares with, and can articulate with, all the other members of the same language group and which, moreover, will ultimately negate his life in the same way that it does theirs. In effect, by rejecting discourse he declares that he is no longer a human being.

It should be acknowledged that this attempt to take the category of death into the territory of discourse ethics to establish a normative core framed in terms of universalism, has inevitably meant that the largely absent category of narrative has had to be smuggled into the argument. That this is readily accomplished by foregrounding death is explicit to all of the foregoing. However, it is not the case that discourse ethics troubles itself with narrative and death in this manner, or that it in any way feels the need to provide such a basis for its universalist claims. Democratic and libertarian values are its prerequisites, not values that it generates. In being self-evident truths, it is not necessary to establish their normative status. That this has, nevertheless, been attempted is the result of two external considerations. One is the introduction of a category that itself covers territory that is normally seen as beyond the range of a single coherent category, and the other is to provide a framework that will allow, later, further comments as to narrative and truth, which defy pacific principles and reengage with violence and the Leninist arguments of the previous chapter and before.

The first consideration has either been established already or it is not to be established at all. It is the claim that death has a unique conceptual status and that it combines and reconciles two pairings, each made up of

two (normally) mutually exclusive elements. The first pairing is practical
and worldly (at least in intent) and is made up of the claims of the individual and the group. It first surfaced in this book in respect of the utopian
paradigm of Marxist humanism. Death is the only concept that can philo-
sophically underpin the reconciliation of these elements.

The second pairing is theoretical, in a paradoxical manner, and is also
implicit in all of the foregoing. It is that death, as *the* universal category,
is both transcendental and empirical in that it is an expression of qualities
that lie outside of our own worldly experience *and* an utterly, corporeally
realized, presence in the material world. Death is thus a bridge between
the empirically worldly and the transcendentally otherworldly. It is the
incontrovertible expression that we live our lives in an ambivalent temporality in that we are defined both by our life span *and* by a temporal place
in something bigger. Thus in the context of theoretical argument, it is
suggested that were death paid more attention it might enable a reconciliation between empirical problem solving and normative validation in that
it is the one category that might be called empirically transcendental or,
indeed, transcendentally empirical.

Clearly, the argument with respect to the unique conceptual character
of death is very generalized. It might be said to be so generalized as to have
little practical purchase. The only response to this objection, which has
hitherto been possible, has involved an appeal to the explanatory power
of narrative. The incessant insistence on the coupling of narrative—in
respect of both its form (the duality made up of the singular and the collective) and its teleology—with death is an expression of this. Narrative is
then to effect some kind of qualitative enrichment. This, after all, has been
the premise of each of the preceding chapters. The question then arises
whether narrative and death can generate something specifically normative that goes beyond the observations already made in respect of fascism.
Certainly, there is more to be said of a more concrete nature about narrative and truth in the context of violent social life. That is, it would be a
mistake to infer from the remarks already directed toward fascism that the
categories foregrounded here imply a form of quietism. They do not. And
this, the second external consideration mentioned above, needs now to be
pursued.

Initially, it might be as well to return to Freudianism. This can be seen
as a sensible strategy for the perverse reason that Freudianism is not sympathetic to the argument made here. Rather, it constitutes the most substantive challenge to the optimistic disposition. Freud, whose jaundiced view of
both the subject and the collective is richly confirmed every day, is a major
obstacle to any utopian focused narrative Weltanschauung. Furthermore,
it is not assumed that this is the case simply because the pessimist is always

proved (in the end) to be right, any more than it is argued that death means that nothing (in the end) matters. Particularly debilitating—and incontrovertible—is the Freudian emphasis in tribal/collective matters on processes of exclusion, of forms of regulation and taboo that constitute both the unstable individual psyche and social organization. In short, the endogamy-exogamy binary pair expresses in part the real nature of collective life. Neither can this be seen as an untroubled celebration of Kantian universalism regarded as an (arbitrary) principle expressed in the categorical imperative and allegedly inferable from a study of aesthetics, nor does it pay due respect to universalism as a category that can free the individual from a self-obsessed Weltanschauung in the manner that has been suggested here. All too often we come together because we only feel safe when we circle the wagons

On one level this is just something that has to be faced and made the best of. Exclusion and intolerance are formative aspects of human history—or, as Freud says, civilization ("Kultur"). After all, it is not unreasonable to assume that the human psyche is unlikely to become an unambiguously beautiful thing. That possibility has functioned here solely as a hypothetical utopian telos whose role—admittedly one of unparalleled importance—has been to introduce forms of judgment and evaluation with respect to (often violent) emancipatory action.

Nonetheless, the Freudian dialectic of endogamy and exogamy reminds us that we are placed in a dangerous world. For however much this is explained in grim retrospective terms, and however attractive pessimism may be in that it protects our intellectual reputations when everything goes belly-up, progress in terms of expanding respect for human rights and freedom from arbitrary suffering is as much on the agenda as the inevitability of various forms of trauma. Auschwitz can no doubt be explained, along with everything else, by the fundamentals of the Oedipal drama, but it is not itself an inevitable result of it, any more than acts to alleviate the sufferings of the poor in the Third World are the *unambiguous* result of repressed fantasies twisted into their opposites by, let us say, sublimated guilt. However jaundiced its general disposition, Freudianism does not and cannot exclude the *fact* of benevolent acts, no matter how it may choose to account for them. True, what is employed here is a loose notion of dialectics. But it is enough for us to see in the endogamy-exogamy pairing and all the intolerance that it expresses, the potential to express its opposite, namely a charitable praxis (no matter how contaminated the motivation) toward those who are excluded.

And although exclusion maintains its attractions, circling the wagons in both multicultural domestic societies and in international relations has become an increasingly counterproductive, even forlorn, strategy.

Belonging and exclusion are becoming more complex and important, and thereby profoundly more dangerous. Furthermore, the problematic encounter with that which we have successfully excluded in the past, but which now comes back to haunt us, will also reset parameters that enable new normative judgments, in that we will be forced to acknowledge that previous strategies were corrupt. Which is to say that the narratives that gave them meaning were also corrupt. However, before this matter is pursued any further, more should be said of the category of universalism, not least because the endogamy-exogamy pairing is also an expression of one of the problems generated by universalism and the across the board "respect" that it implies.

Clearly universalism is a category that of itself is (impossibly) nebulous. Given that its implications are absolute, it is easily rejected as being worthless in that in including everything, it says nothing. This, however, is not an insurmountable problem. The ethical baggage of universalism is best appreciated when it is violated in allegedly ethical terms—terms that themselves have paid due attention to the across the board (moral) behavior universalism requires. That is, its normative implications are valuable because they collide with practical considerations. Nor should it be glibly concluded that "practical" is *just* a synonym for a form of rationalization that, as a result, must be seen as invalidating the lofty universal enterprise. Practical problems, the working out of the best possible narrative, are not an exercise in unbending religious probity. Small sins may be just as likely to send the sinner to hell as great ones, but small or great compromises do not invalidate progress. Universalism is an expression of the utopian drive, not a demand for impeccable behavior in the here and now.

Universalism when put into a normative context, mirrors a key dichotomy that has already surfaced. In the previous chapter, two forms of fairness were proposed with respect to sporting narratives. One was concerned with following the rules; the other with violating them in order to attain a higher form of fairness that was, moreover, understood—if not welcomed—by all the participants. This was underpinned in the same chapter when Brecht (and Lenin) were employed to validate, in oppressive societies, a violation of (universal) human rights in the short term to effect improvements in the long. That "embracing the butcher" is dangerous does not alter the fact that in small as well as in great things that is exactly how the world works. Marcuse puts this unavoidable unpleasantness clearly: "One is thrown back on the inhuman calculus which an inhuman society imposes: weighing the number of victims and the quantity of their sacrifice against the expected (and reasonably expectable) achievements."[4] It is "merely" a question of deciding what short term distasteful actions are permissible and on what basis. There is, after all, an unmistakable epistemological link between the parent taking mild punitive action against the child and the nation undertaking warfare, no matter that any statement that brackets them seems shockingly disproportionate.

The same duality was also emphasized in the chapter on Marxist humanism regarding historically conditional systems of legal rights—and thereby legal repressions—and a deeper sense of universal human rights. This is much the same as the duality between absolute values and practical politics that cropped up in the first chapter with respect to the Treaty of Waitangi in New Zealand, and the (anti-slavery) American Declaration of Independence and the (pro-slavery) US Constitution. The duality turns out to be abrasive, rather than unproblematic.

What emerges from this is a complex nexus of ethical considerations faced by each individual, irrespective of whatever normative values are motivating him. That is, it is not simply a matter of exposing the conditional and contaminated character of the more superficial term (regulated fairness, conditional liberation, legal rights compromised by unequal social relations, etc.,) to the radiant light of fundamental universal axioms so that the "contaminations" may be burnt away, allowing peace to reign, the more creative football team to win, a fair deal for everyone, and—no doubt—a guarantee that no child will be chided because there will be no need. Rather, it is necessary to see to what extent the rights and legal systems that are now enjoyed reflect adequately the universalist values that underpin them. The question of expectation then becomes critical. To what extent is progressive change possible and what price can be paid for it? For change delayed may result in subsequent violence considerably more bloody than was necessary had greater radicalism and courage been shown earlier.

The American Civil War and Emancipation is a particularly rich example. It not only places two forms of morality in instructive conflict—a lesser one (the South had, with respect to slavery and states' rights, the explicit articles of the Constitution on its side) and a higher one (the North fought, among other things, for the deeper, more amorphous principles of the Declaration of Independence). It also foregrounds an issue of such fundamental weight that the apologists of negative liberty or piecemeal incremental progress would have difficulty in arguing their case. Moreover, it also implicitly poses the question: Might it not have been avoided and the Union preserved and the slaves freed nevertheless? For neither winners nor losers had cause to be happy; the losers because they lost (saw their culture trashed and were to be tarred thereafter as of lesser worth), and the winners because the price had been too high. Even former slaves, especially those who remained in the South, did not enjoy the benefits it was imagined emancipation would bring, while the heavy losses in the black regiments fighting for the Union must also be paid due regard.

The chief reason why it is not unfair to put the question as to how all this might have been avoided concerns the particular democratic credentials of the United States. It is not enough simply to point out that US democracy was deeply flawed, as contemporary European visitors liked to observe. At the time the United States had, relative to other Western societies, claim to a higher status as a democratic nation. Furthermore, it might be argued that it was exactly this status, underpinned by law and moral axioms, that should have enabled it to address the cancer in its body politic effectively and with much smaller loss of life. That it was not able to do so should compel us to see the democratic and universalist struggle as a constant. That is, it is dangerous to assume that we have moved on in that these problems just do not apply any more. The incrementalists want to believe that violent action is off the agenda, and we can all engage in "talk" because circumstances have changed, and we have advanced to a point where violence is no longer necessary. The chief difficulty with this does not lie in the irony that such theoreticians are always forced to argue that we enjoy the advantages of the violent liberationist struggles of the past in that we no longer need recourse to just that kind of struggle. After all, that position could be justified on impeccably evolutionary and narrative grounds, although it would require a Whig or progressive notion of history of a rather more sunny disposition than theorists of this sort are normally able to stomach. But the chief problem with the argument from progress is that it confuses theoretical and empirical matters. It confuses the two sorts of moral argument mentioned already, in that in celebrating a particular advance—an advance that is empirically real and morally admirable, such as the abolition of slavery—it imagines that the deeper universalist normative position is decisively strengthened and thus invulnerable. This assumption is dubious, as the Black Codes passed by Southern states in the years following their defeat and the Jim Crow laws that took force toward the end of the nineteenth century make clear. As to the contemporary position of African Americans, alone a glance at prison statistics and sentencing practices in American courts is cause enough to obliterate an untroubled Whig interpretation.

Still, there may be some cause for optimism. Certainly, the parameters have changed in recent decades in that the topography on which these issues play out has become more expansive. Hunkering down with our own clan is less likely to be effective. The end of the Cold War has generated a host of contradictory changes in that it has made the world more complex and has enabled a greater range of intricate interactions, whether ostensibly benign or explicitly malevolent. The game of international politics has become pluralistic, the new rules are not clear, and State Department theorists who argued that we live in a unipolar world could not have chosen more misleading terminology. This is a misinterpretation that, whatever one may think of the complex schema of his model(s) for "civilizational" conflict and his distrust of domestic multiculturalism, Samuel P. Huntington has thoroughly exploded.

However the matter is hardly lacking in dreadful contradictions. For instance, the relaxation of the psychological and materially coercive strictures once forced on well-nigh every nation by the hegemony of the two superpowers, has facilitated exceptional cruelties. Nothing, for instance, has better expressed the fear of the alien element domestically secreted, than the butchery that followed the collapse of Yugoslavia. Without listing specific examples, what is most striking is the multifaceted range on which barbarism and the fear of the all too familiar and present "exotic" worked itself out. Moreover, the degree to which this messy terrain became chaotic and irrational is unmistakable. It is interesting that Huntington, who naturally enough sees in these struggles a powerful exemplar of his model (of what happens in "fault line states" when civilizations clash), is forced to acknowledge "anomalies." The United States allied itself with Arab nations in the interests of Islamic Bosnia, and Russia supported sanctions against fellow Orthodox Serbs. What certainly did tell, however, is the dreadful power of the endogamy-exogamy pairing—what Huntington calls "them and us"—and though he never mentions Freud, it is the Freudian agenda that he is writing large when he observes: "Civilizations are the ultimate human tribes, and the clash of civilizations is tribal conflict on a global scale."[5]

But the opposite is also enabled by the same history. Not, that is, that some people have become better despite others becoming worse, but that the change in the topography has also facilitated the appeal to universal values. The grand phrases of past declarations conferring universal human rights have more force when the citizens of democratic countries that have committed themselves ideologically to such pronouncements, see that the previous obstacles to the realization of these goals are, apparently, no longer there. This is a Weltanschauung that Western governments who, while not always happy with the consequences, are obliged to fuel and encourage. Declaring that democracy has triumphed and that "we" have been proved to be not only the material winners but also the moral victors, is to declare simultaneously that all sorts of things are now possible that were not before. More than even that, it is to declare that injustices that had to be endured due to Realpolitik, are now, theoretically at least, intolerable.

When Jimmy Carter was inaugurated president in 1977, the Cold War still determined the rules and set the points of international relations.

When he announced he intended to pursue an ethical foreign policy, he was derided not merely by political experts and commentators but also by large sections of the general public. Furthermore, events—his critics felt—proved them right. Now Western leaders make exactly these claims. Their voting publics demand poverty be alleviated (even eradicated), that Third World debt be written off, that the planet be saved, and so forth, and the politicians set up initiatives ostensibly to reach all these goals while happily taking advantage of pop stars who sprinkle them with a little glitter and street cred. It is much too easy to see this as the result of unintentional hypocrisy on the part of Western populations that enjoy gains dependent on the exploitation they otherwise condemn, notably with respect to the natural resources of Third World countries. In fact, they remain trapped in a double discourse expressive of a double morality. That they see at the moment no discrepancy—or less discrepancy than before—between legitimate self-interest and universal charity should, perhaps, be welcomed as a clear-sighted recognition that a window of opportunity is present, which allows a degree of dialectical reconciliation it would be irresponsible to ignore. It then becomes a private matter to what extent one deplores sweated labor in poor countries but buys the textiles and footwear produced there nonetheless. That is, even the individual who takes advantage of the obvious rationalizations in these matters, can still play a real and legitimate role in a narrative designed to eradicate poverty.

In short, we are compelled to deal with morality in two discrete narrative frameworks. That is between, on the one hand, a morality focused on an explicit goal that, underpinned by universalist values, is normatively attractive, and on the other the means to bring this about. In the second framework, morality escapes the universal disposition it enjoys in the first in that it accepts the *fact*—no weaker term is permissible—of dialectical life and concludes, when necessary, that little emancipatory progress will be possible without violent action. However, it does not escape the ethical challenge of the universalist position, in that it must justify not only its objectives but its time frame on the basis of universalist principles. It is compelled to set forth its temporally limited narrative program in terms of telos and means—which is to say in explicit terms with regard to the cost in misery and loss of life to all those involved. Even so, it need not in all cases meet the terms it sets itself if it is to avoid being ditched, although that possibility must be increased by the fact of (interim) failure. But it must lay its parameters out. To the extent that any program fails, its promulgators are obliged to convince the population that the failure is explicable in terms that do not contradict the ethical universalism on which the program's objectives are based. That is, they are compelled to establish again that the goal is still reachable and to explain the manner in which it is now to be attained. What they should not be allowed to do—and what politicians most want to do in matters of this sort—is to claim, under the guise of common sense and seeming intellectual modesty, that they really cannot know when things will start to get better, but are sure that at some point they will. This is to employ an enfeebled form of narrative and, in effect, to ask for a moral blank check. But if good reason can be given for the efficacy of any program (let us say on the basis of contemporary analysis and historical precedence), then by virtue of this alone there is reason to demand clarity as to the price that must be paid in both material and temporal terms for that program to succeed. Furthermore, there is nothing per se preventing politicians from speculating publicly from the word "go" on setbacks, even failure. Alternative narratives—including capitulation—are always in play, and the population must simply decide as best it can if it is prepared to continue to support a policy that causes suffering and kills for a telos that is repeatedly postponed.

This requires a degree of openness not only unattractive to politicians and military men, but also to civilian populations who increasingly do not have the appetite for it. It is to demand a degree of responsibility that politicians assume is beyond the public and from whose burden, therefore, the public must be disencumbered. The result is a media culture that deals either in lies or benign contemporary myth-making. Almost all narratives are now sold to the public in fairy-tale terms in which two-dimensional good and bad spirits competitively struggle and neither virtue nor the outcome are (initially) in doubt. This is the case whether it is an administration putting an argument for war or a television report on a natural disaster. Until the number of dead or the flood waters reach levels it was assumed they never would, extreme forms of benevolent reductionism are practiced. Of course, it is the case that any argument that comes to terms with a complex world involves reductionism to some degree. Historical reality is always more elaborate than our, hopefully rational, accounts of it. However, it is the ability to keep a plurality of possibilities in play that best facilitates reevaluation and the chance of changing course. This further enables the advocates of any particular narrative action to make moral claims tenable in a given, practical context.

For instance, as military policy fails, no strategy is more shoddy or, in respect of its empirical consequences, more dangerous than the celebration of a one-dimensional metanarrative that supposedly sweeps all others from the field. As things start to go belly-up, the cry that "There is no alternative" becomes louder. This claim is, literally, never true...except in respect of death. It also turns out to be an interim phase before a further, yet more unethical, step is taken: politicians and military chiefs start to talk of an "exit strategy." But you do not need a strategy to exit. You simply go. Mass bombing civilians (as in Vietnam) in order to engineer a fig-leaf peace-deal, which in fact trumpets the coming defeat and the loss of everything that had hitherto been deemed impossible to forgo, amounts to the dereliction of not only the deeper notion of morality but also the contingent or strategic one as well. It is a double degeneracy.

A further matter surfaces when we consider both notions of morality. There is always the danger that the more immediate but superficial notion attendant on strategies employed to realize fundamental principles, will in turn colonize and corrupt those principles. American arguments justifying torture (while claiming it is not) and the Stalinist murder of the recalcitrant because they do not conform, illustrate this. Another example, one that also recalls the question of slavery in the United States and the Treaty of Waitangi in New Zealand, will put the matter in a less belligerent context. And it will give it a different form. It will again show the contingent notion colonizing the deeper one, but in this case because the deeper one is exposed as bogus. The danger here, is that this leads to a major flunk—a failure of intellectual and moral courage. This is what happened in Germany when the problem of asylum seekers became acute.

Throughout the 1980s and the early 1990s, the number of asylum seekers coming to the Federal Republic increased to the point where social order was threatened and discontent among the indigenous population grew. To solve this problem the CDU (Christian Democratic Union) led government, employing the language of moral responsibility, insisted on a change to Article 16 of the Fundamental Law (the Grundgesetz). And it was duly amended on May 26, 1993. But the Fundamental Law was, and is, exactly that: a statement of universal and inviolable principle. Moreover the asylum provision was never intended as strategic. It was unconditional. To amend it to keep out the people it was designed, presumably, to let in was clearly a contradictory act.

Furthermore, the manner by which this was engineered was an intellectual and ethical swindle. It would have been honorable and healthy to have faced the fact that the Federal Republic could not sensibly pursue an unconditional open-door policy. Ultimately no country can. As a consequence it would have been necessary to admit that an ethical axiom was empirically unsustainable and that it should never have been put in a legal context. In fact, in that context it was exposed as bogus and thus the Germans found themselves in a bind made up of a careless mix of grand principle and (im)practical politics. Clearly, it was necessary to find a new basis on which certain asylum seekers would be let in and others refused. Given that this would have been an arbitrary regulation (a lottery perhaps, or a first come first served approach), it would have required a fundamental

epistemological shift. But this was not done. Instead the Fundamental
Law was maintained as an apparent universalist principle while a trick was
devised to get around the difficulty. A notion of a "safe third country" was
contrived. All countries with which Germany shared a land-border were
then defined as being of this type. Consequently Germany had no duty
to accept asylum seekers at the relevant crossing points; they had already
reached safety.

This might seem a neat finesse, but it is to be regretted in that it confuses, deliberately, principle with practicality.[6] It also infects the status of
the Fundamental Law in that should at some time any neighboring country lose its democratic status, mass entry from that country could not be
legally prevented and the problems that follow from confusing deep-seated
principle with practical regulations would resurface. And given that the
population is inclined to hope that this issue has now been definitively
resolved, its reappearance would be likely to breed more malignant forms
of xenophobia. In general, however, the story in its own rather modest way
indicates the difficulty that populations have in disabusing themselves of
their would-be impeccable self image. Better to hold on to the illusion
of absolute values with respect to human rights than face up to complex
reality.

But the German example should also be seen in terms of narrative
goals. There will be certain normative positions that are unusually vulnerable to narrative pressure, while others, being deep-seated axioms are
(theoretically) atemporal. Universal suffrage and legal equality guaranteed
to all citizens are sustainable in their own terms, even though miscarriages
of justice occur. After all, it is precisely because they are seen as miscarriages that they do not threaten the fundamental axiom. However, the
German regulation as to asylum seekers was not of this sort. While being
impeccably universal in its intentions, it had an inbuilt narrative telos:
the worldwide end of persecution. In enshrining this in practical policy—
thereby making that policy impractical—it was exposed by narrative as a
moral fraud. It is pity that legislators ignored this when it came to devising
a solution.

The German example can be fruitfully compared to the examples
already mentioned. The Treaty of Waitangi made promises with regard
to land, fisheries, and so forth, that could not be kept and were never
intended to be kept. The US Declaration of Independence, meanwhile,
asserted human rights that could well have been honored—although at
some considerable cost. After all, to get around them one needed not only
the Constitution but also the Supreme Court, notably in the Dred Scott
decision of 1857. Article 16 of the German Constitution, however, was neither one nor the other. It asserted a principle that had a universal (global)

term of reference, but was to be realized within the parameters of one nation. If the framers thought this tenable, they were wrong.

Although there is a powerful argument for setting goals that cannot be reached (that is to say, the argument for utopianism), those goals of themselves have no narrative and thereby no empirical terms of reference. Rather, they find expression on a lesser and always conditional level through practical laws and public policies. These laws and policies have attainable objectives, which are explicable and concrete and can be used (should they be reached) to evaluate the wisdom of the original policy. They address the degree to which that policy has succeeded within its own parameters, and—most important of all—the degree to which that policy following its realization can still be seen as reflective of the utopian norms. Should the goals and objectives prove unattainable and even the attempt to reach them evaluated as of little productive worth, they serve as guides to any future attempts to tackle the same problem. They may, of course, also provide ammunition for those who, whether for reasons of self-interest or of principle, question the initial goals.

Nevertheless, it is these would-be practical laws and policies that are truly narrative in character and it is in this manner that they are understood by the actors. Setting "reachable" goals is how policy makers—elected or otherwise—manipulate and manage public opinion and secure, should they need it, willing cooperation. However, as the public in democracies becomes more cynical and thereby more sophisticated in that it becomes used to objectives not reached, the tenor and praxis of political life becomes increasingly complicated, and more skilled strategies of propaganda evolve. It is today a commonplace that large sections of the electorate simply do not vote because they have been too often disappointed in these matters. In the United States, voting figures are so low that the nation's democratic credentials are open to question. And this although American politicians spend hundreds of millions of dollars to get people to the polling booths. However, the abuses this leads to, and the adept manner in which politicians are able to manipulate the various groups of citizens who *do* vote, is not, in the first instance, the critical issue here. More important is the need to set attractive goals to seduce the electorate. Ironically this is best understood in respect of failure.

One way of dealing with narrative failure is fiction. But it is fiction successfully sold—at least temporarily—as fact. Failure is flipped into its opposite for purposes of public consumption. A public that is paradoxically both jaded and predisposed to prefer conspiracy theories over common sense, is easily manipulated. Under these conditions the opportunities for narrative inventiveness are maximized, and events that are fraudulent can be successfully sold as genuine. A classic case is the toppling of the Saddam Hussein statue in Baghdad's Fardus Square on April 9, 2003.

The statue was toppled "live." It was, apparently, a spontaneous act that could, subsequently, be ideologically colonized. But even here it should be acknowledged that there are pictures of an empty square immediately before the show began, which suggest that the business may have been staged. Nonetheless, in being live it was also "real"...history in the making and so forth. However, in lasting for several hours, largely because the people who were supposed to topple the statue did not have the strength, or the numbers, or the technology to do so, it gradually became an artificial production requiring the customary suspension of disbelief on the part of the audience. And yet, while the farce was made clear in that an American armored vehicle had to help and an over patriotic US soldier screwed up the symbolism by placing the "stars and stripes" around the statue's head (later he had to climb back up and remove it), the moment the statue came down all of the anomalies were, momentarily, erased. Then a few hundred (at most) Iraqi men ran over to it and beat it with the souls of their shoes while well-informed TV reporters portentously informed us that beating something with the soul of your shoe is a powerful sign of Iraqi contempt. In short, the act of arriving at the desired goal canceled out the hiccups on the way there. And now those who had seen what they had wanted to see, namely the prewritten narrative getting to the prewritten goal, behaved like theatergoers bored to death by the performance but so pleased that it is over they applaud all the more loudly and tell each other how wonderful it has been. Moreover it is entirely possible that, for the moment at least, they are sincere.

Events such as the Fardus Square show remind us of the power of fiction to create benevolent narratives that not only compensate us for the pain of real life but enable us to regard, however temporarily, that life as something other than it is. In *Wag the Dog*, a dazzling film from 1997, a president facing reelection and about to be embroiled in a sex scandal, is saved by a media expert and a Hollywood producer who invent a Balkan War and an American soldier in enemy hands. Watching it for the first time you might feel that on occasion writer David Mamet and director Barry Levinson laid on the satire with too broad a brush. But you would be mistaken. As the years go by, *Wag the Dog* increasingly looks more like reportage and less like parody.

And this brings us back to something we have not yet finally given up on: aesthetics. Even if the preceding arguments have not permitted the deduction (as opposed to the inference) of anything intrinsically normative from aesthetics *alone*, and even if many of the doubts as to the Kantian celebration of beauty cannot be circumvented, aesthetics remains a terrain whose messiness is peculiarly attractive. There one willingly gets bogged down. But the encounter with aesthetics has been highly loaded in that it has been determined by the notion of narrative. In the first instance, it is claimed that storytelling is axiomatically the closest we get to truth... which is to say, to reality. That is, that realism, as was argued most directly in the previous chapter, should be seen as a narrative phenomenon shaped by a plurality of competing and potentially explanatory stories. In the present chapter, this claim is most explicitly and ambitiously underpinned by the appeal to death as both a fact and a category. And in the second instance, it is inferred from this that the notion of goals is essential if the teleological trope is to have any meaning. That is, both stories and goals are bracketed and much of the immediate discussion has been concerned to isolate utopian (unreachable) goals from strategic goals that reflect them imperfectly in that they attempt some expression of utopian ideals in empirical life. In this context, the earlier chapter on Freud might be seen as troubled by the overdetermining role of a singular story (albeit one with a limitless variety of expressions) for which the goal is a pregiven and unavoidable destiny, while the remarks on Kant in chapter 5 are important because his teleology, despite his elaborate taxonomy of aesthetic forms, is all telos (ultimately a deductible argument for the existence of God) and thereby indifferent to the practice and meaning of storytelling.

But the feeling does not go away that aesthetics, at least in respect of narrative, realism, and death, implies even more. It is clear from the forgoing discussion, however, that whatever might be inferred would hardly be very dependable in the short term. The plurality of storytelling and the highly sophisticated strategies of propaganda generate circumstances under which delusion, counterfeit, and sham are, initially at least, maximized. Narrative plurality underpins strategies that make even simple empirical truth judgments difficult. And this is additionally underpinned by a general media-based culture in which dominant ideology is so removed from lived lives that there is in many cases either a suspicious indifference to it—which easily breeds an intolerant no-nonsense bigotry—or a recourse to absurd inventiveness in which no story is too far-fetched not to be believed. The multiple narrative form seems, then, to generate a mesh of difficulties.

There is no way round this problem. One cannot argue for plurality and then complain that there is a lack of straightforward no-nonsense answers. Nevertheless, it does not follow from this that the dynamic multinarrative structure is wholly divested of values in that all stories are equally valid and we can choose randomly, untroubled by normative considerations. Two arguments, already mentioned and always heavily implicit, are relevant here. The first is the argument for testing and the second, and more difficult, is an argument drawn from the notion of narrative richness.

The argument for testing is self-evidently dependent on goals. It has already been discussed with respect to lesser and conditional narratives that are expressive of deeper normative and utopian values yet set goals that are, theoretically, reachable. The complex manner in which goals reached, and those not reached, are employed to evaluate the narratives, along with the deeper utopian values that imperfectly invest those narratives, is clearly crucial. However, before turning to narrative richness something more might be said about the argument for testing with respect to narrative outcomes. This will have the advantage of putting the problems that narrative richness generates into a wider historical context. Pluralism not only forces us to concede we are stuck on messy terrain. It is also a further indication that singular grand theories should be treated with suspicion. Consider one, albeit extremely important, example: the greater intellectual richness of Kuhn as opposed to Popper. This seems to be a particularly useful, if somewhat ironic, example as Kuhn is accused of getting into epistemological difficulties (his sharpest critics even accuse him of opening the door to scientific relativism—something he rightly denies[7]), while Popper has proved hugely influential precisely because he lays out a narrative account of progress in which the practice of testing (the principle of "falsifiability") takes us unproblematically on and upward, step by unambiguous step.

But the Popperian narrative leans to a singularity and, stringently pursued, would lead to a process whereby numerous babies would be thrown out with their bathwater. Implicit is the feeling that revolutionary action (while impermissible in social life, where change has to be timid and piecemeal) is the ideal in intellectual life (Popper's "great or heroic science"[8]). As a result, in intellectual matters single anomalies ideally require fundamental acts of rewriting. But when it comes to political and social affairs, there is a crisis of courage and the oppressed are left trapped in scenarios likely to prolong their misery. The chief value of this approach probably lies in its challenge to the powerful to establish the probity of their opinions. And while this is a positive characteristic, it is also an expression of a remorseless drive toward hard and fast verdicts as though the world was structured as one grand narrative, albeit experienced in a multitude of small things. In laying out the challenge to find fault (a single fault, such as Popper's single nonwhite swan, is enough) as the basis for reevaluation across the board, it simplifies reality seductively

On the other hand, Kuhn explains how knowledge is carried forward on broad and contradictory fronts. He reminds us how we cannot free ourselves from ambiguities (or anomalies) and, above all, how explanations can be both right and wrong, progressive and reactionary at the same time. Were we to keep this dynamic model in mind (and we should respect Kuhn's regret that he used the atemporal term "paradigm"[9]) we would have cause to take a more sophisticated view of the goals we set ourselves, aware that we will gain and lose over a broad topography. This would more likely teach us the value of trial and error as a plural and nondogmatic activity in which we would be regularly challenged to redefine our notion as to the relationship between that which is desirable and that which is attainable and, consequently, to consider the type and degree of imperfection that, following our actions, we would be prepared to tolerate. Furthermore, in being plural his approach is also preferred here for the—admittedly partial—reason that it is more easily married to realism as defined and employed in the previous chapter. In being plural it is also richer.

The argument drawn from narrative richness has, self-evidently, its roots in narrative plurality. But it is not identical with it. It is expressed in powerful commonsense terms when we acknowledge that things could be otherwise. Nothing is more formative of our imaginative (or repressed) lives than the awareness of that which is not the case, or has not (yet) been done, or now never will be done. Certainly we may confront this lack on a richer and more seductive level through conventional aesthetics; but it is hardly dependent on books, and the theater, and so forth. As both an emotional pull and as an intellectual speculation it is a lived part of the subject's daily life no matter how mundane that life may be. If most of us today are Willy Lomans that does not deny us the authenticity of a Lear, even if our blunders are less mighty and our suffering less thunderous.

However, the same "subjunctive" sense of what could be otherwise has been foregrounded with respect to the grander historical narrative. As such it is an antidote to extreme forms of pessimism or teleological naivete. The best exemplar of the former is the total loss of faith following the crimes of the twentieth century; of the latter the belief that history has conceptually reached the final phase viewed as a universally triumphant socioeconomic system. In the first case, the loss of faith following Auschwitz does not work solely because it is too demanding and too simple, although it is both. It fails because it is the ultimate celebration of an event that is thought to make further events worthless. It is no accident that Adorno invokes nuclear obliteration. In the second case, one notes that Fukuyama was keen on events as long as they were disabused of their customary historical significance. There were no longer any fundamental "what ifs" for Fukuyama. In that Adorno and Fukuyama lean toward a singularity there is, consequently, a further similarity between them. Neither wants to (nor should want to) go any further; Adorno because he has lost heart after seeing that everything has gone to the dogs, and Fukuyama because there is not really any need to succumb to further doubts as to fundamental historical truth. In this they are the least plural of thinkers, although Adorno has to make a colossal effort to willfully blind himself to the multifarious reality that surrounds him. Ultimately he fails and that, if anything, saves him. An increasingly troubled Fukuyama, meanwhile, is forced to acknowledge a world that is more complex and unstable than would be the case were the triumph of liberal democracy as clear to others as it is to him.

On the other hand, despite all his taxonomic precision, Samuel P. Huntington, like Kuhn, is aware that history moves forward on a board and complex front. He pays due regard to both narrative and plurality. As a result he does not give us either history as catastrophe or history as a riddle solved. But perhaps the diagram of the multipolar and multicivilizational world on page 245 of *The Clash of Civilizations*, illustrates more than he intends. Namely, that his supposedly explanatory, ordered schema, does homage to the fact that history, like his diagram, is very untidy indeed.

However, given that Huntington in respect of contradictions explicitly uses the Kuhnian term "anomalies," something should be said about the telling differences between them. Huntington, despite what he may think, cannot give anomalies the same status they have in Kuhn's account of the development of scientific knowledge. For Huntington, an anomaly is external to the systemic explanation he is laying out. It is extrinsic. True, if there were enough of them the explanatory model would (in the best Kuhnian fashion) fall apart. But they are unwelcome, and must, as in the case of the breakdown of Yugoslavia after Tito's death, be explained away. However, for Kuhn anomalies are intrinsic. They are evidence of the scientific probity of the explanatory model and the driving forces of its change. Thus, anomalies have a key role in establishing the instability and transitory nature of the model, which, as a result, emerges as a *dynamic* construct in which the adjective takes precedence over the noun. Certainly Huntington is imaginative enough as to consider future developments, but his vivid dystopian speculation at the end of *The Clash of Civilizations* is there solely to validate the model as it stands, not to suggest how it might be dismantled, let alone exposed as false.

Yet it should be admitted that this comparison between Kuhn and Huntington is in a key sense improper. Kuhn is dealing with the nature of change using abstract (if testable) knowledge merely as his raw material. Essentially it is only the dynamic practices that count. Huntington, however, is explaining the empirical world in the context of the structure of global struggles. Any such undertaking, in that it must explain the world as a set of constructs no matter how dynamically they may collide, will inevitably have to give a great many hostages to fortune as to how those constructs, even assuming they exist in the manner Huntington defines, develop.

But irrespective of how generously the net of narrative richness may be cast, no matter that it comprehensively ensnares both the grand

narrative and the imaginative life of the humblest individual, it does
not of itself give us any normative reason to set it higher than narrative paucity. A narrative that celebrated—as much classical literature
does—an incident-rich epic tale of slaughter and adventure might well be
regarded as inferior to a domestic story of a poor, but morally grounded,
woman trying to maintain standards in the grand house of rich relatives. Furthermore, it is possible to make a strong case for the aesthetic
virtue of the unpalatable. If aesthetics is indeed seen as expressive of
drives and repressions, a violent, sadistic, and/or fascist aesthetic praxis
might logically be regarded as the most potent and true expression of the
imaginative life of the subject. Aesthetics would then be regarded as the
royal road whereby the unconscious was unlocked. What then poured
out of it would be evaluated as axiomatically virtuous simply because it
is telling a truth not normally told. All of this would certainly allow us to
maintain a crude normative status for aesthetics dependent on teeming,
unrestricted heterogeneity, but enlightened normative values would only
be present ironically.

Nor can the notion of narrative richness be based on the principle that
the more narrative there is the truer the discourse will be, it being impossible to overegg the pudding...although, as was argued in chapter 3, it is
certainly the case that to forgo narrative en bloc is to end up in a blind
alley. Rather, narrative richness illustrates the importance of alternatives
played off against each other in a manner that may, following the previous
chapter, be called Brechtian. It underpins the arguments on which choices
are made, and in turn must evoke the range and significance those choices
have in the destinies of fictive characters. And on this basis it is clear that
Mansfield Park is not placed, as a result of formal considerations, in an
inferior position to a plot-rich picaresque novel. Whatever normative value
is then inferred from the conjunction of narrative and truth in the context
of aesthetics is wholly dependent on the nature of those choices. And it is
here that death is seen, conceptually and functionally, as the critical category, not least because it will permit of some normative inference.

The argument for the special status of death begins, as this book did,
with its bedrock vindication of narrative. Hemingway talks of "true-story"
telling. This implies goals and goals imply utopian thinking. Of decisive
significance has been the additional claim that death (Hemingway's self-
evident goal) has a peculiar (truthful) narrative status because it, paradoxically, allows the individual to spring the boundaries of his own temporal
experience of the world. This has been paralleled in the last pages by the
notion of narrative richness which has also been shown to be equally applicable to the imaginative life of the individual and the grander history of
the tribe.

Whatever normative inferences are then subsequently produced out of aesthetics are a consequence of this parallel. If, as has been argued in this chapter, death logically demands a respect on the part of the individual for the lives of others, then narrative richness demands the same. And, as was illustrated with Austen and Brontë in chapter 3, this can be strikingly evident even when the social terrain and the events described seem exceptionally constricted. Therefore, it is not surprising that aesthetics as both a narrative and an imaginative activity attains, as a category, a normative gloss, irrespective of whether the stories it tells are life-enhancing or life-despairing.

But aesthetics is not restricted to what is customarily regarded as "art," let alone high art. Sport, as we have seen, has a privileged place. But this is not because one wants to divest aesthetics of formal characteristics so that the net can be cast, on postmodern principle, in as wide and nonhierarchical a manner as possible. Rather, sport takes on a special role because it is productive of (utopian) telos; it is the one characteristic—dynamic and formal—that is given precedence over all other aesthetic considerations. And narrative significance crops up here for the last time because it has yet to be fully exhausted of meaning.

In sport, telos, competing stories, and aesthetic satisfaction are exceptionally present. Of particular importance has been fairness, divided into a conditional notion obedient to rules, and a deeper and ideal notion that may legitimately violate them because the story it tells is more aesthetically satisfying and thereby fairer. In view of the argument laid out in this chapter, it is now inferred that the *aesthetic* superiority of the deeper narrative is no less expressive of its normative superiority than the universal values it enshrines. This can be best illustrated when the phenomenon of the impeccable narrative is once again considered, but this time in respect of its violation.

Sport realizes objective judgments that make it possible to evaluate the success of the narrative that triumphs and the failures of the ones that did not. Times run, distances thrown, heights jumped, and so forth, are not interpretative matters. Nor are points scored, although here, because the narrative is so obviously more complex, the aesthetic richness is much greater and encourages players and spectators to not only imagine how things might have been otherwise, but also to conclude that, in particular circumstances, it would have been more aesthetically/morally satisfying if they had been. This also explains why sports that pit players or teams in direct aggressive/creative confrontation (such as football) are more popular than track and field where the rival competitors have parallel or sequential noncombative roles. Moreover, the narrative richness that is produced by sports such as football often makes its aesthetic character most clear in that it longs for perfection. As was mentioned in the previous chapter, there is a utopian moment—that is of the perfect narrative having apparently triumphed—which is clear from the language and reactions of those involved. And yet even this perfection may be trumped. Greater accomplishments, more blissful victories, are always possible. That sports fans should express a longing for the utopian telos—which indeed will make several of them, when they believe they have reached that point, declare that they could now die happy—is indicative of how deeply ethical the aesthetic narrative can be. This is best appreciated when the narrative form is betrayed.

There are certain so-called sports that aim at a false telos and a fake utopia. They are arbitrarily judged by teams of supposed experts and marks are awarded for categories with titles such as "artistic impression." The business has become so disreputable that the terminology is frequently altered in the forlorn hope that changes in packaging will disguise the intrinsic fraud. The consequence of these arbitrary marking systems has been a litany of cheating. But this has not been cheating (Maradona-like) in the service of the deeper notion of aesthetic fairness. Rather, it has been motivated by nationalist corruption and/or bribery, and constitutes an attempt to undermine *both* rule-obedient and aesthetically deep-seated forms of fairness.

Above all, these types of "sports" (ice-dancing, rhythmic gymnastics, synchronized swimming, etc.,) permit absolute perfection. In this, they allow the spectators to imagine that an indisputable, and not to be exceeded, utopian point has been attained. Such is the power of this—although even the most naive spectator knows it is fake—that judges are put under massive pressure by spectators to award the perfect (absolute) score. The most famous case occurred when the ice-dancers Jane Torvill and Christopher Dean scored perfect 6.0s in all categories for their "Bolero" routine during the 1984 Winter Olympics in Sarajevo. Although this is a (aesthetic and normative) betrayal of sport, it is remarkably potent. The fiction thus cobbled together has garnered substantial TV audiences who get all the pleasure of art reduced to kitsch (costumes, music are a feature) while claiming, fraudulently, that the business has the authenticity (that is the *realism*) of sport.

The growth of these entertainment sports is, however, a product of utopian, narratively shaped, longing, in that they reveal how easily we are seduced by apparent perfection packaged in a *reachable* telos, even though death, and narrative, and utopia have been manifestly debased. Above all, these fake sports trivialize aesthetics—that extrinsic glue that binds death, narrative, and utopia, while not being a necessary part of any of them. In doing so, fake sports unintentionally reveal the deep productive nature of aesthetics and the moral superiority of true narrative fairness.

However, it is possible for popular culture, independent of sport, to tackle narrative, truth, universalism, and rich fulfilled lives. One example will serve. It is the last anecdotal illustration of this book and although a modest one, it does not shortchange its overriding themes.

Robin and Marian (1976) is a beguiling film directed by Richard Lester and written by James Goldman. At first sight it is merely a romantic comedy with a poignant ending. In fact, although never portentous, it is somewhat more. It is another go at narrative made beneficent in that the actors get a second chance. Just as Anne Elliot in *Persuasion* is allowed to repeat the story so as not to make the mistakes she made the first time and thereby attain an implicit triumph over death, so are Robin Hood and Maid Marian allowed another attempt at happiness following his return to Sherwood Forest after a career in the service of King Richard. The glamor of the previous adventure-rich history is the constant commentary of the, apparently, more mundane story as the two lovers cope with being old. A deal of light wit is in play. When Sean Connery carries the very petite Audrey Hepburn across a river he is quite convinced she has put on a few pounds.

However Lester cannot resist the heroic narrative and the old adventures are repeated. And given that the narrative is beneficent, there is no option but to repeat them triumphantly. The climax is a massive fight between Robin and the Sheriff of Nottingham, which ends with Robin victorious but wounded. Marion duly tends him in her cell high in an isolated tower. However she chooses to kill him, and also takes the poison herself. He does not realize what is going on until he has drunk and is, at first, horrified. But then he sees the justice of the *Liebestod* she has engineered. He admits that the day has been perfect, that he will never have such a day again. Like her, he knows there is no further narrative that they can play out that will be comparable, and therefore sees in a death chosen for him in a timely way the perfect utopian moment. Lester and Goldman even get away with Sean Connery shooting an arrow out of the window of the cell to mark the place where he will be buried.

Death, freely chosen when there is no conventionally accepted reason why it should be chosen, has seldom had a more benign aesthetic expression. We, of course, are hardly obliged to do likewise, not least because their narrative is most assuredly not ours. And having no lived recourse to impeccable invented narratives, it is highly unlikely that we will ever experience telos in such a form. The choices we make as to the narratives of own lives will be both more mundane and more complicated. In the meantime we might question Solzhenitsyn's bleak judgment as to the intentions of God, the status of humanism, and, above all, the nature of death. For death is the great universal that makes us human, disposed to realize not only our own destinies as best we can but to respect those of others. It gives us goals, both subjective and tribal, and forces us to vindicate what we do to reach them. Therefore, it is able to make out of us creatures that are always to some degree creative. And when all these qualities come together, it also challenges us to be moral.

Notes

1 AN OVERVIEW

1. Adorno, Theodor. *Negative Dialectics* Translation by Dennis Redmond 2001 (from the web) http://members.efn.org/~dredmond/ndtrans.html. "Dying Today" pp. 361–366.
2. Benjamin, Walter. "Der Erzähler. Betrachtungen zum Werk Nikolai Lesskows" in Sebastain Kleinschmidt *Allegorien, kulturelle Erfahrung. Ausgewählte Schriften* 1920–1940 Verlag Philipp Reclam jun. Leipzig (1984), pp. 390–391, my translation.
3. Ricoeur, Paul. *Time and Narrative* University of Chicago Press, Chicago (1984) Vol. 1, p. 4.
4. Ibid. (Vol. 1) pp. 110–111.
5. Ibid. (Vol. 3) p. 115.
6. Benjamin (1984) op cit., p. 390, my translation.
7. Peukert, Detlev J. K. "Der Genesis der 'Endlösung' aus dem Geiste der Wissenschaft" in *Zerstörung des moralischen Selbstbewußtseins: Chance oder Gefährdung. Praktische Philosophie in Deutschland nach dem Nationalsozialismus.* Herausgegeben von Forum für Philosophie, Bad Homburg. Suhrkamp, Frankfurt am Main (1988) pp. 30–33.
8. Fukuyama, Francis. *The End of History and the Last Man* The Free Press, New York (1992) p. XI.
9. White, Hayden. *Metahistory. The Historical Imagination in Nineteenth-Century Europe* John Hopkins University Press, Maryland (1973) p. XI.
10. Jameson, Fredric. *The Political Unconsciousness. Narrative as a Socially Symbolic Act* Methuen, London (1981) p. 289.
11. Althusser, Louis. *Essays in Self Criticism* NLB, London (1976) p. 107.
12. See, for instance, Eagleton, Terry. *Marxism and Literary Criticism* Methuen, London (1977) pp. 56–57.
13. Marx, Karl. "Economic and Philosophical Manuscripts" in *Karl Marx: Early Writings* introduced by Lucio Colletti. Harmondsworth, (1975) p. 365. Quoted Eagleton (1990) p. 204.
14. Anderson, Perry. *In the Tracks of Historical Materialism* NLB (1980) pp. 82–83.

15. Ibid., p. 246.
16. See, for instance, Baxandall L. and Morawski S., *Marx and Engels on Art and Literature* Telos Press, St. Louis Milwaukee, WI (1973).
17. Eagleton, Terry. *Against the Grain. Essays 1975–1985* Verso, London (1986) p. 2.
18. Eagleton, Terry. *Criticism and Ideology* NLB, London (1976) p. 175.
19. See note 13.
20. Eagleton, Terry. *The Ideology of the Aesthetic* Basil Blackwell, Oxford (1990) p. 224.
21. See Selsam, H. and Martel, H. (eds.) *Reader in Marxist Philosophy* International Publisher, New York (1980) pp. 202–204.
22. Brooks, Jeffrey. *Thank You Comrade Stalin! Soviet Public Culture from Revolution to Cold War* Princeton University Press, Princeton, New Jersey (2000) p. 109.
23. Ibid., p. 112.
24. Berlin, Isaiah. *Conversations with Isaiah Berlin* Edited by Ramin Jahanbegloo. Peter Halban, London (1992) p. 143.
25. Ibid., p. 203.
26. Judt, Tony *Reappraisals: Reflections on the Forgotten Twentieth Century* The Penguin Press, New York (2008) pp. 116–127.
27. Eagleton, Terry (1986) op. cit., p. 84.
28. However, see Rose, Margaret A. *Marx's Lost Aesthetic. Karl Marx and the Visual Arts* Cambridge University Press (1984) for an alternative account emphasizing thematic links between early aesthetics and Marx's later ideas, especially with regard to alienation.
29. Ricoeur (1984) op. cit. (Vol. 1) p. 124. My emphasis.
30. Ibid. (Vol. 1) p. 37. It is interesting in this context that Ricoeur quotes Frank Kermode to the effect that "to develop a character means more narration, and to develop a plot means enriching a character." Frankly, I am not convinced of this but I imagine many traditional literary critics are.
31. Jameson, Fredric. *The Ideology of Theory. Essays 1971–1986. Vol. 1. Situations of Theory* University of Minnesota Press, Minneapolis (1988) pp. 102–103.
32. Ricoeur (1984) op. cit. (Vol. 1) p. 124.
33. See, for instance, Rother, Rainer. *Die Gegenwart der Geschichte. Ein Versuch über Film und zeitgenössische Literatur* J. B: Metzlersche Verlagsbuchhandlung, Stuttgart.(1990) p. 4 and p. 150.
34. Ricoeur (1984) op. cit. (Vol. 2) p. 28.
35. Lyotard, Jean-François. *The Postmodern Condition: A Report on Knowledge* Manchester University Press, Manchester (1984) p. XXIV.
36. Belsey, Catherine and Moore, Jane. (eds.) *The Feminist Reader: Essays in Gender and the Politics of Literary Criticism* Basingstoke, Macmillan http://www.macmillaneducation.com/ Education (1989) p. 14.
37. See Toril, Moi. *Sexual and Textual Politics: Feminist Literary Theory* Methuen, London (1985) p. 163.
38. See "Women's Time" in *The Kristeva Reader* Eited by Toril Moi. Basil Blackwell, Oxford (1986) p. 191.

39. Ibid., p. 192.
40. Irigaray, Luce. *This Sex Which Is Not One* Cornell University Press, Ithaca (1985) p. 24.
41 Ibid., p. 24.
42. Cixous, Hélène. "The Laugh of Medusa" in *New French Feminisms. An Anthology* Marks, Elaine and de Courtivron, Isabelle. (eds.) University of Massachusetts Press (1980) p. 256.
43. Ibid., p. 246.
44. Ibid., pp. 259–260.
45. Ibid., pp. 252–253.
46. Ibid., p. 252.
47. Humm, Maggie. *A Reader's Guide to Contemporary Feminist Literary Criticism* Harvester, England (1994) p. 296.
48. See Marks, Elaine and de Courtivron, Isabelle (1980) op. cit., p. 153.
49. See Eagleton, Mary (ed.) *Feminist Literary Theory. A Reader* Basil Blackwell, Oxford, England (approved) (1990) p. 231.
50. Benstock, Shari. (ed.) *Feminist Issues in Literary Scholarship* Indiana University Press, Bloomington and Indianapolis, Indiana (1987) p. 52.
51. Ibid., p. 117.

2 Marxist Humanism

1. Jameson, Fredric. *The Ideology of Theory. Essays 1971–1986 Vol. 1: Situations of Theory.* University of Minnesota Press, Minneapolis (1988) p. 110.
2. *The New York Review of Books*: June 11, 2009.
3. Daniel, Yergin and Joseph, Stanislaw. *The Commanding Heights: The Battle Between Government and the Marketplace That Is Remaking the Modern World* Simon and Schuster, New York (1998). Quoted in "The New Demon" by Benjamin M. Friedman *The New York Review of Books*: October 8, 1998.
4. Hegel, G. W. F. *Reason in History* The Library of Liberal Arts, Bobbs-Merrill, New York (1953) p. 54.
5. Ibid., pp. 50–51.
6. See Selsam, H. and Martel, H. (eds.) *Reader in Marxist Philosophy* International Publisher, New York (1980) p. 305.
7. Marx, Karl. and Engels, Friedrich. *The German Ideology* Lawrence and Wishart, London (1977) p. 54.
8. Cohen, Gerald Allan. *Karl Marx's Theory of History. A Defense* Clarendon Press, Oxford (1978) p. 133.
9. Marx and Engels. (1977) op. cit., p. 117.
10. Ibid., p. 54 emphasis added.
11. Auxter, Thomas. *Kant's Moral Teleology* Mercer University Press, Macon GA (1982) pp. 6–7.
12. Ibid., p. 169.

13. Ibid., p. 78.
14. Ibid., p. 10. The reference is to "Die Metaphysik der Sitten" *Kants gesammelte Schriften* Volumes 1–9 Berlin. Königliche Preussische Akademie der Wissenschaften. (1902.) Volume 6, p. 386.
15. Ibid., (Auxter) p. 173.
16. Hegel (1953) op. cit., p. 83, emphasis added.
17. Dowling, William, C. *Jameson, Althusser, Marx: An Introduction to the Political Unconscious* Methuen, London (1984) p. 55.
18. Althusser, Louis. *Essays in Self Criticism* NLB, London (1976) p. 49.
19. Ibid., p. 53.
20. Ibid., p. 107.
21. Engels's letter to Joseph Bloch (1980) quoted in Selsam, H. and Martel, H. p. 204.
22. Lukács, Georg. *History and Class Consciousness* The MIT Press, Cambridge, MA (1977) p. 27. My emphasis.
23. Ibid., p. 66.
24. Lyotard, Jean-François and Thébaud, Jean-Loup. *Just Gaming Minneapolis (1985)* p. 59.
25. See Selsam, H. Martel, H. (1980) op. cit., p 289 and passim.
26. Ibid., p. 308. My emphasis
27. Ibid., p. 305.
28. Eagleton, Terry. *The Ideology of the Aesthetic* Basil Blackwell, Oxford (1990) p. 371.
29. Habermas, Jürgen. "Erläuterungen zum Begriff des kommunikativen Handelns' (1982) in *Vorstudien und Ergänzungen zur Theorie des kommunikativen Handelns* Suhrkamp Frankfurt am Main (1984) p. 606. My translation.
30. Ibid., p. 606. My translation.
31. Apel, Karl-Otto. "Ist die Ethik der idealen Kommunikationsgemeinschaft eine Utopie?" in *Utopieforschung: Interdisziplinäre Studien zur neuzeitlichen Utopie* Herausgegeben von Wilhelm Voßkamp, Metzler – Stuttgart (1982) Band 1 p. 344. He points out that as every participant in the discourse is compelled to "anticipate" an "ideal form of communication" a transcendental element expressive of a utopian ideal is unavoidable. My translation.
32. Kuhlmann, Wolfgang. "Philosophie und Rekonstruktive Wissenschaft: Bemerkungen zu Jürgen Habermas' Theorie des kommunikativen Handelns" in *Zeitschrift für philosophische Forschung* 40 (1986) p. 232. My translation.
33. Ibid., p. 230. My translation.
34. Ibid., p. 234. My translation.
35. Eagleton, Terry. *After Theory* Allen Lane, London (2003) p. 169.
36. Habermas, Jürgen. *Glauben und Wissen Suhrkamp* Verlag, Frankfurt am Main (2001). All further references are in parenthesis in the text. Translations are mine.
37. Behind Habermas's article is a paper on cloning by the philosopher Peter Sloterdijk: "Regeln fur den Menschenpark : Ein Antwortschreiben zum Brief über den Humanismus" (Rules for the Human Theme-Park: A Reply to

the Letter on Humanism) July 1998. This caused a considerable furore, but Habermas at first took no public position. However, Sloterdijk published a letter (Die Zeit, September 2, 1999) accusing Habermas of agitating against him. The tone of the letter has been called petulant: "you have talked about me with numerous people, never with me."

38. See Frankfurter Allgemeinen Zeitung. May 31, 2003 and Borradori, Giovanna. *Philosophy in a Time of Terror: Dialogues with Jürgen Habermas and Jacques Derrida* University of Chicago Press, Chicago (2003).

39. The full quotation in the original is: "Dass der Gott, der die Liebe ist, in Adam und Eva freie Wesen schafft, die ihm gleichen, muss man nicht glauben, um zu verstehen, was mit Ebenbildlichkeit gemeint ist. Liebe kann es ohne Erkenntnis in einem anderen, Freiheit ohne gegenseitige Anerkennung nicht geben."

40. Dews, Peter. *Logics of Disintegration* Verso, London (1987) p. 242.

41. See point 37.

42. See Chapter 1, note 13

43. Kuhlmann (1986) op. cit. p. 231, goes to some pains to point out that by permitting a "fallibility" principle Habermas is inevitably caught in a trap whereby he cannot ground any of his claims for discourse ethics unambiguously, including— paradoxically—the fallibility principle itself. That is, it too must be seen as potentially fallible.

44. Popper, Karl. "Utopia and Violence" in The *Hibbert Journal* 16, January 2, 1948, p. 115.

45. Berlin, Isaiah. *Conversations with Isaiah Berlin* Edited by. Ramin Jahanbegloo. Peter Halban, London (1992) p. 106.

3   Women and Writing

1. Nye, Andrea. *Feminist Theory and the Philosophies of Man* Croom Helm, London (1988) p. 199.

2. Irigaray Luce. *This Sex Which Is Not One* Cornell University Press, Ithaca (1985) p. 68.

3. Ibid., p. 87.

4. Ibid., p. 24.

5. Ibid., p. 213.

6. Cixous, Hélène "The Laugh of Medusa" in *New French Feminisms. An Anthology* Marks, Elaine and de Courtivron, Isabella (eds.) University of Massachusetts Press USA (1980) p. 260.

7. Gilbert, Sandra M. and Gubar, Susan. *The Madwoman in the Attic* Yale University Press, New Haven, CT (1979).

8. Auden, W. H. *Selected Poems* Edited by Edward Mendelson, Great Britain Faber and Faber (1979) pp. 150–51.

9. Gilbert and Gubar (1978) op. cit., p. 360.

10. Showalter, Elaine. *A Literature of Their Own: British Women Novelists from Brontë to Lessing* Princeton University Press New Jersey (1977) p. 28.
11. Woolf, Virginia. *A Room of One's Own (from the* web) Chapter 4.
12. Woolf, Virginia. *The Common Reader* (from the web) Chapter 14.
13. Moers, Ellen. *Literary Women* The Women's Press London (1978) pp. 157–158.
14. Said, Edward. *Culture and Imperialism* Alfred A. Knopf. New York (1994) p. 96.
15. Barthes, Roland. "The New Citroen" in *Mythologies* Jonathan Cape, London (1972) p. 88f.
16. Woolf, Virginia. *A Room of One's Own (from the* web) Chapter 4.
17. Moers (1978) op. cit., p. 71.
18. Mitchell, Juliet. "Gender and Genre" in *Feminist Literary Theory. A Reader* Edited by Mary Eagleton, Basil Blackwell, Oxford (1990) p. 101.
19. Jacobus, Mary. *Reading Woman. Essays in Feminist Criticism* Columbia University Press, New York (1986) see "The Buried Letter": *Villette.*
20. Woolf , Virginia. *The Common Reader* (from the web) Chapter 14.
21. Moers (1978) op. cit., p. 81.
22. Woolf Virginia. *Women and Writing* Introduction by Michele Barrett. The Women's Press, London (1979) p. 129.
23. Humm, Maggie. *A Reader's Guide to Contemporary Feminist Literary Criticism* Harvester, England (1994) p. 208.
24. Furman, Nelly. "The Politics of Language: Beyond the Gender Principle?" in *Making a Difference: Feminist Literary Criticism* Edited by Greene, Gayle and Coppéla, Kahn, Methuen, London and New York (1985) p. 67.
25. Mitchell, Juliet in Mary Eagleton (1990) op. cit., p. 101.
26. Jacobus (1986) op. cit., p. 202.
27. Felski, Rita. *Beyond Feminist Aesthetics. Feminist Literature and Social Change* Harvard University Press, Cambridge MA (1989) p. 19.
28. Ibid., p. 80.
29. Kaplan, Cora. "Pandora's Box: Subjectivity, Class and Sexuality in Socialist Feminist Criticism" In Greene and Kahn (1985) op. cit., p.148.

4   Freud

Sources and translations for the Wolf Man and *Totem* and *Taboo*

A. In the case of the Wolf Man the collection prepared in English by Muriel Gardiner is used:

The Wolf-Man by the Wolf-Man with the Case of the Wolf-Man by Sigmund Freud
    Edited by Muriel Gardiner, Basic Books, New York (1971). This is indicated in the text proper by G followed by page number.

The German original is referred to below: see Footnote 22 for details.
The reference for the Wolf Man case in the Standard Edition, Hogarth Press is
Vol 17,: pp. 7–122.

B. In the case of *Totem and Taboo* the Standard Edition is, in general, used: Vol
13,: pp. 1–162. This is indicated in the text proper as F followed by page number.
However, in several places I have used my own translation. When this occurs it is
footnoted and references are given for both the English, as above, and the German.
The German edition used is:

Sigmund Freud. *Totem und Tabu. Einige Übereinstimmungen im Seelenleben der
Wilden und der Neurotiker* Fischer Bücherei, Frankfurt am Main (1970). This is
indicated in the notes below as Freud (1970).

1. Freud, Sigmund. *Standard Edition* Hogarth Press Vol. 2, p. 160. London (1964).
2. Freud, Sigmund. *Die Traumdeutung* Studienausgabe Band II Fischer
   Taschenbuch Verlag, Frankfurt am Main (2000) pp. 21–23. My translation.
3. Freud, Sigmund. *The Complete Letters of Sigmund Freud to Wilhelm Fliess
   1887–1907* Masson, Moussaieff (Editor and translator.) Harvard University
   Press, Cambridge, MA (1985) p. 243.
4. See note A above.
5. Kant, Immanuel. *The Critique of Judgment* in "Great Books of the Western
   World" (Editor in Chief, Robert Maynard Hutchins) Vol. 42, "Kant".
   Translated by James Creed Meredith, Encyclopedia Britannica Inc., Chicago
   (1952) 85, pp. 588–589.
6. Masson (1985) op. cit., p. 11. My emphasis.
7. Freud (2000) Band II op. cit., p. 320.
8. Ibid., p. 346.
9. Ibid., p. 524.
10. Masson (1985) op. cit., p. 398.
11. See *The Purloined Poe: Lacan, Derrida and Psychoanalytic Reading* Edited
    by John P. Muller and William J. Richardson, Maryland John Hopkins
    University Press (1988). For the Wolf Man's reference to Dupin, see Gardiner
    (1971) pp. 146–147.
12. Spence, Donald P. *The Rhetorical Voice of Psychoanalysis. Displacement of
    Evidence by Theory* Harvard University Press USA (1994) p. 89.
13. Masson (1985) op. cit., pp. 264–266.
14. Ibid., pp. 270–273.
15. Crews, Frederick. *The Critics Bear It Away: American Fiction and the Academy*
    Random House, New York (1992) pp. 8–9.
16. See Spence (1994) op. cit., pp. 87–8, pp 181–2. and Spence, Donald,
    P. *Narrative Truth and Historical Truth. Meaning and Interpretation in
    Psychoanalysis* Norton and Co., New York (1982).
17. Brooks, Peter. *Reading for the Plot. Design and Intention in Narrative* Clarendon
    Press, Oxford (1984) p. 277.
18. Freud (2000) Band II op. cit., p. 266. My translation.
19. Ibid., p. 269.
20. Freud employed the jig-saw analogy himself. See, for instance, *Standard
    Edition* Vol. 3, p. 205 and Vol. 23,: p. 17.

21. See Spence (1994) op. cit., pp. 38–39.
22. The original German is not quite as bold as the standard translation above. Freud talks of his doubts concerning the acceptance of such an observation of the child's and not "of this observation." Nonetheless, the caveat above regarding the invalidity of implying that the interpretation is anything other than his discovery remains. See Freud, Sigmund *Zwei Kinderneurosen Studienausgabe Band VIII*. S Fischer Verlag, Frankfurt am Main (2000) p. 158.
23. See note 3.
24. See Freud (2000) Band VIII op. cit., p. 169.
25. These objections can certainly be avoided if it is assumed that Serge unconsciously inserted the scene, just as he, presumably, suppressed the sight of the primal scene so that he had no conscious memory of it. However, I suggest that the passage quoted above in the text reads as though the act of "insertion" were knowing.
26. In this instance, the standard translation employed above underlines my argument rather more than the original. Freud does not employ here either the word "fact" or any direct synonym. Rather he uses the third person singular: "That our little boy...produced a stool is to be judged as establishing," and so forth. Nonetheless, it is clear that even this formulation is dependent on the production of the stool having the status of an undisputed given. See Freud (2000) Band VIII op. cit., p. 195. My translation.
27. See *Freud's Case Studies* Edited by Barry Magid, The Analytic Press, London (1993) for accounts of how the fathers of Dora and "Little Hans" actively colluded with Freud in the analyszes. Although it should be noted that Dora's father would have been disappointed that Freud believed her when she claimed that the father's friend was trying to seduce her. However, the hermeneutic activity is preserved in that Freud concluded that Dora unconsciously desired the seduction attempt.
28. Freud, Sigmund. *Moses and Monotheism* Standard Edition (1964) Vol. 23, p. 131.
29. Naturally no such evidence can exist, therefore it is scarcely legitimate of us to demand that it be produced. Yet, it should not be forgotten that evidence in the case of Freud can never be direct. It is always the product of a process of interpretation based on the principle that what one superficially sees is misleading. The danger for the Freudian analyst/sociologist/anthropologist is that he will prove to be naive and literal. To be shown to be interpreting at anything approaching the level of the self-evident is to fail to get at the hidden scientific truth. One would, axiomatically, be wrong. For instance, in the Wolf Man dream night signifies day, the stillness of the wolves the violence of the parents' actions, the prominent tails the missing (i.e., castrated) "maternal" penis, and so forth.
30. See note B above.
31. See Freud (1970) op. cit (see note B above) p. 158.
32. By the time he has got to *Moses and Monotheism* (late 1930s) Freud feels able (compelled) to question the (literal) single event. Summarizing *Totem and*

Taboo, he writes: "The story is told in an enormously condensed form, as though it happened on a single occasion, while in fact it covered thousands of years and was repeated countless times during that long period." Standard Edition Vol. 23,: p. 81. This may be more credible, but it should be noted that Freud will not give up the fundamental assumptions of *Totem and Taboo*, no matter how violently he has been criticized. He is merely giving us the primal scene repeated. It is still the same scene. Freud's problem with *Moses and Monotheism* is the increased anthropological knowledge of the intervening 25 years. Some concessions are now necessary. For instance, he suddenly acknowledges the possibility of a matriarchy, which he slips in following the initial, if now plural, "act" of parricide. See *Standard Edition* Vol. 23,: p. 132. But the fundamental notions on which the Oedipal trauma rests remain uncontested, despite the criticisms of others.

33. The standard English translation turns the German impersonal pronoun "One will object to this that ..." into the simple "To this it may be objected that." However, the original is clearer with respect to the manner in which someone (the reader?) is doing the objecting. See Freud (1970) op. cit., p. 177, and F p. 160, note B above.

34. The standard English translation once again does not do justice to the manner in which Freud moves from voice to voice, employing doubt only to extinguish it with grand formulations. See: Freud (1970) op. cit., p.179 and F p. 161.

35. Benjamin, Walter. "Über den Begriff der Geschichte" in *Allegorien kultureller Erfahrungen Ausgewählte Schriften 1920–1940* Verlag Philipp Reclam jun. Leipzig (1984) pp. 160–161.

36. Marcuse, Herbert. *Eros and Civilization. A Philosophical Inquiry into Freud* Beacon Press, Boston, MA (1955) p. 58.

37. Ibid., p. 93.

38. Ibid., p. 143.

39. See Freud (1970) op. cit. On p. 39, he suggests a possible "inherited psychical element." By p. 176, he is compelled to assert that a part of the psychic material has to be passed down from "generation to generation," and that "no generation is in a position to hide meaningful psychic precedents from the coming one." My translations.

40. *Standard Edition* Vol. 23: 98–100 and Footnote 102.

41. Ibid., pp. 257–266.

42. Freud, Sigmund. *Civilization and Its Discontents* The International Psychoanalytical Library No 17. Translated by Joan Riviere, edited by James Strachey, Hogarth Press, London (1973) p. 62.

43. Ibid., p. 23.

44. Ibid., p. 50.

45. Ibid., p. 49.

46. Ibid., p. 50.

47. Ibid., p. 52.

48. Brooks (1984) op. cit., p. 278.

49. Spence (1982) op. cit., p. 187.

5 PHILOSOPHY AND FATHERLAND

1. Adorno, Theodor. *Negative Dialectics* Translation by Dennis Redmond 2001 (from the web) URL http://members.efn.org/~dredmond/ndtrans.html Hereafter in the text above (ND followed by section number). In this case (ND 313–315).

2. Kuhn, Thomas S. *The Road Since Structure. Philosophical Essays 1970–1993* with an autobiographical interview. Edited by James Conant and John Haugeland. University of Chicago Press, Chicago and London (2000) p. 98 and p. 115.

3. Kant, Immanuel. *The Critique of Judgement* (from the web) The translation is by James Creed Meredith. Hereafter the section number is given in parentheses, as here (§ 8). If there is no section number a page reference is given for *Great Books of the Western World* (Editor in Chief, Robert Maynard Hutchins) Vol. 42. Translated by James Creed Meredith, Encyclopedia Britannica Inc., Chicago (1952).

4. Freud, Sigmund. *Die Traumdeutung* Studienausgabe Band II, Fischer Taschenbuch Verlag, Frankfurt am Main (2000) p. 90.

5. Horkheimer, Max und Adorno, Theodor. *Dialektik der Aufklärung* S. Fischer Verlag, Frankfurt am Main (1969) p. 106. My translation.

6. See chapter 2 note 12.

7. See note 1.

8. See Williams, Raymond. *Drama from Ibsen to Brecht* Chatto and Windus, London (1971) pp. 277–290 and: Williams, Raymond. *Politics and Letters* NLB and Verso Editions, London (1981) p. 218f.

9. Bloch et al. *Aesthetics and Politics* Translation Editor Ronald Taylor. Verso, London (1980) p. 194.

10. Horkheimer, Max und Adorno, Theodor. (1969) op. cit. See "Nachwort".

11. Ibid., p. 289.

12. Bloch et. al. (1980) op. cit., p. 147.

13. Beetham, David. *Marxists in the Face of Fascism* Manchester University Press Manchester (1983) p. 110.

14. Ibid., p.18.

15. Later Adorno was to rationalize this in a passage written in 1935 and added to *Minima Moralia*. See Adorno, Theodor, *Minima Moralia*, Translator Dennis Redmond (from the Web) Section 123. http://www.efn.org/~dredmond /MinimaMoralia.html

16. Ibid., Section 143.

17. Schopenhauer, Arthur. *The World as Will and Representation* New York, Dover (1966) Vol. 1, pp. 262–263.

18. Nietzsche, Friedrich. *The Birth of Tragedy out of the Spirit of Music* (from the web) http://records.viu.ca/~johnstoi/nietzsche/tragedy_all.htm Translation prepared by Ian C. Johnston of Malaspina University-College, Nanaimo, BC Canada. Revised 2003. Section 5.

19. Ibid., Section 22.

20. Habermas, Jürgen. "Wege der Detranszendentalisierung.Von Kant zu Hegel und zurück" in *Wahrheit und Rechtfertigung: Philosophische Aufsätze*. Suhrkamp, Frankfurt am Main (1999).
21. Ibid., p. 195. My translation.
22. Ibid., pp. 226–227.
23. Nietzsche, Friedrich. *On the Genealogy of Morals. A Polemical Tract* (from the web) http://records.viu.ca/~johnstoi/nietzsche/genealogytofc.htm prepared by Ian Johnston of Malaspina University-College, Nanaimo, BC Canada. From First Essay, Section 16. The original German is "Napoleon, diese Synthesis von Unmensch und Übermensch."
24. Robespierre, Maximilien. "The Cult of the Supreme Being" in *The Internet Modern History Sourcebook* (from the web). http://www.fordham.edu/halsall/mod/robespierre-supreme.asp No translator given, but © Paul Halsall. August 1997.
25. "Noch einmal: Zum Verhältnis von Theorie und Praxis" in Habermas (1999) op. cit., p. 331. My translation.
26 Nieztsche (Note 23) op. cit., First Essay, Section 11.
27. Ibid., Second Essay, Section 23.
28. Hoffmann, Peter. *Claus Schenk Graf von Stauffenberg und seine Brüder* Deutsche Verlags-Anstalt, Stuttgart (1992) pp. 337–338.
29. See, for instance, Berlin, Isaiah. "The Decline of Utopian Ideas in the West" in *The Crooked Timber of Humanity: Chapters in the History of Ideas* John Murray, London (1990) where the Kantian element in this Sturm und Drang celebration of the Will and the native is underlined.
30. Fichte, Johann Gottlieb. *Addresses to the German Nation* Thirteenth Address (from the web). Source given is Johann Gottlieb Fichte *Addresses to the German Nation George A. Kelly (ed.) New York: Harper Torch Books, (1968)* pp. 190–198.
31. Ibid.
32. Ibid.
33. Craig, Gordon A. *The Politics of the Prussian Army 1640–1945* Oxford, Clarendon Press (1955) p. 48.
34. Ibid., p. 239f.
35. For the Nazis and the total work of art see, in particular: Zimmerman, Michael E. *Heidegger's Confrontation with Modernity. Technology, Politics and Art Indiana* University Press, Bloomington (1990) p. 101 passim.
36. Benjamin, Walter. "Das Kunstwerk im Zeitalter seiner technischen Reproduzierbarkeit" (Zweite Fassung) in Sebastain Kleinschmidt *Allegorien, kultureller Erfahrung. Ausgewählte Schriften 1920–1940* Verlag Philipp Reclam jun. Leipzig (1984) p. 433. My translation.
37. Nevin, Thomas. *Ernst Jünger and Germany. Into the Abyss, 1914–1945* Duke University Press, Durham, NC USA (1996) p. 45.
38. Fischer, Klaus P. *History and Prophecy. Oswald Spengler and the Decline of the West* Peter Lang, New York (1989) p. 39.
39. Jünger quoted Nevin (1996) op. cit., p. 74.

40. Wolin, Richard. *The Seduction of Unreason. The Intellectual Fascination with Fascism from Nietzsche to Postmodernism* Princeton University Press, New Jersey (2004) p. 57.
41. Spengler quoted in Fischer (1989) op. cit., p. 114.
42. Ibid., p. 119.
43. Ibid., pp. 117–118.
44. Heldt, Guido. "Hardly Heroes: Composers as a Subject in National Socialist Cinema" in *Music and Nazis. Art under Tyranny, 1933–1945* Edited by Michael H. Kater and Albrecht Riethmüller. Laaber-Verlag, Laaber (2003) p. 129.
45. See Hoffman (1992) op. cit., p. 448.
46. Kater, Michael H. and Riethmüller, Albrecht (eds.) *Music and Nazis. Art Under Tyranny, 1933–1945* Laaber-Verlag, Laaber (2003) p. 22.
47. On November 6, 1932, the last election before Hitler was appointed chancellor the KPD received 16.9% of the vote. See: Fowkes, Ben. Com*munism in Germany Under the Weimar Republic Macmillan,* London (1984) p. 169.
48. Ibid., p. 177. Fowkes records that in one month there were over 600 meetings in one district of Berlin alone. The comrades were exhausted. p 177.
49. Gallas, Helga. *Marxistische Literaturtheorie. Kontroversen im Bund proletarisch-revolutionärer Schriftsteller* Luchterhand, Neuwied und Berlin (1971) p. 94.
50. Ibid., p 69.
51. Ueding, Gert. "Ernst Blochs Philosophie der Utopie" in *Utopieforschung. Interdisziplinäre Studien zur neuzeitlichen Utopie* Band 1 Herausgegeben von Wilhelm Voßkamp. Metzler, Stuttgart (1982) p. 297. My translation.
52. Lepenies, Wolf, *The Seduction of Culture in German History* Princeton University Press, New Jersey (2006) p.150.
53. Eckermann, Johann Peter in: Johann Wolfgang Goethe. *Sämtliche Werke nach Epochen seines Schaffens* Münchner Ausgabe. Hg. v. Karl Richter u.a. Band 19. München, Wien (1986) p. 632. My translation.
54. Hoffmann (1992) op. cit., pp. 217–218.
55. Ibid., pp. 180–181.
56. Ibid., p. 448.

6 REALISM

1. Aristotle. *Poetics* from Part XVIII. Translated by S. H. Butcher (from the web). http://www.gutenberg.org/files/1974/1974-h/1974-h.htm
2. Ibid. Parts XXIII and XXIV.
3. Willett, John. *Brecht on Theatre. The Development of An Aesthetic* Methuen, London (1984) p. 23.
4. Ibid., p. 190.
5. See Barthes, Roland and Savran, David. "The Dolls of Bunraku." in Diacritics Vol. 6, No. 4. Winter (1976) pp. 46–47.

6. Demetz, Peter. *Brecht: A Collection of Critical Essays* Prentice-Hall Inc., New York (1962) p. 8.

7. Althusser, Louis. *Essays in Self Criticism* NLB, London (1976) p. 52..

8. See Dial. J. *The Contribution of Marxism to Bertolt Brecht's Theater Theory: The Epistemological Basis of Epic Theater and Brecht's Concept of Realism* Dissertation Harvard (1975) p. 50f.

9. Willett (1984) op. cit., p. 15.

10. Brecht, Bertolt. *Plays Vol. 1* Eyre Methuen, London (1970) p. 115.

11. Eagleton, Terry. *The Ideology of the Aesthetic* Basil Blackwell, Oxford (1990) p. 350.

12. BBA 110/31 and109/22. Although there are published accounts of the *Fatzer* project, I have used here the numbers from the Bertolt Brecht Archives (BBA followed by book and page) because the source material is so massive, chaotic, and contradictory. But no distinction has been made between the photocopies of the original documents and typed volumes of transcriptions when the archive numbers are the same. All translations are mine.

13. Fatzer: BBA 110/47.

14. Ibid., 822/105.

15. Ibid., Fatzer: BBA 109/7. For the Kranllieder see 9–302.

16. Ibid., Fatzer: BBA 109/35–36.

17. Willett (1984) op. cit., pp. 46–47.

18. Iljin, M. *Naturgewalten und Menschenmacht* Mundus Verlag, Basel (1945) pp. 172–173.

19. Brecht, *Bertolt Gesammelte* Werke Suhrkamp, Frankfurt am Main (1967) pp. 1007–1008. The imagery of rain, water, and stream is ubiquitous in Brecht. For a discussion of this, see Rilla, P. "Brecht from 1918 to 1950" in Witt, H. (ed.) *Brecht as They Knew Him* Seven Seas Publishers, Berlin DDR (1977) p. 125f.

20. Willett (1984) op. cit., pp. 266–270.

21. Ibid., pp. 100–101 and see also the "Horace" story, p. 270.

22. Willett (1984) op. cit., p. 4.

23. See Hornby, Nick. *Fever Pitch* Penguin Books, England (2000) p. 113.

24. Barthes, Roland. *Mythologies* Jonathan Cape, London (1972) pp. 15–16.

25. Hornby (2000) op. cit., pp. 178–179.

26. Ibid., p. 194.

27. Apel, Karl-Otto. 'Die ethische Bedeutung des Sports in der Sicht einer universalistischen Diskursethik' in *Diskurs und Verantwortung* Suhrkamp, Franfurt am Main (1988) p. 238. My translation.

28. Brecht, Bertolt. *The Measures Taken, and Other Lehrstücke* Eyre Methuen, London (1977) p. 18. I have, however, sometimes used my own translation. The German original is in Brecht (1967) op. cit., Vol. 2. As the play is so short no further page references are given.

29. Fischer, Ruth. *Stalin and German Communism. A Study in the Origins of the State Party* Harvard University Press, Cambridge, MA. (1948) p. 618.

30. Pike, David. *Lukács and Brecht* University of North Carolina Press, Chapel Hill, London (1985) p. XIV.

31. Kurella, Alfred. "An Experiment with Not Quite Adequate Means" in *Literatur der Weltrevolution* (1931) No. 4, pp. 100–109.
32. Mittenzwei, Werner. *Bertolt Brecht von der 'Massnahme' zu 'Leben des Galilei'* Aufbau-Verlag Berlin and Weimar (1977) see pp. 55–60.
33. Esslin, Martin. *Brecht: A Choice of Evils* Eyre and Spottiswoode, London (1959) pp. 138–140. My emphasis.
34. Merleau-Ponty, Maurice. *Humanism and Terror. An Essay on the Communist Problem* Beacon Press, Boston (1971) p. 109.
35. Ibid., p. 110.
36. Brecht, Bertolt. *Diaries 1920–1922* Eyre Methuen, London (1979) p. 36.
37. Lenin, Vladimir Ilyich. *Collected Works* Lawrence and Wishart, London (1960 onwards) Vol. 12, pp. 425–428.
38. Ibid., Vol. 31, p. 70. See also p. 28 for the importance of retreating.
39. Ibid., p. 24.
40. Ibid., pp. 79–80.
41. It is central to the argument—as far as Brecht is concerned—that his desire to return to the Teaching Play form is a confirmation of how crucial the issues (political and aesthetic) he was then dealing with are. With regard to Brecht seeing The Measures Taken as the model for the theater of the future, see Wekwerth, Manfred. Schriften. Arbeit mit Brecht Berlin DDR (1975) pp. 78–79.
42. Apel (1988) op. cit., p. 219.
43. Ibid., p. 242.
44. Ibid., p. 230.
45. Koestler, Arthur. "On Disbelieving Atrocities" (1944) in *The Yogi and the Commissar and Other Essays* Jonathan Cape, London (1945) reprinted (1971) p. 98.
46. See Wills, Garry. "Fringe Government" in *The New York Review of Books* Vol.ume LII No.umber 15, October 6 (2005) pp. 46–50.

7 DEATH

1. Aristotle. *Poetics* from Part XV. Translated by S. H. Butcher (from the web). http://www.gutenberg.org/files/1974/1974-h/1974-h.htm
2. Marcuse, Herbert. *One Dimensional Man—Studies in the Ideology of Advanced Industrial Society* (1964) Chapter 8. (from the web). http://www.marcuse.org/herbert/pubs/64onedim/odm8.html
3. Voltaire, François Marie Arouet *Treatise on Tolerance* Chapter 1 (from the wWeb). http://www.constitution.org/volt/tolerance.htm
4. Marcuse, Herbert. *Counterrevolution and Revolt* Beacon Press Books, Boston, MA (1972), p. 53.
5. Huntington, Samuel P. *The Clash of Civilizations and the Remaking of World Order* Touchstone Books, Simon and Schuster, New York (1998) p. 207.

6. This certainly troubled some German commentators. Friedrich E. Schnapp, for instance, remarked that, "it is clear that in the case of Article 16a the Constitution had been changed in a disturbing manner in order that it can be employed to solve a political dispute." See *Grundgesetz-Kommentar Band 1: Articles 1–19* Grundgesetz 5th Edition (2000). (v. Münch and Kunig editors) p. 1001. My translation.
7. Kuhn, Thomas S. *The Structure of Scientific Revolutions* Second Edition, International Encyclopedia of United Science. Vol. 2, No. 2. University of Chicago Press , Chicago, Illinois (1970) p. 206.
8. Popper, Karl. "The Problem of Demarcation" Part II of "Replies to my Critics" in Schilpp, P. A. (ed.) *The Philosophy of Karl Popper* Open Court, La Salle, Illinois (1974) p. 981.
9. See chapter 5 note 2.

Bibliography

Adorno, Theodor. *Negative Dialectics* (from the web) Translation by Dennis Redmond 2001. http://members.efn.org/~dredmond/ndtrans.html
———. *Minima Moralia* (from the web) Translator Dennis Redmond 2005. http://www.efn.org/~dredmond/MinimaMoralia.html
Althusser, L. *Essays in Self Criticism* NLB, London (1976).
Anderson, Perry. *In the Tracks of Historical Materialism* NLB, London (1980).
Apel, Karl-Otto. "Ist die Ethik der idealen Kommunikationsgemeinschaft eine Utopie?" in *Utopieforschung: Interdisziplinäre Studien zur neuzeitlichen Utopie* Herausgegeben von Wilhelm Voßkamp, Metzler, Stuttgart (1982).
———. *Diskurs und Verantwortung* Suhrkamp, Franfurt am Main (1988).
Aristotle. *Poetics* (from the web) Translated by S. H. Butcher. http://www.gutenberg.org/files/1974/1974-h/1974-h.htm
Auden, W. H. *Selected Poems* Edited by Edward Mendelson, Faber and Faber London (1979).
Auxter, Thomas. *Kant's Moral Teleology* Mercer University Press, Macon GA (1982).
Barthes, Roland. *Writing Degree Zero and Elements of Semiology* Beacon Press, Boston, MA (1967).
———. *Mythologies* Jonathan Cape, London (1972).
———. *Diacritics: A Review of Contemporary Literature* Winter (1976) Vol. 6, No. 4.
———. *Image-Music-Text* Selected and translated by Stephen Heath, Fontana/Collins (1977).
Baxandall L. and Morawski S., *Marx and Engels on Art and Literature* Telos Press, St. Louis Milwaukee, WI (1973).
Beetham, David. *Marxists in the Face of Fascism* Manchester University Press (1983). Manchester.
Belsey, Catherine and Moore, Jane. (eds.) *The Feminist Reader: Essays in Gender and the Politics of Literary Criticism*, Macmillan Education Basingstoke, UK (1989).
Benjamin, Walter. *Allegorien, kultureller Erfahrung. Ausgewählte Schriften 1920–1940* Edited by Sebastian Kleinschmidt Verlag Philipp Reclam jun. Leipzig (1984).
Benstock, Shari. (ed.) *Feminist Issues in Literary Scholarship* Indiana University Press, Bloomington (1987).

Berlin, Isaiah. *Against the Current. Essays in the History of Ideas* The Hogarth Press, London (1980).

———. *The Crooked Timber of Humanity: Chapters in the History of Ideas* John Murray, London (1990).

———. *Conversations with Isaiah Berlin* Edited by Ramin Jahanbegloo. Peter Halban, London (1992).

Bernauer, James and Rasmussen, David, (eds.) *The Final Foucault* MIT Press. Cambridge, MA (1988).

Bloch, Ernst. *Geist der Utopie* Zweite Fassung (1923) Suhrkamp, Frankfurt am Main (1964).

———. *Abschied von der Utopie?* Editor Hanna Gekle. Suhrkamp, Frankfurt am Main (1980).

Bloch, Ernst; Adorno, Theodor; Benjamin, Walter; Brecht, Bertolt; Lukács Georg; Jameson, Fredric (Afterword) . *Aesthetics and Politics* Translation Editor Ronald Taylor. Verso, London (1980).

Borradori, Giovanna. *Philosophy in a Time of Terror: Dialogues with Jürgen Habermas and Jacques Derrida* University of Chicago Press, Chicago (2003).

Brecht, Bertolt. *Gesammelte Werke* Suhrkamp, Frankfurt am Main (1967).

———. *Plays Vol 1* Eyre Methuen, London (1970).

———. *The Measures Taken, and Other Lehrstücke* Eyre Methuen, London (1977).

———. *Diaries 1920–1922* Eyre Methuen, London (1979).

———. *Poems* Eyre Methuen, London (1979).

Brooks, Jeffrey. *Thank You Comrade Stalin! Soviet Public Culture from Revolution to Cold War* Princeton University Press New Jersey (2000).

Brooks, Peter. *Reading for the Plot. Design and Intention in Narrative* Clarendon Press, Oxford (1984).

Carlier, J. C. "Roland Barthes's Resurrection of the Author and the Redemption of Biography" in *Roland Barthes* Sage Masters of Modern Social Thought. Gane, Mike and Gane, Nicholas Sage Publications, London (2004).

Cixous, Hélène. "The Laugh of Medusa" in *New French Feminisms. An Anthology* Marks, Elaine and de Courtivron, Isabelle (eds.) University of Massachusetts Press (1980).

Cohen, Gerald Allan. *Karl Marx's Theory of History. A Defense* Clarendon Press, Oxford (1978).

Cole, David. "What Bush Wants to Hear" in *The New York Review* Volume LII Number 18, November 17 (2005) pp. 8–12.

Craig, Gordon A. *The Politics of the Prussian Army 1640–1945*, Clarendon Press, Oxford (1955).

Crews, Frederick. *The Critics Bear it Away: American Fiction and the Academy* Random House, New York (1992).

Currie, Mark. *Postmodern Narrative Theory* St. Martin's Press, New York (1998).

Dangerfield, George. *The Strange Death of Liberal England 1910–1914* (1935). First Perigree Printing, New York (1980).

Day, Gary (ed.) *Readings in Popular Culture: Trivial Pursuits* Macmillan, London (1990).

Demetz, Peter. *Brecht: A Collection of Critical Essays* Prentice-Hall Inc., New York (1962).

――――. *Marx, Engels and the Poets* Prentice-Hall Inc. New York (1967).

Dews, Peter. *Logics of Disintegration* Verso, London (1987).

Dial. J. *The Contribution of Marxism to Bertolt Brecht's Theater Theory: The Epistemological Basis of Epic Theatre and Brecht's Concept of Realism* Dissertation, Harvard (1975).

Dowling, William C. *Jameson, Althusser, Marx: An Introduction to the Political Unconscious* Methuen, London (1984).

Eagleton, Mary (ed.) *Feminist Literary Theory. A Reader* Basil Blackwell, Oxford, England (1990).

Eagleton, Terry. *Criticism and Ideology* NLB, London (1976).

――――. *Marxism and Literary Criticism* Methuen, London (1977).

――――. *Against the Grain. Essays 1975–1985* Verso, London (1986).

――――. *The Ideology of the Aesthetic* Basil Blackwell, Oxford (1990).

――――. *After Theory* Allen Lane, London (2003).

――――. *Why Marx Was Right* Yale University Press USA (2011).

Emslie, Barry. "Bertolt Brecht and Football, or Playwright versus Playmaker" in *Readings in Popular Culture: Trivial Pursuits* Day, Gary (ed.) Macmillan, London (1990).

Esslin, Martin. *Brecht: A Choice of Evils* Eyre & Spottiswoode, London (1959).

Felski, Rita. *Beyond Feminist Aesthetics. Feminist Literature and Social Change* Harvard University Press, Cambridge MA (1989).

Fichte, Johann Gottlieb. *Addresses to the German Nation* (from the web). http://archive.org/details/addressestothege00fichuoft The source given is Johann Gottlieb Fichte *Addresses to the German Nation* George A. Kelly (ed.) New York: Harper Torch Books (1968).

Fischer, Klaus P. *History and Prophecy. Oswald Spengler and the Decline of the West* Peter Lang, New York (1989).

Fischer, Ruth. *Stalin and German Communism. A Study in the Origins of the State Party* Harvard University Press (1948).Cambridge, MA.

Foucault, Michel. "The Ethic of Care for the Self as a Practice of Freedom" in *The Final Foucault* James Bernauer and David Rasmussen (eds.) MIT Press. Cambridge, MA (1988).

Fowkes, Ben. *Communism in Germany Under the Weimar Republic* Macmillan, London (1984).

Freud, Sigmund. *Standard Edition* Hogarth Press London (1953–74).

――――. *Die Traumdeutung* Studienausgabe Band II, Fischer Taschenbuch Verlag, Frankfurt am Main (2000).

――――. *Totem und Tabu. Einige Übereinstimmungen im Seelenleben der Wilden und der Neurotiker* Fischer Bücherei, Frankfurt am Main (1970).

――――. *The Wolf-Man by the Wolf-Man with The Case of the Wolf-Man by Sigmund Freud* Edited by Muriel Gardiner. Basic Books, New York (1971).

Freud, Sigmund. *The Complete Letters of Sigmund Freud to Wilhelm Fliess 1887–1907* Masson, Moussaieff (ed. and translator) Harvard University Press, Cambridge, MA (1985).

———. *Zwei Kinderneurosen* Studienausgabe Band VIII. S Fischer Verlag, Frankfurt am Main (2000).

Friedman, Benjamin M. "The New Demon" in *The New York Review:* October 8, 1998 p.35.

Fry, Northrop. *Anatomy of Criticism* Princeton University Press, Princeton, NJ (1957).

Fuegi John. "Russian 'Epic Theater' Experiments and the American Stage" in *The Minnesota Review* New Series 1, Fall pp. 102–112 (1978).

Fukuyama, Francis. *The End of History and the Last Man* The Free Press, New York (1992).

———. *Trust. The Social Virtues and the Creation of Prosperity* The Free Press, New York (1995).

Furman, Nelly. "The Politics of Language: beyond the gender principle?" in *Making a Difference: Feminist Literary Criticism* Greene, Gayle and Kahn, Coppéla (eds) Methuen, London and New York (1985).

Gallas, Helga. *Marxistische Literaturtheorie. Kontroversen im Bund proletarisch-revolutionärer Schriftsteller* Luchterhand, Neuwied und Berlin (1971).

Gane, Mike and Gane, Nicholas. (eds.) *Roland Barthes* Sage Masters of Modern Social Thought. 3 volumes. Sage Publications, London (2004).

Gardiner, Muriel. (ed.) *The Wolf-Man by the Wolf-Man with The Case of the Wolf-Man by Sigmund Freud* Basic Books, New York (1971).

Geras, Norman. *Marx and Human Nature: Refutation of a Legend* NLB and Verso, London (1983).

Gilbert, Sandra M. and Gubar, Susan. *The Madwoman in the Attic* Yale University Press, New Haven, CT (1979).

Goethe, Johann Wolfgang. *Sämtliche Werke nach Epochen seines Schaffens.* Münchner Ausgabe. Hg. v. Karl Richter u.a.Band 19 München, Wien (1986).

Goldhagen, Daniel. *Hitler's Willing Executioners* Knopf, New York (1996).

Greene, Gayle and Kahn, Coppéla (eds.) *Making a Difference: Feminist Literary Criticism* Methuen, London and New York (1985).

Habermas, Jürgen. "Erläuterungen zum Begriff des kommunikativen Handelns" (1982) in *Vorstudien und Ergänzungen zur Theorie des kommunikativen Handelns* Suhrkamp Frankfurt am Main (1984).

———. *Wahrheit und Rechtfertigung: Philosophische Aufsätze* Suhrkamp Frankfurt am Main (1999).

———. *Glauben und Wissen* Suhrkamp Verlag, Frankfurt am Main (2001).

Hegel, G. W. F. *Reason in History* The Library of Liberal Arts, Bobbs-Merrill, New York (1953).

Heldt, Guido. "Hardly Heroes: Composers as a Subject in National Socialist Cinema" in *Music and Nazis. Art Under Tyranny, 1933–1945* Kater, Michael H. and Riethmüller, Albrecht (eds.) Laaber-Verlag, Laaber (2003).

Hoffmann, Peter. *Claus Schenk Graf von Stauffenberg und seine Brüder* Deutsche Verlags-Anstalt, Stuttgart (1992).

Horkheimer, Max und Adorno, Theodor. *Dialektik der Aufklärung* S. Fischer Verlag, Frankfurt am Main (1969).

Hornby, Nick. *Fever Pitch* Penguin Books, London England (2000).

Humm, Maggie. *A Reader's Guide to Contemporary Feminist Literary Criticism* Harvester, England (1994).

Huntington, Samuel P. *The Clash of Civilizations and the Remaking of World Order* Touchstone Books, Simon and Schuster New York (1998).

Iljin, M. *Naturgewalten und Menschenmacht* Mundus Verlag, Basel (1945).

Innes, Christopher. *Erwin Piscator's Political Theater* Cambridge University Press (1972).

Irigaray, Luce. *This Sex Which Is Not One* Cornell University Press, Ithaca (1985).

Jacobus, Mary. *Reading Woman. Essays in Feminist Criticism* Columbia University Press, New York (1986).

Jameson, Fredric. *The Political Unconsciousness. Narrative as a Socially Symbolic Act* Methuen, London (1981)

———. *The Ideology of Theory. Essays 1971–1986. Vol. 1. Situations of Theory* University of Minnesota Press, Minneapolis (1988).

Judt, Tony. *Reappraisals: Reflections on the Forgotten Twentieth Century* The Penguin Press, New York (2008).

Kant, Immanuel. *The Critique of Judgment* in *Great Books of the Western World* (Editor in Chief, Robert Maynard Hutchins) Vol. 42, Translated by James Creed Meredith, Encyclopaedia Britannica Inc., Chicago (1952).

Kaplan, Cora. "Pandora's Box: Subjectivity, Class and Sexuality in Socialist Feminist Criticism" *Making a Difference: Feminist Literary Criticism* Edited by Greene and Kahn Methuen, London and New York (1985).

Kater, Michael H. and Riethmüller, Albrecht (eds) *Music and Nazis. Art under Tyranny, 1933–1945* Laaber-Verlag, Laaber (2003).

Kay, Jonathan. *Among the Truthers. A Journey Through America's Growing Conspiracist Underground* Harper/HarperCollins New York (2011).

Koestler, Arthur. *The Yogi and the Commissar and Other Essays* London (1945) reprinted (1971). Jonathan Cape

Kristeva, Julia. *The Kristeva Reader* Moi, Toril (ed.) Basil Blackwell, Oxford (1986).

———. *Interviews* Edited by Ross Mitchell Guberman Columbia University Press New York (1996).

Kuhlmann, Wolfgang. "Philosophie und Rekonstruktive Wissenschaft: Bemerkungen zu Jürgen Habermas' Theorie des kommunikativen Handelns" in *Zeitschrift für philosophische Forschung* 40 (1986).

Kuhn, Thomas S. *The Structure of Scientific Revolutions* Second Edition, International Encyclopedia of United Science. Volume 2 Number 2. University of Chicago Press Chicago, Illinois (1970).

———. *The Road Since Structure. Philosophical Essays 1970–1993* with an autobiographical interview. Edited by James Conant and John Haugeland. University of Chicago Press Chicago, Illinois (2000).

Kurella, Alfred. "An Experiment with Not Quite Adequate Means" in *Literatur der Weltrevolution* (1931) No. 4, pp. 100–109.

Lechte, John. *Julia Kristeva* Routledge, London and New York (1990).

Lenin, Vladimir Ilyich. *Collected Works* Lawrence and Wishart, London (1960 onwards).

———. *What is to be Done?* Progress Publisher, Moscow (1973).

Lepenies, Wolf. *The Seduction of Culture in German History* Princeton University Press New Jersey (2006).

Lübbe, Hermann. "Verdrängung? Über eine Kategorie zur Kritik des deutschen Vergangenheitsverhältnisses" in *Zerstörung des moralischen Selbstbewußtseins: Chance oder Gefährdung. Praktische Philosophie in Deutschland nach dem Nationalsozialismus.* Herausgegeben von Forum für Philosophie, Bad Homburg. Suhrkamp, Frankfurt am Main (1988).

Lukács, Georg. *History and Class Consciousness* The MIT Press, Cambridge, MA (1977).

———. *The Historical Novel* Merlin, London (1989).

Lukes, Steven. *Marxism and Morality* Oxford University Press Oxford (1987).

Lyotard, Jean-François. *The Postmodern Condition: A Report on Knowledge* Manchester University Press, Manchester (1984).

Lyotard, Jean-François and Thébaud, Jean-Loup. *Just Gaming* University of Minnesota Press Minneapolis (1985).

MacCabe, Colin "The Revenge of the Author" in *Roland Barthes Sage Masters of Modern Social Thought.* Gane and Gane (eds.) Vol. III Sage Publications, London (2004).

Magid, Barry (ed.) *Freud's Case Studies* The Analytic Press, London (1993).

Marcuse, Herbert. *Eros and Civilisation. A Philosophical Inquiry into Freud* Beacon Press, Boston, MA (1955).

———. *One Dimensional Man—Studies in the Ideology of Advanced Industrial Society* (1964) (From the web) http://www.marcuse.org/herbert/pubs/64onedim /odm8.html

———. *Counterrevolution and Revolt* Beacon Press Books, USA Boston, MA (1972).

Marks, Elaine and de Courtivron, Isabelle (eds.). *New French Feminisms. An Anthology* University of Massachusetts Press (1980).

Marx, Karl 'Economic and Philosophical Manuscripts' in *Karl Marx: Early Writings*, introduced by Lucio Colletti, Harmondsworth, UK (1975).

Marx, Karl and Engels, Friedrich. *The German Ideology* Lawrence and Wishart, London (1977).

Masson, Moussaieff. (Editor and translator.) *The Complete Letters of Sigmund Freud to Wilhelm Fliess 1887–1907* Harvard University Press, Cambridge, MA (1985).

McPherson, James, M. "The Art of Abraham Lincoln" in *The New York Review* Volume XXXIX Number 13, July 16 (1992) pp. 3–5.

Merleau-Ponty, Maurice. *Humanism and Terror. An Essay on the Communist Problem* Beacon Press, Boston, MA (1971).

Mitchell, Juliet. "Gender and Genre" in *Feminist Literary Theory. A Reader.* Eagleton, Mary (ed.) Basil Blackwell, Oxford (1990).

Mittenzwei, Werner. *Bertolt Brecht von der 'Massnahme' zu 'Leben des Galilei'* Aufbau-Verlag Berlin and Weimar (1977).

Moers, Ellen. *Literary Women* The Women's Press London (1978).

Moi, Toril. *Sexual and Textual Politics: Feminist Literary Theory* Methuen, London (1985).

Muller, John, P. and Richardson, J. William. (eds.) *The Purloined Poe: Lacan, Derrida and Psychoanalytic Reading* MD (1988). John Hopkins University Press, Maryland.

von Münch and Kunig (eds.) *Grundgesetz-Kommentar Band 1: Articles 1–19* Grundgesetz Fifth Edition (2000).

Nevin, Thomas. *Ernst Jünger and Germany. Into the Abyss, 1914–1945* Duke University Press, Durham, NC (1996).

Nietzsche, Friedrich. *The Birth of Tragedy out of the Spirit of Music* (from the web: http://records.viu.ca/~johnstoi/nietzsche/tragedy_all.htm) Translation prepared by Ian C. Johnston of Malaspina Uiniersity-College, Nanaimo, BC, Canada. Revised 2003.

———.*I: The Case Of Wagner II: Nietzsche Contra Wagner III: Selected Aphorisms* Translated By Anthony M. Ludovici Third Edition T. N. Foulis 13 & 15 Frederick Street Edinburgh and London 1911 (from the Web) http://www.gutenberg.org/files/25012/25012-h/25012-h.html

———. *On the Genealogy of Morals. A Polemical Tract* (from the web) http://records.viu.ca/~johnstoi/nietzsche/genealogytofc.htm Prepared by Ian Johnston of Malaspina University-College, Nanaimo, BC, Canada.

de Nooy, Juliana. *Derrida, Kristeva, and the Dividing Line. An Articulation of Two Theories of Difference* Garland Publishing, Inc., New York and London (1998).

Norris, Christopher. *What's Wrong with Postmodernism. Critical Theory and the Ends of Philosophy* Harvester Wheatsheaf, Hemel Hempstead (1990).

Nye, Andrea. *Feminist Theory and the Philosophies of Man* Croom Helm, London (1988) p. 199.

Peukert, Detlev J. K. "Der Genesis der 'Endlösung' aus dem Geiste der Wissenschaft" in *Zerstörung des moralischen Selbstbewußtseins: Chance oder Gefährdung. Praktische Philosophie in Deutschland nach dem Nationalsozialismus.* Herausgegeben von Forum für Philosophie, Bad Homburg. Suhrkamp, Frankfurt am Main (1988).

Pike, David. *Lukács and Brecht* University of North Carolina Press, Chapel Hill, London (1985).

Piscator, Erwin. *The Political Theatre* Eyre Methuen, London (1980).

Popper, Karl. "Utopia and Violence" in *The Hibbert Journal* 16, January 2, 1948.

———. "Replies to my Critics" in *The Philosophy of Karl Popper* Schilpp, P. A. (ed.) Open Court, La Salle IL (1974).

———. *Unended Quest: An Intellectual Autobiography* Open Court, La Salle, IL, 1982; revised edition published by Routledge, London, (1992).

Ricoeur, Paul. *Time and Narrative* University of Chicago Press, Chicago, IL (1984).

Rilla, P. "Brecht from 1918 to 1950" in *Brecht as They Knew Him* Witt (ed.) Seven Seas Publishers, Berlin DDR (1977).

Robespierre, Maximilien. "The Cult of the Supreme Being" in *The Internet Modern History Sourcebook* (from the web). http://www.fordham.edu/halsall /mod/robespierre-supreme.asp No translator given, but © Paul Halsall. August 1997.

Robinson, Paul. *Freud and His Critics* University of California Press Berkeley, California (1993).

Rose, Margaret A. *Marx's Lost Aesthetic. Karl Marx and the Visual Arts* Cambridge University Press Cambridge (1984).

Rother, Rainer. *Die Gegenwart der Geschichte. Ein Versuch über Film und zeitgenössische Literatur* J. B: Metzlersche Verlagsbuchhandlung, Stuttgart (1990).

Said, Edward W. *Culture and Imperialism* Alfred A. Knopf, New York (1994).

Schilpp, P. A. (ed.) *The Philosophy of Karl Popper* Open Court, La Salle IL (1974).

Schnapp, Friedrich E. *Grundgesetz-Kommentar Band 1: Articles 1–19* Grundgesetz 5th Edition (2000). (v. Münch and Kunig editors) p. 1001.

Schopenhauer, Arthur. *The World as Will and Representation* Dover New York (1966).

Selsam, H. and Martel, H. (eds.) *Reader in Marxist Philosophy* International Publisher, New York (1980).

Showalter, Elaine. *A Literature of Their Own: British Women Novelists from Brontë to Lessing* Princeton University Press New Jersey (1977) p. 28.

Smith, Anna. *Julia Kristeva: Readings of Exile and Estrangement* J. W. Arrowsmith Ltd., Great Britain (1996).

Spence, Donald, P. *Narrative Truth and Historical Truth. Meaning and Interpretation in Psychoanalysis* Norton and Co. NY (1982).

———. *The Rhetorical Voice of Psychoanalysis. Displacement of Evidence by Theory* Harvard University Press Cambridge, MA (1994).

Storr, Anthony. *Music and the Mind* Harper and Collins, London (1997).

Taylor, William, L. "The Nominee" in *The New York Review* Volume LII Number 15, October 6 (2005) pp. 31–32.

Trotsky, Leon. *On Literature and Art*, Pathfinder Press Inc., New York (1970).

Ueding, Gert. "Ernst Blochs Philosophie der Utopie" in *Utopieforschung. Interdisziplinäre Studien zur neuzeitlichen Utopie* Band 1. Voßkamp Wilhelm (ed.) Metzler, Stuttgart (1982).

Voltaire, François Marie Arouet. *Treatise on Tolerance* (from the web). http://www .constitution.org/volt/tolerance.htm

Vorenberg Michael. *Final Freedom: The Civil War, the Abolition of Slavery, and the Thirteenth Amendment* Cambridge University Press, Cambridge, England (2001).

Voßkamp, Wilhelm. (ed.) *Utopieforschung. Interdisziplinäre Studien zur neuzeitlichen Utopie* Band 1. Metzler, Stuttgart (1982).

Wekwerth, Manfred. *Schriften. Arbeit mit Brecht* Berlin DDR (1975).

White, Hayden. *Metahistory. The Historical Imagination in Nineteenth-Century Europe* John Hopkins University Press, Maryland (1973).

———. 'The Question of Narrative in Contemporary Historical Theory' (1984) in *The Content of Form. Narrative Discourse and Historical Imagination* John Hopkins University Press, Baltimore, MD (1987).

Willett, John. *Brecht on Theater. The Development of an Aesthetic* Methuen, London (1984).

Williams, Raymond. *Drama from Ibsen to Brecht* Chatto and Windus, London (1971).

———. *Politics and Letters* NLB and Verso Editions, London (1981).

Wills, Garry. *Lincoln at Gettysburg: The Words that Remade America* Simon and Schuster, New York (1992).

———. "Fringe Government" in *The New York Review* Volume LII Number 15, October 6 (2005) pp. 46–50.

Witt, H. (ed.) *Brecht as They Knew Him* Seven Seas Publishers, Berlin DDR (1977).

Wolin, Richard. *The Seduction of Unreason. The Intellectual Fascination with Fascism from Nietzsche to Postmodernism* Princeton University Press New Jersey (2004).

Woolf Virginia. *Women and Writing* Introduction by Michele Barrett. The Women's Press, London (1979).

———. *A Room of One's Own* (from the web) http://gutenberg.net.au /ebooks02/0200791.txt

———. *The Common Reader* (from the web) http://gutenberg.net.au /ebooks03/0300031.txt

Yergin, Daniel and Stanislaw, Joseph. *The Commanding Heights: The Battle between Government and the Marketplace That Is Remaking the Modern World* Simon and Schuster, New York (1998).

Zimmerman, Michael E. *Heidegger's Confrontation with Modernity. Technology, Politics and Art* Indiana University Press, Bloomington, Indiana (1990).

Index

The two title terms of this book are not directly indexed as they are ubiquitous and central to the argument of the whole. However, for the coupling between *narrative* and *truth* the reader should look in particular at *aesthetics, death and universalism, Marxist Humanism, normative values, realism (& narration),* and *teleology.*